Portfolio Learning

Barbara L. Cambridge

Indiana University Purdue University Indianapolis

Anne C. Williams

Indiana University Purdue University Indianapolis

Prentice Hall, Upper Saddle River, New Jersey 07458

Library of Congress Cataloging-in-Publication Data

Cambridge, Barbara L., (date)
Portfolio learning / Barbara L. Cambridge, Anne C. Williams.
p. cm.
ISBN 0-13-299819-X
1. English language—Rhetoric. 2. Portfolios in education—United States. 3. Report writing. I. Williams, Anne, (date) II. Title.
PE1408.C278 1998 97-22725
808'.042—dc21 CIP

Editorial Director: Charlyce Jones Owen
Acquisition Editor: Leah Jewell
Editorial Assistant: Patricia Castiglione
Developmental Editor: Marcia Muth
Director of Production and Manufacturing: Barbara Kittle
Managing Editor: Bonnie Biller
Production Liaison: Fran Russello
Project Manager: Linda B. Pawelchak
Manufacturing Manager: Nick Sklitsis
Prepress and Manufacturing Buyer: Mary Ann Gloriande
Cover Director: Jayne Conte
Cover Design: Pat Wosczyk
Electronic Art Creation: Asterisk Group
Marketing Manager: Rob Mejia
Copy Editing: Susan Korb
Proofreading: Geoffrey Hill

This book was set in 11/13 Times Roman by The Clarinda Company and was printed and bound by Hamilton Printing Company. The cover was printed by Phoenix Color Corp.

© 1998 by Prentice-Hall, Inc.
Simon & Schuster/A Viacom Company
Upper Saddle River, New Jersey 07458

All rights reserved. No part of this book may be reproduced, in any form or by any means, without permission in writing from the publisher.

Printed in the United States of America
10 9 8 7 6 5 4 3 2 1

ISBN 0-13-299819-X

Prentice-Hall International (UK) Limited, *London*
Prentice-Hall of Australia Pty. Limited, *Sydney*
Prentice-Hall Canada Inc., *Toronto*
Prentice-Hall Hispanoamericana, S.A., *Mexico*
Prentice-Hall of India Private Limited, *New Delhi*
Prentice-Hall of Japan, Inc., *Tokyo*
Simon & Schuster Asia Pte. Ltd., *Singapore*
Editora Prentice-Hall do Brasil, Ltda., *Rio de Janeiro*

Contents

Preface

Portfolio Learning invites you to learn from producing, collecting, analyzing, and assessing writing. You will write in both informal and formal ways about your own ideas and the ideas of others and receive responses as you write and revise your papers.

ASSUMPTIONS OF THIS TEXTBOOK

This book offers you a special approach to learning to write. Portfolio learning is based on assumptions that you might like to know as you start your course.

1. You are in control of topics and sources.

   This textbook assumes that you will learn by choosing topics and sources that are significant to you. You will practice many techniques to help you discover what you want to write about and what sources might be useful.

2. You need time to discover your ideas and synthesize them with the ideas of others. In this process you collaborate with your teacher and your classmates.

This book assumes that you learn from taking time to discover your own ideas, to place them in the context of other people's thinking, and to generate new ideas from the synthesis of the two. Techniques for engaging with other writers and readers are an integral part of this textbook.

In this portfolio class, your relationship to your teacher and to your classmates may be different from that in other classes you've taken in high school or college. Your instructor functions as a "guide by your side." If past English teachers have dictated your topics, formats, and grades, you will probably be glad for a knowledgeable, empathetic teacher who will help you decide on and assess your work throughout the course. In addition, your classmates and you become guides for one another. Decisions for choosing topics, revising drafts, and selecting portfolio contents will be easier because you collaborate with other writers in your class.

3. Making mistakes can be productive.

Portfolio learning assumes that you will learn more and be better able to represent your learning if you have many chances to write and revise. You may do some writing that ultimately does not work, for example, ideas that never get developed, paragraphs that don't fit with the others in a paper, or entire drafts that are best left unfinished. In a portfolio, you get to reflect on why something did not work and to show in other pieces of writing what you learned from the problem. In portfolio learning, you can fail without penalty because the failure becomes positive when you use it to improve. In portfolio learning, you can apply new insights to former writing any time during the term.

4. A body of work represents your learning better than a single piece of writing does.

Your portfolio composed of multiple kinds of writing will show more about you as a writer and learner than any one piece of writing can do. Your portfolio will contain writing that you did as you decided on a topic, as you tried different perspectives on the topic, and as you revised your paper. Even better than a stack of finished papers, your portfolio will demonstrate your writing process, your own assessment of that process, and the products that result from it.

5. Your writing in this course is part of a lifetime of writing.

You build in this course on your previous writing experience and look ahead to writing in the future. This awareness of your developing literacy is emphasized in composing a literacy autobiography, revising continuously, and creating a portfolio. The portfolio represents past and current learning and can be modified and expanded as you learn in the future. You undoubtedly hear often about lifelong learning: portfolio learning supports that idea in process and format.

ORGANIZATION OF THIS TEXTBOOK

The table of contents reveals an organization that imposes a sequence on writing, only because books are typically sequential. The writing process is often not so orderly, however, because writers may write ideas in notes, compose a draft of a paper, scout for other people's ideas on the subject, drop certain paragraphs and revise others, reorganize the main sections, and revise again. In other words, as a writer you may need help with revising both before and after you want advice about organization.

Your teacher and your class, therefore, may choose to use chapters in this book out of their sequential order. You may skip a chapter and return to it later. You may jump ahead to one section of a later chapter even when you are working your way through early chapters. Feel free to browse in the book, to alight on a helpful section, and then to return to earlier sections. Going through the book systematically makes sense, but so does using various chapters and sections as the subjects they treat come up in your class.

NUMBER AND KINDS OF PAPERS SUGGESTED IN THIS TEXTBOOK

In this book you will meet Justin Cooper who produced drafts of five papers, three of which he completed for his portfolio. This example is not a model to follow: it is one example of one way that your class might proceed.

Although your class may do the same kinds of writing that Justin does, your instructor may have other assignments for you to complete. You may do more research-based papers, or you may write a formal argument. You may write more essays, or a letter to the editor may be included in your assignments. The book is written so that your class has flexibility if you want it in number and kinds of papers, but you may also write five papers very similar to those that Justin does. Portfolio learning allows for flexibility in assignments to meet the needs of your class and its context.

USE OF THIS TEXTBOOK WITH OTHER BOOKS

Your class may use this textbook with other books. For example, you may want a handbook that explains in detail points of grammar, usage, punctuation, and style. If your instructor wants you to read more pieces of writing by professional authors to explore topics, perspectives, or stylistic options, you may have a book of readings to accompany *Portfolio Learning*. If your school emphasizes writing argument, you may have a book on logic and kinds of argument. In other words, you may use *Portfolio Learning* along with other books or with other materials that fit the context of your course.

On the other hand, your teacher may rely little on other textbooks and prefer to rely on the writing of students in your class to illustrate points about purpose, audience, focus, organization, and grammar. This textbook supports such an approach by using an extended student example throughout the book and multiple shorter examples within chapters.

Portfolio Learning is designed for flexibility. Partnered with other texts or with student writing from your class, it supports multiple course designs.

COLLABORATIVE PRODUCTION OF *PORTFOLIO LEARNING*

This textbook was produced through the cooperation of many people. From the patient encouragement of our first editor, Nancy Perry; through the systematic, persistent, and supportive assistance of our editorial guide, Marcia Muth; to the enthusiastic support of our editors, Charlyce Jones Owen, Leah Jewell and Linda Pawelchak, we have benefited from wonderful editorial guidance.

The following reviewers sent us honest, reflective, and helpful comments as we revised and revised this book: Richard Batteiger, Oklahoma State University; Cheryl Forbes, Hobart and William Smith Colleges; Joe Potts, California State University, Long Beach; Jeff Sommers, Miami University, Middleton Campus; and Wendy L. Wright, El Camino Community College.

Our students who have taught us during our entire careers about how to teach and how to learn deserve our sincere thanks. We especially appreciate the students who allowed us to use their work in this book.

Our colleagues who have over time collaborated in developing curricula, new teaching practices, and ways to support one another as professionals and as persons are present in this book.

Our children, who listened to us and wrote for us during the entire birthing of this book, enrich our professional and personal lives. We thank Andy, Bethany, Darren, and Emily.

We are thankful for each other. Collaborating on any extensive project tests empathy, mutual respect, and commitment to the purpose of the project. Our collaboration has strengthened our understanding of our teaching, our writing, and ourselves.

Finally, we are thankful that you will use this book for inspiration and instruction about writing. We would be delighted to hear from you with suggestions about the book, examples of your writing, or alternative ways of dealing with the writing issues in the book. Please send your ideas or pieces of writing to us through our publisher. Your ideas may be the wellspring for the next edition of *Portfolio Learning!*

Barbara L. Cambridge
Anne C. Williams

CHAPTER 1
Exploring Your Role as a Portfolio Learner and Writer

Welcome to a class in which you will create a portfolio that demonstrates your many roles, goals, and accomplishments as a learner and a writer. You may have heard of portfolios before primarily in terms of artists, who collect and arrange their best artwork to show others what they have created. In this class, you will generate a similar collection of writings amplified by your own reflections on what you have produced. Unlike classes in which each piece of work is completed and evaluated as a single instance of your learning, this class assumes that you are better represented by a variety of written pieces that show the diversity of your accomplishment. As you work with this variety of pieces, you learn through the portfolio process more about yourself as a thinker, writer, and learner.

You will create two versions of the portfolio during this class. Your Working Portfolio consists of a collection of your works-in-progress during the term; your Course Portfolio is a collection of work that shows learning at the end of the term.

A Working Portfolio contains a variety of learning documents, most of which you will produce through writing experiences in this textbook. For example, in this chapter you will write dialogue journal entries. In later chapters you will write paper proposals, Writer's Statements, drafts of papers, and revised drafts. In addition, you will receive written responses from readers, prepare final papers, and do periodic self-assessments. As you write during this term, you will keep all your writing in a Working Portfolio. What you learn from writing early in the semester can be applied to later writing; likewise, what you learn from later writing can inform revisions of your earlier writing. This process is the foundation of portfolio learning.

As the term progresses, you will assemble a Course Portfolio. This final portfolio will contain selected pieces of writing, based on criteria generated by your college or university, your teacher, or yourself. As you make decisions about revision in later chapters, you will choose drafts from your Working Portfolio and a format for your Course Portfolio. As you begin your writing course, however, you will be focused on your Working Portfolio.

The Working Portfolio functions at the center of your portfolio learning. Made up of a variety of documents representing your work and your own and others' responses to your writing, it is the locus of your learning. Returning to work done earlier in the course, drawing comparisons between papers you have written at different times, and analyzing your own and others' responses to your work provide the basis for the kind of learning offered by a portfolio class.

As you create documents for your Working Portfolio and add to documents that will become a part of others' Working Portfolios, you will find yourself playing a variety of roles. At times you will be the writer, struggling to express your ideas in a way that will help others to understand who you are and what you think. Within the writer role is the self-learner: you learn through your writing and through encountering your own ideas as you produce work. Within the writer role is also the self-critic: you play the part of every writer who both loves and hates his work. And, at various times, you will be the reader, providing feedback to others about their drafts and responding to other writers' questions and self-critiques. At still other times, you will take on the roles of apprentice and expert.

One reason that portfolio learning makes sense is that it mirrors life, in which we each play multiple roles and have multiple goals. Think about the context for the roles that you will take in this writing course by considering the roles you fulfill outside the course.

IDENTIFYING MULTIPLE ROLES

Listening during the last presidential campaign, I was struck by our desire for idealized leaders: people who can please all constituencies, solve impossible dilemmas, and never tire. We want people who have not made mistakes, who relate to everyone, and who are informed about all subjects. We certainly do not want someone who admits to uncertainty, to a changing viewpoint over time, or to living paradoxically.

But all of us are more complex than we realize. Sometimes we explain this complexity by saying that we play many roles. For example, I am an English professor, past president of a national professional organization, a mother of two sons, chairperson of the administrative board of my church, and friend to many people from my past and present. I tend to be very organized but often procrastinate about writing that I don't want to do. I'm good at conducting meetings but not so good at housework. While I sometimes accept growing older, I struggle with the youthful images demanded of women by American culture. When I am doing my best professional work, I am often afraid that I'm not doing my best parenting. My roles intersect sometimes, and I'm simultaneously unsure of one and confident in another.

You, too, are a complex person with many roles. You may be a college student, a parent, an employee, a friend, an aunt or uncle, and a citizen. How are you defined in each of these roles? What determines when you will be labeled daddy rather than chemistry student, daughter rather than taxpayer, aunt rather than waitress, or boyfriend rather than drummer?

When you are in a certain situation within a certain culture, one of your roles may be foregrounded. For instance, if you are babysitting for a friend's baby, it is more important at that moment that you are a caregiver than that you are also a political science major. You continue to be a political science major as you change the baby's diaper, but it's essential then that you focus on adjusting the diaper, not on understanding the electoral college. Just as you will often simultaneously be apprentice and expert in your writing class, it is appropriate to highlight the former when you are listening to a professional writer and the latter when you are responding to another student having difficulty with something you have mastered.

Although this multiplicity of roles may seem obvious, we may forget that we are really a collection of what some people call subject positions. That is, although we may seem to be the actor in a situation, we are simultaneously being acted upon. Our roles are defined for us at the same time that we are defining them.

For example, you may study very hard for your biology test and influence the outcome by that study, but your professor also controls the outcome by the questions asked, the method of response demanded, and the method of grading. Other factors influence both you and the professor. The professor may be at risk within his department because he gave too many high grades last term. You may be tired from working overtime at your office. The test paper may be blurred because the copier was overheated as the tests were reproduced. Many covert and overt factors influence our positions at any one time.

In a recent writing class in which I was a member, students and teachers were to write an introduction about themselves. The following entry contains my exact words of explanation to the class about the way in which my role as parent had superseded my role as writer the night of our introduction assignment.

> My choices last night about writing were influenced by several parts of my life. I returned home at 6:15 p.m. and quickly ironed my younger son's clothes for the school's honors awards ceremony that was to begin at 7:00 p.m. My older and younger sons were honored, about which this proud mom felt good.
>
> But then the evening deteriorated. Earlier that day my older son had had his car towed from an illegal parking space on a college campus. After he'd paid

> earlier in the day, he noticed that he had been charged for three days' storage, when his car had been at the gas station for about four hours. When we returned to the station to get the charge corrected, we were both subjected to verbal abuse, culminating in the station manager telling my son, "F___ you!"
>
> My choice when I returned home at 10:00 p.m. was to write a letter to the gasoline company's regional manager or to write the introduction for this class. I decided I should write the letter.
>
> In that situation I chose to foreground my role as parent over my role as class member. By not letting the incident pass, I modeled for my sons that they need not take such abuse without remonstrance to authorities who can cultivate change, that anger has an outlet not only in abusive oral language but also in reasonable and emotional written language, and that I support them in negative as well as positive circumstances.

Interestingly, my role as writer was enacted in the letter writing but also in my use of this incident now to illustrate a point in this book. While a certain role is getting the most attention, another role may be enacted simultaneously. Our complex roles intermingle.

PRACTICE WITH ROLES

Think about the roles that you enact all the time. First write answers to the following questions, and then discuss your answers with your classmates. You may want to discuss in small groups so that everyone who wants to has a chance to speak.

1. What happens when you tell your friends or extended family members that you are a college student? What do they think you do and learn as a student? How does what they say and think about you influence your sense of your role as a student?
2. How are you different as a college student than you were as a high school student, whether you were in high school last year or twenty years ago? Is your role in the classroom different? What circumstances create that difference?
3. List all the roles that you have right now. Draw arrows between roles that influence one another. For example, your role as a pizza delivery person probably influences your role as a student because it both adds money for tuition and subtracts from possible study time.
4. Who decided which course(s) you are taking this term? List everyone and everything that influenced your being in the class(es) that you are. Were any of the influences in conflict? How did you deal with all the influences?
5. In what part of your life are you in most control? Describe that part of your life. Now consider what factors actually influence your ability to keep control. Are you simultaneously in and not in control?

RECOGNIZING INFLUENCES ON YOUR ROLE AS A COMPOSITION STUDENT

As you start your Working Portfolio, you will write about topics and in forms that are partly dependent on the context in which you write. For example, your college or university has created a way to determine that you belong in a particular class. If all students take the same beginning composition course, the university may have decided that students of every background and every degree of writing experience need this course to prepare for university work. If students are assigned to different composition courses, placement may be based on SAT scores, a multiple choice test, or a writing sample. Raters of a writing sample use standards such as grammar and punctuation, organization and focus, or creativity and logic. On the basis of whatever standards are in effect, students are placed into an appropriate composition class or even exempted from the course. The university has made conscious choices about who is placed in what class.

But why has the university made such choices? The reasons may be multiple. A university that admits all applicants may create a spectrum of classes to serve all students including at-risk and honors students, or it may decide students must perform in mainline classes or fail. The university may have insufficient funds to offer a spectrum of courses or to accommodate as many students as want to enroll. On the other hand, the university may have developed well-differentiated classes designed to acculturate students into academic writing. Multiple factors influence policies.

Your role as a composition student is partly dependent on the way in which your college or university decides to offer you writing classes. The contents of your portfolio will reflect the kind of class in which you are placed. For example, if you are in a developmental class, you may need to include pieces in your portfolio that demonstrate you are ready for the next composition course.

Your School's Goals for Your Composition Course

A critical component of portfolio learning is understanding the context for that learning. You will not be writing individual papers that have little or no connection to one another or to the setting in which you write them. You will write in an overtly rhetorical situation, that is, a situation in which you will be most successful if you understand the context for your writing. That context is made up of the purposes of your writing, the audiences for your writing, and your own relationship to those purposes and audiences.

Your role as a composition student is partly dependent on the purposes and goals that your college or university has for you. Many colleges and universities require a writing course as or soon after a student enrolls. Why? Some writing faculty will tell you that the main point of your writing class is finding your voice, that is, enabling you to express your own views and perspectives. You need to know that what you have to say and how you say it are important, that you have the freedom and the responsibility to talk about what you want to talk about.

Other people in the university may tell you that you are in a composition class to prepare for writing in the university. When you enter a history class in which a book review is due, you must know how to describe and evaluate the book. When you write an essay test in philosophy class, you must know how to make an argument. When you construct a survey in sociology class, you must have the editing skills to make each item clearly understood.

Still other people may tell you that you need both to develop your own voice and to learn the conventions of academic writing. They contend that a composition course prepares you to speak up with your own ideas and feelings and prepares you to deal with the ideas and feelings of others in the field of study that you plan to enter.

What are the goals of the writing course in which you are enrolled? You need to know what you will be working toward in your course. If your syllabus does not include goals for your course or your teacher has not provided institutional goals, you might want to seek them out. Don't be surprised or upset if the goals are multiple, for example, enabling you to find your own voice and teaching you the possible voices of the historian or engineer or psychologist. But you deserve to know the influences that are coming to bear on you through the expectations of the institution, the department that is offering this course, and your professor. For your portfolio you will want to prepare papers that enable you to meet the goals of the course.

Each student in a recent course I taught interviewed five people about the purpose of a beginning writing course. Each talked with a student who had taken such a course, a professor who teaches a subject other than writing, a writing professor, a non-college-educated person, and a college graduate. Charlotte found that all her interviewees valued communication, but for different reasons. A writing instructor said, "Communication is a major portion of education. Communication of ideas is easily accomplished with writing." An assistant vice-president of data processing for a local bank stated that "a good writing course teaches you to think, be creative, work with others. It teaches you to get your ideas across." An accounting student, while emphasizing the need for good communication skills to make one "a more marketable commodity," also said that "how you express yourself says a lot about you as a person." A teacher of second grade students stated that "in education you are a role model for those you are teaching. In the inner city, the teacher is the only view of the standard way of speaking and writing for some children." And a retired homemaker with no college education said emphatically, "The difference between ignorance and stupidity is that ignorance can be changed and stupidity can't be. Reading what you want and writing what you want should be considered a privilege. Anything that would help a person both speak and write so you can better communicate with others in the world should be encouraged." Charlotte concluded that her interviewees valued professional, personal, and societal goals for writing courses.

As you continue to think about institutional and personal goals for studying writing, you can record and reflect on your thinking in a dialogue journal. In a dialogue journal you explore your thinking and the responses from others to that thinking. During this course you will identify, analyze, and assess your own goals in dialogue journal entries. These entries about your goals will go into your Working Portfolio for reference throughout the term.

KEEPING A DIALOGUE JOURNAL

A personal journal, which you may have kept in other classes or for your own pleasure, is a notebook in which you record your thoughts and ideas in progress. Unlike a diary in which you report events of a day, a journal is a place for thinking through a subject or a feeling, for practicing a tone of voice, or for beginning to build an argument in favor or against something. Because the journal contains evolving ideas, you do not need to worry about spelling, organization, or introductions and conclusions in a journal entry. You can even use shorthand or drawings. Because you are writing primarily for yourself in a personal journal, you need not be concerned with other readers.

A dialogue journal, on the other hand, assumes that you will have readers for your entries and that you will read and respond in writing to other writers' journals. Conversation is the mode of dialogue journals. Because you will have readers, you need to eliminate extensive shorthand, but the assumption still is that you are experimenting with ideas and forms. Readers will be asked to react and respond to your writing, not to edit spelling, punctuation, and sentence structure. Part of the writer's fun with a dialogue journal is trying out ideas; the reader can enjoy responding with any questions, suggestions, or thoughts that the writing evokes.

You will want a notebook for your dialogue journal. You may choose a three-ring binder so that you can take out journal entries to use for material for your papers and add printouts if your class does journal entries on the computer, or you may prefer a spiral notebook. In your notebook, divide each page to make a place for your own writing on one side of the page and for a response on the other side. Draw a line down the page approximately three quarters of the way across the page to separate your entry and the response. Dating an entry enables you later to know when it was you had the thought; asking readers to date and sign their responses provides context for the responses.

For instance, the following entries were written on the first day of a composition class that was exploring the role of the university. The journal writer is Julie, a student who had a nursing background, reared children and did volunteer work, and now has returned to the university to explore formal learning again.

Julie wrote in the left column in response to the question "What is a university?" Nancy, a classmate, responded to Julie's thoughts in the right column.

Julie's Journal Entry and Response

University has many meanings for me. It is certainly a place one goes for higher learning after high school. It is also something of a mind-set: a way of thinking about what we want to do with our lives and pursuing courses to reach that goal. It evokes feelings of excitement and eagerness. 8/27	A very interesting opinion. Makes me feel bad I was so sarcastic in my writing! As if I was taking for granted what I have benefitted from IUPUI. Very nice definition and "look" through your eyes. Nancy 8/27

PRACTICE WITH DIALOGUE JOURNALS

Set up a dialogue journal that you will use throughout the term. The first writing in your journal will concern the goals for your writing class of different people, including yourself.

Answer the following questions in your dialogue journal. Ask at least one other person to respond to your entry. Remember to leave space on the page for your reader to write.

1. Ask your classmates about their goals for your composition course. Collect as many answers as possible, but at least five. Are the answers the same or different? Do any individuals have more than one answer? How will these goals affect the class?

2. Try the assignment that Charlotte and her classmates did, interviewing five people outside your class about the goals of an introductory composition course. What can you conclude from the variety of answers that you received? What can you learn from the ideas of the people whom you interviewed?
3. Look in the bulletin that describes the requirements of the department or of the college in which you are enrolled or hope to enroll. Does the bulletin say that you are required or encouraged to take a composition course? Are reasons provided for the requirement? If not, what can you infer from other requirements or suggestions about the importance of writing?

DEFINING YOUR GOALS FOR THIS COURSE

You, too, may have your own goals for this class. Yes, the course is probably required, but beyond the legitimate goal of passing the class, you will need to fashion some objectives for yourself. Many influences, including your multiple roles, affect your goals: as a student you may be taking so many classes that you worry about carving out special time for this one, as an employee you may be changing jobs and needing to change your study times, or as a writer you may know that you often have problems organizing your ideas. Your various roles at this particular time will influence the goals that you set.

No two people in a writing class will have identical goals. Even if you and another student both want to focus on using enough details, you may be working toward short story writing and she toward writing legal briefs. If you are concerned about spelling, you may only need to learn to do a computer spellcheck, whereas your classmate must be convinced to use a dictionary regularly. You may want to learn about writing introductions, and another student may have trouble with conclusions. You may want to learn about using metaphor, but your classmate may not even recognize that term.

In the kind of writing class supported by this book, you will be able to work toward your own goals. In your Course Portfolio you will have the opportunity to show how you have made progress toward those goals in your own way. As you start the term and begin your Working Portfolio, you can benefit from establishing your individual goals. Perhaps reading the collective and individual goals of another class will help your thinking.

The following goals were established by students in a beginning composition course. The class members brainstormed, revised, and came to consensus on a set of class goals; then each person wrote individual goals. The following description of class goals and of individual goals was subsequently included in the syllabus for direction during the term. Here's how a portion of the syllabus read.

Class Goals—Composition I

We have agreed on these class goals toward which we will work and against which we will periodically check our progress.

1. To help one another to become better writers through offering and receiving constructive suggestions and in-depth examination of writing styles.
2. To become more critical readers of our own and others' work by learning to analyze and to evaluate.
3. To hone thinking skills by exploring and discovering ideas through writing about them.
4. To write in a variety of genres.
5. To build a repertoire of strategies to use in different writing situations.
6. To refresh and expand technical use of grammar in writing.
7. To gain a vision of ourselves as writers who are aware of and in control of processes and techniques to achieve varied purposes.
8. To consider each class session as an opportunity for progress individually and as a class.
9. To generate a portfolio of pieces that demonstrate our interests and abilities as writers conscious of our own processes.
10. To work hard but to have some fun, too.

Individual Goals

In addition to class goals, we each have generated personal goals for the course. We are committed to helping one another work toward these individual goals as well as the class goals and will use both for evaluating progress during and at the end of the semester.

Tami

1. To understand where details are important. No over- or under-dramatizing.
2. To take it upon myself to learn more about correct punctuation, especially quotations in dialogue.
3. To find a balance between art and writing. I tend to get artsy, as if everyone else can see what's in my

mind. I also tend to get wordy through getting too artsy.

4. To find and understand my own writing style.
5. To not be intimidated by my own true feeling and emotions when writing.
6. To improve verbal communication skills when offering comments about work.

Patti

1. To develop more self-discipline in completing written projects on time in all classes in order to avoid panic-stricken efforts at the last minute.
2. To experiment with new ideas and forms in writing. To look for new directions, test the limits, consider different possibilities for my imagination.
3. To try to write in a less formal, more conversational style.

Other students generated their own lists of objectives for the semester. As they exchanged paper drafts during the term, they then expected their classmates to refer to their individual goals. Dialogue journal exchanges about drafts and other work of the class went into Working Portfolios so that writers could refer to them as they revised their work and as they created new papers.

PRACTICE WITH SETTING GOALS

In your dialogue journal, answer whichever of the following questions your class or your instructor decides will help you analyze your goals. Ask a person who has not read your writing previously to respond to your answers.

1. How does or could a syllabus work for you? Do you have a syllabus in your writing class, or do you have syllabuses in other classes? Does having a syllabus clarify the reasons for the course? If you have had syllabuses in classes previously, have they accurately reflected the course? How often have you seen objectives on a syllabus?
2. Brainstorm a list of goals with other members of your class. On which goals can the class agree? How can you keep those goals in mind throughout the course?
3. Do any of the class goals conflict with the goals of the professor or of the institution? What can you do about the conflict? If the class's, the professor's, and the institution's goals are harmonious, how do you account for the similarities?

4. List your goals for this composition class for this semester. Be as specific as you can. How will you be able to tell if you have progressed toward these goals?
5. Interview a professor or an administrator in your school. Ask her what a student in the composition course in which you are enrolled should learn. How do the expectations of your interviewee compare to your goals for yourself in this course? Are they compatible? Contradictory? In what ways?
6. Write about the forces that may contribute to your achieving your goals. Then write about the forces that may work against your making progress toward your goals. How will you deal with these latter forces?

Setting goals recognizes your individuality; a multitude of cultural influences affect your needs and wants at a given time. For example, you may have as a goal to assert opinion: this is the first time that you have lived away from your dominant father who didn't care about your ideas. You may have as a goal to use standard English: you realize that the dialect you used in your rural high school may interfere with your aim of becoming an elementary school teacher in a suburban school. You may, conversely, want to explore the uses of dialect in writing: your high school teacher valued standard English so much that you felt alienated from writing and from readers who would discredit your own dialect.

If you are coming to college as a recent high school graduate or as a working person, you may simply want practice in writing. A research study recently showed that high school students engage in about fifteen minutes of writing per day, including time writing notes to friends. Even if your high school experience was richer in writing, it may have been only in English class or only creative or research report writing. Likewise, on your job you may do little writing, or perhaps you have done only one type of writing for several years. Practice in writing is, therefore, a reasonable goal.

Setting and working toward goals is empowering. Setting a realistic goal forces you to take into account abilities, circumstances, and influences. You must acknowledge that many forces play into your decisions, some of which control you and some of which you control. Regarding the composition course solely as something imposed on you by the university or even as something provided you by the university gives over the power to shape what you do in the course solely to the university. Recognizing that you are influenced by decisions of your school, you, nonetheless, can make your own uses of the course. The intersection of university expectations and of your own expectations shapes your reality as a student in this portfolio learning class.

USING DIALOGUE JOURNAL ENTRIES AS BACKGROUND FOR WRITING A PAPER

This chapter introduces you to one kind of writing that will appear in your Working Portfolio: dialogue journal entries. You have already begun to write dialogue journal entries and will extend their use. After you have read an essay in which an author reveals his story of becoming a writer, you will write further entries on the way to writing a proposal for a paper in which you will tell your own literacy story, your own account of how you have become the kind of writer you are today.

You have already begun exploring your thoughts through dialogue journal entries; however, those entries may be extended to a multitude of other subjects. On the same class day that Julie wrote her definition of the university, she made another entry in response to the question "What is one topic that you are currently interested in?" Judy, another classmate, responded.

Julie's Journal Entry and Response

One topic I am particularly interested in is death and dying, particularly the contemporary views on how we deal with the issue. I do volunteer work with a hospice program, including at-home care and bereavement, and I see the benefit of the openness which the program encourages.	Where is the hospice? I am also interested in death and dying with dignity.
Since my mother died two years ago, having faced surgery and a diagnosis of terminal illness, I have learned a great deal about the subject. 8/27	A loss does make you more compassionate. Judy 8/27

Julie was starting to explore both her reasons for being at a university and topics about which she might write. Through responses to her two dialogue journal entries, she learned that she had a more serious attitude than another class member, that a classmate would take her approach seriously enough to question her own sarcastic attitude, that a reader would be willing to look through her eyes at a topic, that she would have at least one reader interested in knowing more about dying with dignity, that one classmate shares her background in nursing, and that a reader was able to apply a generalization to her specific example about her mother. In the few minutes involved in writing and responding in a dialogue journal, Julie began to discover some things about herself and about the potential audience for her writing.

PREPARING TO TELL YOUR LITERACY STORY

Through accumulating dialogue journal entries on various topics, you build a base for writing papers for your class. Entries that deal with your past, present, and future writing can contribute to your own sense of yourself as a literate person. When writers decide to write about their evolving literacies, they compose what is often called a literacy autobiography.

Portfolio learning in this class assumes that you have written in the past and that you will continue to write in the future. You will be asked to think about what has been valuable in helping you to write in past schooling and in your workplace, and you will be asked to think ahead to writing that you predict you will do in the future. Understanding your past roles and goals and anticipating future ones helps you understand your current moves toward greater literacy. The creation of a portfolio in this class will enable you to become a better writer through practice, revision, self-assessment, and connection to your ongoing literacy story. What you write and what you learn from that writing will affect who you are and what you become.

Some writers have chosen to tell parts of their literacy stories. The following piece of writing by Scott Russell Sanders explains the literacy story in which he finds himself as a professional essayist. Read the essay with an ear open for the goals that Sanders has for himself as a writer. Mark passages that seem important to you in understanding the role of both the essayist and the essay. Although the essay may refer to writers whom you don't yet know, let yourself enjoy what Sanders is revealing about his own writing.

After you read the essay, you will write in your dialogue journal in order to sort through your reactions to the essay. If writing as you read helps you collect your thoughts, you may want to set up a dialogue journal page to use as you read. You could jot down interesting perspectives, confusing passages, or ideas that stimulate your thinking about your own writing history. Be thinking about the influences from your past that would be important enough to include in your own literacy autobiography.

The Singular First Person

by Scott Russell Sanders

The first soapbox orator I ever saw was haranguing a crowd beside the Greyhound Station in Providence, Rhode Island, about the evils of fluoridated water. What the man stood on was actually an upturned milk crate, all the genuine soapboxes presumably having been snapped up by antique dealers. He wore an orange plaid sports coat and matching bow tie and held aloft a bottle filled with mossy green liquid. I don't remember the details of his spiel, except his warning that fluoride was an invention of the Communists designed to weaken our bones and thereby make us pushovers for a Red invasion. What amazed me, as a tongue-tied kid of seventeen newly arrived in the city from the boondocks, was not his message but his courage in delivering it to a mob of strangers. I figured it would have been easier for me to jump straight over the Greyhound Station than to stand there on that milk crate and utter my thoughts.

To this day, when I read or when I compose one of those curious monologues we call the personal essay, I often think of that soapbox orator. Nobody had asked him for his two cents' worth, but there he was declaring it with all the eloquence he could muster. The essay, although enacted in private, is no less arrogant a performance. Unlike novelists and playwrights, who lurk behind the scenes while distracting our attention with the puppet show of imaginary characters, unlike scholars and journalists, who quote the opinions of others and shelter behind the hedges of neutrality, the essayist has nowhere to hide. While the poet can lean back on a several-thousand-year-old legacy of ecstatic speech, the essayist inherits a much briefer and skimpier tradition. The poet is allowed to quit after a few lines, but the essayist must hold our attention over pages and pages. It is a brash and foolhardy form, this one-man or one-woman circus, which relies on the tricks of anecdote, conjecture, memory, and wit to enthrall us.

Addressing a monologue to the world seems all the more brazen or preposterous an act when you consider what a tiny fraction of the human chorus any single voice is. At the Boston Museum of Science an electronic meter records with flashing lights the population of the United States. Figuring in the rate of births, deaths, emigrants leaving the country and immigrants arriving, the meter calculates that we add one fellow citizen every twenty-one seconds. When I looked at it recently, the count stood at 249,958,483. As I wrote that figure in my notebook, the final number jumped from three to four. Another mouth, another set of ears and eyes, another brain. A counter for the earth's population would stand somewhere past five billion at the moment, and would be rising in a blur of digits. Amid

From *Secrets of the Universe* by Scott Russell Sanders. © 1991 by Scott Russell Sanders. Used by permission of Beacon Press, Boston.

this avalanche of selves, it is a wonder that anyone finds the gumption to sit down and write one of those naked, lonely, quixotic letters-to-the-world.

A surprising number do find the gumption. In fact, I have the impression there are more essayists at work in America today, and more gifted ones, than at any time in recent decades. Whom do I have in mind? Here is a sampler: Wendell Berry, Carol Bly, Joan Didion, Annie Dillard, Stephen Jay Gould, Elizabeth Hardwick, Edward Hoagland, Phillip Lopate, Barry Lopez, Peter Matthiessen, John McPhee, Cynthia Ozick, Paul Theroux, Lewis Thomas, Tom Wolfe. No doubt you could make up a list of your own—with a greater ethnic range, perhaps, or fewer nature enthusiasts—a list that would provide equally convincing support for the view that we are blessed right now with an abundance of essayists. We do not have anyone to rival Emerson or Thoreau, but in sheer quantity of first rate work our time stands comparison with any period since the heyday of the form in the mid-nineteenth century.

Why are so many writers taking up this risky form, and why are so many readers—to judge by the statistics of book and magazine publication—seeking it out? In this era of prepackaged thought, the essay is the closest thing we have, on paper, to a record of the individual mind at work and play. It is an amateur's raid in a world of specialists. Feeling overwhelmed by data, random information, the flotsam and jetsam of mass culture, we relish the spectacle of a single consciousness making sense of a portion of the chaos. We are grateful to Lewis Thomas for shining his light into the dark corners of biology, to John McPhee for laying bare the geology beneath our landscape, to Annie Dillard for showing us the universal fire blazing in the branches of a cedar, to Peter Matthiessen for chasing after snow leopards and mystical insights in the Himalayas. No matter that they are sketchy, these maps of meaning are still welcome. As Joan Didion observes in her own collection of essays, *The White Album,* "We live entirely, especially if we are writers, by the imposition of a narrative line upon disparate images, by the 'ideas' with which we have learned to freeze the shifting phantasmagoria which is our actual experience." Dizzy from a dance that seems to accelerate hour by hour, we cling to the narrative line, even though it may be as pure an invention as the shapes drawn by Greeks to identify the constellations.

The essay is a haven for the private, idiosyncratic voice in an era of anonymous babble. Like the bland burgers served in their millions along our highways, most language served up in public these days is textureless, tasteless mush. On television, over the phone, in the newspaper, wherever humans bandy words about, we encounter more and more abstractions, more empty formulas. Think of the pabulum ladled out by politicians. Think of the fluffy white bread of advertising. Think, lord help us, of committee reports. By contrast, the essay remains stubbornly concrete and particular: it confronts you with an oil-smeared toilet at the Sunoco station, a red vinyl purse shaped like a valentine heart, a bow-legged dentist hunting deer with an elephant gun. As Orwell forcefully argued, and as dictators seem to agree, such a bypassing of abstractions, such an insistence on the concrete, is a politically subversive act. Clinging to this door, this child, this grief, following the zigzag motions of an inquisitive mind, the essay renews language and clears trash from the springs of thought. A century and a half ago, in the rousing manifesto entitled *Nature,* Emerson called on a new generation of writers to cast off the hand-me-down rhetoric of the day, to "pierce this rotten diction and fasten words again to visible things." The essayist aspires to do just that.

As if all these virtues were not enough to account for a renaissance of this protean genre, the essay has also taken over some of the territory abdicated by contemporary fiction. Whittled down to the bare bones of plot, camouflaged with irony, muttering in brief sentences and grade-school vocabulary, peopled with characters who stumble like sleepwalkers through numb lives, today's fashionable fiction avoids disclosing where the author stands on anything. In the essay, you had better speak from a region pretty close to the heart or the reader will detect the wind of phoniness whistling through your hollow phrases. In the essay you may be caught with your pants down, your ignorance and sentimentality showing, while you trot recklessly about on one of your hobbyhorses. You cannot stand back from the action, as Joyce instructed us to do, and pare your fingernails. You cannot palm off your cockamamie notions on some hapless character.

To our list of essay's contemporary attractions we should add the perennial ones of verbal play, mental adventure, and sheer anarchic high spirits. To see how the capricious mind can be led astray, consider the foregoing paragraph, which drags in metaphors from the realms of toys, clothing, weather, and biology, among others. That is bad enough; but it could have been worse. For example, I began to draft a sentence in that paragraph with the following words: "More than once, in sitting down to beaver away at a narrative, felling trees of memory and hauling brush to build a dam that might slow down the waters of time. . . ." I had set out to make some innocent remark, and here I was gnawing down trees and building dams, all because I had let that *beaver* slip in. On this occasion I had the good sense to throw out the unruly word. I don't always, no doubt you will have noticed. Whatever its more visible subject, an essay is also about the way a mind moves, the links and leaps and jigs of thought. I might as well drag in another metaphor—and another unoffending animal—by saying that each doggy sentence, as it noses forward into the underbrush of thought, scatters a bunch of rabbits that go bounding off in all directions. The essayist can afford to chase more of those rabbits than the fiction writer can, but fewer than the poet. If you refuse to chase any of them, and keep plodding along in a straight line, you and your reader will have a dull outing. If you chase too many, you will soon wind up lost in a thicket of confusion with your tongue hanging out.

The pursuit of mental rabbits was strictly forbidden by the teachers who instructed me in English composition. For that matter, nearly all the qualities of the personal essay, as I have been sketching them, violate the rules that many of us were taught in school. You recall we were supposed to begin with an outline and stick by it faithfully, like a train riding its rails, avoiding sidetracks. Each paragraph was to have a topic sentence pasted near the front, and these orderly paragraphs were to be coupled end-to-end like so many boxcars. Every item in those boxcars was to bear the stamp of some external authority, preferably a footnote referring to a thick book, although appeals to magazines and newspapers would do in a pinch. Our diction was to be formal, dignified, shunning the vernacular. Polysyllabic words derived from Latin were preferable to the blunt lingo of the streets. Metaphors were to be used only in emergencies, and no two of them were to be mixed. And even in emergencies we could not speak in the first person singular.

Already as a schoolboy, I chafed against those rules. Now I break them shamelessly, in particular the taboo against using the lonely capital *I*. Just look at what I'm doing right now. My speculations about the state of the essay arise, needless to say, from my own practice as reader and writer, and they reflect my own tastes, no matter how I may pretend to gaze dispassionately down on the question from a hot-air balloon. As Thoreau declares in his cocky manner on the opening page of *Walden:* "In most books the *I,* or first person, is omitted; in this it will be retained; that, in respect to egotism, is the main difference. We commonly do not remember that it is, after all, always the first person that is speaking. I should not talk so much about myself if there were anybody else whom I knew as well." True for the personal essay, it is doubly true for an essay about the essay: one speaks always and inescapably in the first person singular.

We could sort out essays along a spectrum according to the degree to which the writer's ego is on display—with John McPhee, perhaps, at the extreme of self-effacement, and Norman Mailer at the opposite extreme of self-dramatization. Brassy or shy, center stage or hanging back in the wings, the author's persona commands our attention. For the length of an essay, or a book of essays, we respond to that persona as we would to a friend caught up in a rapturous monologue. When the monologue is finished, we may not be able to say precisely what it was about, any more than we can draw conclusions from a piece of music. "Essays don't usually boil down to a summary, as articles do," notes Edward Hoagland, one of the least summarizable of companions, "and the style of the writer has a 'nap' to it, a combination of personality and originality and energetic loose ends that stand up like the nap of a piece of wool and can't be brushed flat" ("What I Think, What I Am"). We make assumptions about that speaking voice, assumptions we cannot validly make about the narrators in fiction. Only a sophomore is permitted to ask if Huckleberry Finn ever had any children; but even literary sophisticates wonder in print about Thoreau's love life, Montaigne's domestic arrangements, De Quincey's opium habit, Virginia Woolf's depression.

Montaigne, who not only invented the form but nearly perfected it as well, announced from the start that his true subject was himself. In his note "To the Reader" at the beginning of the *Essays,* he slyly proclaimed:

> I want to be seen here in my simple, natural, ordinary fashion, without straining or artifice; for it is myself that I portray. My defects will here be read to the life, and also my natural form, as far as respect for the public has allowed. Had I been placed among those nations which are said to live still in the sweet freedom of nature's first laws, I assure you I should very gladly have portrayed myself here entire and wholly naked.

A few pages after this disarming introduction, we are told of the Emperor Maximilian, who was so prudish about exposing his private parts that he would not let a servant dress him or see him in the bath. The emperor went so far as to give orders that he be buried in his underdrawers. Having let us in on this intimacy about Maximilian, Montaigne then confessed that he himself, although "bold-mouthed," was equally prudish, and that "except under great stress of necessity or voluptuousness," he never allowed anyone to see him naked. Such modesty, he reared, was unbecoming in a soldier. But such honesty is quite becoming in an essayist. The very confession of his prudery is a far more revealing gesture than any doffing of clothes.

A curious reader will soon find out that the word *essay,* as adapted by Montaigne, means a trial or attempt. The Latin root carries the more vivid sense of a weighing out. In the days when that root was alive and green, merchants discovered the value of goods and alchemists discovered the composition of metals by the use of scales. Just so the essay, as Montaigne was the first to show, is a weighing out, an inquiry into the value, meaning, and true nature of experience; it is a private experiment carried out in public. In each of three successive editions, Montaigne inserted new material into his essays without revising the old material. Often the new statements contradicted the original ones, but Montaigne let them stand, since he believed that the only consistent fact about human beings is their inconsistency. In a celebration called "Why Montaigne Is Not a Bore" Lewis Thomas has remarked of him that "He (was) fond of his mind, and affectionately entertained by everything in his head." Whatever Montaigne wrote about—and he wrote about everything under the sun; fears, smells, growing old, the pleasures of scratching—he weighed on the scales of his own character.

It is the *singularity* of the first person—its warts and crotchets and turn of voice—that lures many of us into reading essays, and that lingers with us after we finish. Consider the lonely, melancholy persona of Loren Eiseley, forever wandering, forever brooding on our dim and bestial past, his lips frosty with the chill of the Ice Age. Consider the volatile, Dionysian persona of D. H. Lawrence, with his incandescent gaze, his habit of turning peasants into gods and trees into flames, his quick hatred and quicker love. Consider that philosophical farmer, Wendell Berry, who speaks with a countryman's knowledge and a deacon's severity. Consider E. B. White, with his cheery affection for brown eggs and dachshunds, his unflappable way of herding geese while the radio warns of an approaching hurricane.

E. B. White, that engaging master of the genre, a champion of idiosyncrasy, introduced his own volume of *Essays* by admitting the danger of narcissism:

> I think some people find the essay the last resort of the egoist, a much too self-conscious and self-serving form for their taste; they feel that it is presumptuous of a writer to assume that his little excursions or his small observations will interest the reader. There is some justice in their complaint. I have always been aware that I am by nature self-absorbed and egotistical; to write of myself to the extent I have done indicates a too great attention to my own life, not enough to the lives of others.

Yet the self-absorbed Mr. White was in fact a delighted observer of the world, and shared that delight with us. Thus, after describing memorably how a circus girl practiced her bareback riding in the leisure moments between shows ("The Ring of Time"), he confessed: "As a writing man, or secretary, I have always felt charged with the safekeeping of all unexpected items of worldly or unworldly enchantment, as though I might be held personally responsible if even a small one were to be lost." That may still be presumptuous, but it is a presumption turned outward on the creation.

This looking outward helps distinguish the essay from pure autobiography, which dwells more complacently on the self. Mass murderers, movie stars, sports heroes, Wall Street crooks, and defrocked politicians may blather on about whatever high jinks or low jinks made them temporarily famous, may chronicle their exploits, their diets, their hobbies, in perfect confidence that the public is eager to gobble up every least gossipy scrap. And the public, according to sales figures, generally is. On the other hand, I assume the public does not give a hoot about my private life. If I write of hiking up a mountain with my one-year-old boy riding like a papoose on my back, and of what he babbled to me while we gazed down from the summit onto the scudding clouds, it is not because I am deluded into believing that my baby, like the offspring of Prince Charles, matters to the great world. It is because I know the great world produces babies of its own and watches them change cloudfast before its doting eyes. To make that climb up the mountain vividly present for readers is harder work than the climb itself. I choose to write about my experience not because it is mine, but because it seems to me a door through which others might pass.

On that cocky first page of *Walden,* Thoreau justified his own seeming self-absorption by saying that he wrote the book for the sake of his fellow citizens, who keep asking him to account for his peculiar experiment by the pond. There is at least a sliver of truth to this, since Thoreau, a town character, had been invited more than once to speak his mind at the public lectern. Most of us, however, cannot honestly say the townspeople have been clamoring for our words. I suspect that all writers of the essay, even Norman Mailer and Gore Vidal, most occasionally wonder if they are egomaniacs. For the essayist, in other words, the problem of authority is inescapable. By what right does one speak? Why should anyone listen? The traditional sources of authority no longer serve. You cannot justify your words by appealing to the Bible or some other holy text; you cannot merely stitch together a patchwork of quotations from classical authors; you cannot lean on a podium at the Atheneum and deliver your wisdom to a rapt audience.

In searching for your own soapbox, a sturdy platform from which to deliver your opinionated monologues, it helps if you have already distinguished yourself at some other, less fishy form. When Yeats describes his longing for Maud Gonne or muses on Ireland's misty lore, everything he says is charged with the prior strength of his poetry. When Virginia Woolf, in *A Room of One's Own,* reflects on the status of women and the conditions necessary for making art, she speaks as the author of *Mrs. Dalloway* and *To the Lighthouse.* The essayist may also lay claim to our attention by having lived through events or traveled through terrains that already bear a richness of meaning. When James Baldwin writes his *Notes of a Native Son,* he does not have to convince us that racism is a troubling reality. When Barry Lopez takes us on a meditative tour of the far north in *Arctic Dreams,* he can rely on our curiosity about that fabled and forbidding place. When Paul Theroux climbs aboard a train and invites us on a journey to some exotic destination, he can count on the romance of railroads and the allure of remote cities to bear us along.

Most essayists, however, cannot draw on any source of authority from beyond the page to lend force to the page itself. They can only use language to put themselves on display and to gesture at the world. When Annie Dillard tells us in the opening lines of *Pilgrim at Tinker Creek* about the tomcat with bloody paws who jumps through the window onto her chest, why should we listen? Well, because of the voice that goes on to say: "And some mornings I'd wake in daylight to find my body covered with paw prints in blood; I looked as though I'd been painted with roses." Listen to her explaining a few pages later what she is up to in this book, this broody, zestful record of her stay in the Roanoke Valley: "I propose to keep here what Thoreau called 'a meteorological journal of the mind,' telling some tales and describing some of the sights of this rather tamed valley, and exploring, in fear and trembling, some of the unmapped dim reaches and unholy fastnesses to which those tales and sights so dizzyingly lead." The sentence not only describes the method of her literary search, but also exhibits the breathless, often giddy, always eloquent and spiritually hungry soul who will do the searching. If you enjoy her company, you will relish Annie Dillard's essays; if you don't you won't.

Listen to another voice which readers tend to find either captivating or unsufferable:

> That summer I began to see, however dimly, that one of my ambitions, perhaps my governing ambition, was to belong fully to this place, to belong as the thrushes and the herons and the muskrats belonged, to be altogether at home here. That is still my ambition. But now I have come to see that it proposes an enormous labor. It is a spiritual ambition, like goodness. The wild creatures belong to the place by nature, but as a man I can belong to it only by understanding and by virtue. It is an ambition I cannot hope to succeed in wholly, but I have come to believe that it is the most worthy of all.

That is Wendell Berry in "The Long-Legged House" writing about his patch of Kentucky. Once you have heard that stately, moralizing, cherishing voice, laced through with references to the land, you will not mistake it for anyone else's. Berry's themes are profound and arresting ones. But it is his voice, more than anything he speaks about, that either seizes us or drives us away.

Even so distinct a persona as Wendell Berry's or Annie Dillard's is still only a literary fabrication, of course. The first person singular is too narrow a gate for the whole writer to squeeze through. What we meet on the page is not the flesh-and-blood author, but a simulacrum, a character who wears the label *I*. Introducing the lectures that became *A Room of One's Own,* Virginia Woolf reminded her listeners that "'I' is only a convenient term for somebody who has no real being. Lies will flow from my lips, but there may perhaps be some truth mixed up with them; it is for you to seek out this truth and to decide whether any part of it is worth keeping." Here is a part I consider worth keeping: "Women have served all these centuries as looking-glasses possessing the magic and delicious power of reflecting the figure of man at twice its natural size." It is from such elegant, revelatory sentences that we build up our notion of the "I" who speaks to us under the name of Virginia Woolf.

What the essay tells us may not be true in any sense that would satisfy a court of law. As an example, think of Orwell's brief narrative, "A Hanging," which describes an execution in Burma. Anyone who has read it remembers how the condemned man as he walked to the gallows stepped aside to avoid a puddle. That is the sort of haunting detail only an eyewitness should be able to report. Alas, biographers, those zealous debunkers, have recently claimed that Orwell never saw such a hanging, that he reconstructed it from hearsay. What then do we make of his essay? Or has it become the sort of barefaced lie we prefer to call a story?

Frankly, I don't much care what label we put on "A Hanging"—fiction or nonfiction, it is a powerful statement either way—but Orwell might have cared a great deal. I say this because not long ago I was bemused and then vexed to find one of my own essays treated in a scholarly article as a work of fiction. Here was my earnest report about growing up on a military base, my heartfelt rendering of indelible memories, being confused with the airy figments of novelists! To be sure, in writing the piece I had used dialogue, scenes, settings, character descriptions, the whole fictional bag of tricks; sure, I picked and chose among a thousand beckoning details; sure, I downplayed some facts and highlighted others; but I was writing about the actual, not the invented. I shaped the matter, but I did not make it up.

To explain my vexation, I must break another taboo, which is to speak of the author's intent. My teachers warned me strenuously to avoid the intentional fallacy. They told me to regard poems and plays and satires as objects washed up on the page from some unknown and unknowable shores. Now that I am on the other side of the page, so to speak, I think quite recklessly of intention all the time. I believe that if we allow the question of intent in the case of murder, we should allow it in literature. The essay is distinguished from the short story, not by the presence or absence of literary devices, not by tone or theme or subject, but by the writer's stance toward the material. In composing an essay about what it was like to grow up on that military base, I *meant* something quite different from what I mean when concocting a story. I meant to preserve and record and help give voice to a reality that existed independently of me. I meant to pay my respects to a minor passage of history in an out-of-the-way place. I felt responsible to the truth as known by other people. I wanted to speak directly out of my own life into the lives of others.

You can see I am teetering on the brink of metaphysics. One step farther and I will lunge into the void, wondering as I fall how to prove there is any external truth for the essayist to pay homage to. I draw back from the brink and simply declare that I believe one writes, in essays, with a regard for the actual world, with a respect for the shared substance of history, the autonomy of other lives, the being of nature, the mystery and majesty of a creation we have not made.

When it comes to speculating about the creation, I feel more at ease with physics than with metaphysics. According to certain bold and lyrical cosmologists, there is at the center of black holes a geometrical point, the tiniest conceivable speck, where all the matter of a collapsed star has been concentrated, and where everyday notions of time, space, and force break down. That point is called a singularity. The boldest and most poetic theories suggest that anything sucked into a singularity might be flung back out again, utterly changed, somewhere else in the universe. The lonely first person, the essayist's microcosmic "I," may be thought of as a verbal singularity at the center of the mind's black hole. The raw matter of experience, torn away from the axes of time and space, falls in constantly from all sides, undergoes the mind's inscrutable alchemy, and reemerges in the quirky, unprecedented shape of an essay.

Now it is time for me to step down, before another metaphor seizes hold of me, before you notice that I am standing, not on a soapbox, but on the purest air.

PRACTICE WITH DIALOGUE JOURNAL RESPONSES TO READING

If you decided to take notes in a dialogue journal entry as you read, you can use those notes now to answer whichever of the following questions your teacher assigns or you choose. Be sure to leave space on the right of your page or computer screen for classmates to respond. These entries can be a basis for class discussion and provide ideas for your literacy autobiography, which will be discussed in chapter 2.

1. Does Sanders's essay demonstrate different kinds of learning through reading and writing? What kinds of learning? Does your literacy story include any realizations like Sanders's about the value of certain kinds or a certain kind of writing for you?

2. What roles that Sanders alludes to are roles that you fill as well? Do these roles affect you as a writer in the same way that they affect Sanders? What can you learn from Sanders's experience that you might apply to your own?
3. Do you have significant people or events that have influenced you as strongly as the people and events that Sanders includes in his essay? Who are the people, and what effect did they have on you? What were the events, and how did they influence you?
4. In one class students listened to "The First Person Singular" read aloud. They concluded that an essay doesn't work unless the writer is "willing to stick his neck out." What do you think they meant? How does sticking out one's neck apply to writing a literacy autobiography?
5. What would you like to remember from Sanders's essay as you write your own literacy autobiography? Make a dialogue journal entry that explains the points you most want to remember.

   After you have written a draft of your literacy autobiography in the next chapter, return to this entry. At that point, write a dialogue journal response to yourself: how did you use what you learned from Sanders's writing or ideas in your own piece of writing?

With dialogue journal entries in hand, you are now ready to continue your portfolio learning. In chapter 2 you will learn about and practice preliminary writing, analyze a student's first draft of a literacy autobiography, produce your first draft, learn about Writer's Statements, and write a Writer's Statement for your draft. You will then be ready in chapter 3 to examine how to generate more materials to use in the revision of your draft.

WORKING PORTFOLIO UPDATE

As you progress through this course, develop the habit of updating your Working Portfolio regularly. Make sure that all the material you have produced thus far is included in the Working Portfolio and is identified and dated. For instance, in this chapter, you may have produced a variety of documents, including answers to questions, notes for class discussion, your own writing, and responses to others' writing. These entries may discuss your multiple roles, your individual goals for this course, and ideas generated by reading another writer's essay. You may also have lists of other goals, such as a list of the department's or college's goals and a list of class goals. To provide a context for your writing, your Working Portfolio should also contain your course syllabus and any other course materials provided by your instructor.

Remember that you are free to include in your Working Portfolio any other materials that will help you in your writing. For example, you may have received a handout on writing in another class, you may learn from this textbook by outlining chapters as you read them, or you may have written a report at work that shows how you are working on one of your individual goals. Because you can later take out anything that you decide does not belong in your official Course Portfolio, you are smart to keep in your Working Portfolio any materials that might be useful as you do the work of this course.

Watch at the end of each chapter for reminders about your Working Portfolio at that point.

CHAPTER 2
Writing a Draft

When I went to high school many years ago, we were required in English class to write an outline before beginning a paper. Supposedly, we knew before we began writing the paper what we wanted to say, the order of our points, the necessary amount of evidence, and the conclusion. Research findings on writers and writing processes, however, call into question the use of formal outlines before writing papers. One finding reveals that writers rarely do outlines before they write: even in school settings, when twelfth graders were interviewed, the vast majority revealed that they had done the outline *after* writing the paper. A second finding is that writers often learn what they want to say about a topic as they write.

Do these findings suggest that you should launch rapidly into a draft of a paper? Already from practicing with dialogue journal entries, you know that the answer to that question is no. In fact, a basic premise of portfolio learning is that the process, the often lengthy process, of composing a paper includes various kinds of writing before, during, and after drafting. Preliminary writing can be quite useful.

Two decisions you will want to make early in your writing process concern the purpose in writing your paper and the audience for it. Whether you can choose any topic or whether you are assigned a topic, you need to find a purpose and audience for your paper.

DETERMINING PURPOSE

When you identify a purpose for a piece of writing, you identify what you want to accomplish with that piece. You may want to convince your parents that moving from the dorm to an apartment is a good idea. You may want to explain to your boss why flex time scheduling would be better than a standard work week.

Or you may want to show your history professor that you understand the major issues in the continuing dispute over the Vietnam War.

Three methods to discover a purpose for your writing include brainstorming, questioning, and journal entries. These methods can be used whether you have an open or assigned topic.

Brainstorming for Purpose

Brainstorming is one way of generating ideas. When you brainstorm, you make a list of everything that comes to mind. To brainstorm, you turn off that automatic editor inside you that wants to consider whether the topic is a good one or how to spell certain words: you allow yourself to write down anything that occurs to you.

If you are brainstorming for topics, you may generate a list of disparate subjects. For example, Bethany, a freshman living off campus at a large university, needed to come up with a topic for her first essay in a composition class. Sitting in the living room of her apartment, she brainstormed for three minutes, coming up with this list.

Bethany's Brainstorming

```
books
new apartments
living situations
being on my own
different jobs
restaurants
waiting tables
caring for my plant
my cat
my family
favorite material objects
```

Although her teacher had suggested brainstorming for ten minutes, Bethany wrote in her journal, "I saw several things I could write about and decided to quit. I could easily write about waiting tables or about my new apartment because they are both immediate personal concerns."

If you are brainstorming for purposes within a topic, you may discover multiple options. For example, when Dakota was assigned an analysis of Medicare in his political science class, he brainstormed the following list of possible purposes for his particular paper.

Dakota's Brainstorming

```
explain to Grandma about the reasons for possible
  future cuts in her Medicare payments
complain in a letter to the editor about rising
  hospital costs
try to persuade my church to take a stand against
  cuts in Medicare
prepare material for our upcoming debate in speech
  class about views of the major presidential
  candidates on crucial issues
tell other college students in our school paper the
  reasons people my age should care about this
  subject now because it will affect them later
```

Sometimes when you are assigned a topic in a class, you may feel little investment in the topic. By brainstorming for your own purpose within the topic, you take control and make the topic your own.

When Justin was assigned a literacy autobiography with the purpose of helping his classmates understand him as a thinker and a writer, he decided to brainstorm to see what he could get out of the paper. His brainstorming list had five entries.

Justin's Brainstorming for Purpose, Paper 1, Literacy Autobiography

```
explain to myself why I'm in college
remember how I've been influenced by teachers and
  other people to be sure in college I hang around
  people like those who've helped me
convince myself that I am literate
look at my background realistically so I'll make
  good choices in the future
have fun remembering the past
```

Notice that some of the purposes Justin has identified would mesh nicely with the assigned purpose for the paper. Justin could take on two roles, that of learner about himself and that of teacher about himself to others. As long as the purposes complement one another, Justin can write a coherent autobiography.

DETERMINING AUDIENCE

Audience is closely related to the purpose that drives a piece of writing. Sample purposes mentioned so far in this chapter have included consideration of audience: for example, parents to be convinced of the advantages of apartment living, a boss who needs to understand the relative merits of flex time, a professor who wants to know that her students understand the issues surrounding the Vietnam War, and classmates who need to understand Justin to be better readers of his work. Accomplishing a purpose in your writing generally means accomplishing it for a specific audience.

Whether your audience is determined by the circumstance of the writing task, by an assignment, or through your own determination, knowledge about readers can help you make choices about organization, vocabulary, perspective, and examples in your paper.

Guidelines for Questions to Determine Audience

Answers to questions about readers will make choices easier to make as you write your papers. Answering questions like these will assist you in your decision making.

How old are my readers?

Are my readers mostly male or female?

Are my readers well educated?

What vocabulary is familiar or unfamiliar to this audience?

What examples will be understandable?

What do these readers already know about this subject?

Will readers likely be sympathetic or antagonistic to this subject?

What objections might these readers bring to the subject or to my perspective?

What attention span can I expect from these readers about this subject?

Sometimes your writing may have more than one audience. At work, for instance, when you prepare a report for a client, it likely will be read and approved by your supervisor before being sent to your primary audience. When a professor assigns a letter to the editor of your college newspaper, he becomes your secondary audience and the readers of the campus newspaper your primary audience. The professor may want a logical argument or application of a principle from his course, but readers of the newspaper may want to relate your main point to their own ideas. In this instance, you must know both audiences and consider the expectations of both.

Justin's literacy autobiography assignment has three audiences: his teacher, who will read and respond to the paper; his classmates, who hope to learn about Justin through reading the paper; and, because he decided so, himself, as he chooses his individualized purpose for the piece.

In a journal entry about his audience for the paper, Justin described the characteristics of his potential readers.

Justin's Dialogue Journal Entry about Audience for Paper 1, Literacy Autobiography

My audience for the literacy autobiography is the other people in the class. I don't know too much about them yet, but I do know that they are all college students. Most of them are about my age though a couple of the women look older, I don't want to guess about that! They have all graduated from high school, I guess, and they must have read some things, and they would probably have heard of some of the things I read or my mom read to me when I was a little kid. This should be a friendly audience because we have to work together after all, at least I want to know about them. I know I shouldn't be nervous about writing about myself, but I am, even if I know a lot about myself. My teacher talked about primary and secondary audience in class. I guess the class is the primary audience, and my teacher is the secondary audience. I'm also interested in what this paper ends up saying. The teacher will probably look at spelling and if I did the assignment right.

PRACTICE WITH DETERMINING PURPOSE AND AUDIENCE

1. Brainstorm a list of purposes for a paper. You have authority to establish a purpose for your paper even if the topic is assigned. When you have written for five minutes, read your list to yourself. Underline the two purposes that seem most interesting to you. Discuss the reasons for your choices with a classmate. Help one another decide on a primary purpose for the paper.

2. Did an audience emerge as you decided on a purpose for your paper? If not, brainstorm a list of potential audiences for your paper. After you have a list, choose a primary and perhaps a secondary audience. Tell a classmate why you have chosen the audience(s) you have.
3. Write a dialogue journal entry in which you include all that you know about the audience(s) you have chosen. Ask a classmate to respond in your journal with suggestions about other questions you need to answer in order to make good choices as you write your paper.
4. If your assignment is a literacy autobiography, brainstorm a list of events from your life that explain you as a learner and writer. Keep writing as long as you can think of events that seem significant. Then circle those events that you think might best serve your chosen purpose and audience.

   If you have a different assignment, brainstorm items for that topic. Then circle the items that best serve your chosen purpose and audience.
5. Write a dialogue journal entry in which you write about three of the events or items that you circled from your brainstorming list in question 4. Then ask a classmate to write questions about what would interest her as a reader about the events or as a member of your potential audience about the items. Be sure to include in your journal entry the purpose of your paper.

USING PROPOSALS TO FOCUS YOUR IDEAS

Once you have thought about purpose and audience for your piece of writing, you are ready to do a form of preliminary writing that can guide you as you begin a draft of your paper. Some writers compose a proposal in order to specify purpose, audience, perspective, probable evidence, and other features of a future piece of writing. The proposal need not function as a straightjacket, like some formal outlines, but it can provide guidance during the process of writing the paper. The writer can use it to think through ideas about important aspects of the paper. A reader can use it to suggest to the writer other ideas for consideration as the writer begins the paper. The proposal is an initial effort to make some important choices.

For example, Julie wrote a proposal for a paper on returning to school, a topic that emerged from her dialogue journal entries that you read in chapter 1. She had some sure ideas and some uncertainty about the project.

Julie's Proposal

I propose to write a paper that communicates the ways in which life changes and personal growth have contributed

> to my goal of returning to school. I feel a strong desire, if not a need, to share some of the experience of my journey through self-exploration which has led me to this point in my life. It is a personal experience story that may be a motivating factor to someone who is contemplating a search for intellectual fulfillment through college but who may not have the confidence to take the first step, or to a person who needs a change in her life and has not considered this option. Perhaps it may be just an entertaining anecdote of how I developed the yearning for more education after profound changes in my attitude about life.
>
> As a middle-aged woman who has gone through the slow process of rebirth--occasionally exhilarating, often painful--I feel I am an appropriate voice for this topic. I intend to write in an informal manner, lively, enthusiastic, and somewhat introspective. Through college reentry, I have a personal perspective on the topic, with empathy for those who may be experiencing the same situation.
>
> The difficulty with writing about this topic is that it is highly subjective. Not everyone faces this crisis in her life, certainly not in the manner that I did. A few may choose the same path as I but because of the diversity in personalities and background experience, a person may, or may not, identify with or understand the choice I made of pursuing my education.

Julie identifies five points in this proposal: (1) her reason for writing the paper, which is a strong desire to share her story, (2) her possible purpose of motivating persons who lack confidence or inspiration to return to college, (3) her tone, (4) her authority for writing, and (5) a reader obstacle she must consider.

You may state in your proposal your personal motivation for choosing a topic, your perspective, your purpose, your intended audience, possible sources of information, and possible difficulties you will face in your writing. Your instructor may ask you to address areas pertinent to a particular kind of writing. Your resulting proposal can help you focus your ideas as you begin a draft of a paper.

PRACTICE WITH PROPOSALS

1. Write a proposal for a paper that you have been assigned. What is your purpose in writing the piece? Who is your audience? What makes you a particularly good person to write this piece—your experience, your intense interest, or your desire to do well on a particular assignment? Where will you get information?

2. Look back at your writing about your multiple roles. Think about the roles that are most important to you. Write a proposal for a piece in which you would introduce yourself to other students in your class. Why will you include certain roles? What is the central idea that you want to project about yourself? What do you know about your classmates that will influence what you include in your paper?
3. Write a proposal for a paper in which you introduce a person whom you admire. Your purpose is to introduce this person to your classmates. What is the main idea that you want to project about this person? What makes the person worthy of attention and admiration?
4. In chapter 1, I commented that Americans place impossible demands on the president of our country. The person must perform in a multitude of roles with no mistakes and with multiple constituencies in mind. Write a proposal for a piece in which you suggest realistic roles for this governmental leader. Choose an audience who would be interested in this topic. Consider what approach you will take to the subject: a humorous, personal, analytical, or alternate perspective.
5. Write a proposal for a paper that fulfills an assignment for this class or for another class you are taking. Remember the purpose and audience of the paper. What evidence will you need to write the paper? What approach will you take to the topic? What writing schedule will you use to finish the paper for submission on time?

This practice with proposal writing will be useful as you approach writing the first paper for this course. As you write, use a proposal for a guideline but be open to emerging ideas. Writing is a process of discovery, so your writing may reveal a different perspective or focus that will serve your purpose even better than your original idea. Later you can learn more about your writing process by reflecting on how your proposal did or did not help you as you wrote your paper.

Save this practice with proposals in your Working Portfolio. When you have the option for a topic of your own selection during this term, you can return to this set of proposal exercises for ideas about that paper.

WRITING A PROPOSAL FOR YOUR LITERACY AUTOBIOGRAPHY

Justin's first paper is a literacy autobiography. Although you may or may not have the same first assignment, following Justin's process in doing a proposal will illustrate possibilities for your own process.

This part of Justin's assignment began with a proposal for his paper. The primary audience for his paper would be other members of his class, and the purpose of the paper would be to help them understand him as a writer and learner so that they could be better readers of his papers.

The sections of your own paper proposal may be stipulated by your professor, or you may have ideas of your own. The sections suggested here for a literacy autobiography provide a structure or may augment the ideas of your professor, your classmates, or yourself.

Guidelines for a Proposal for a Literacy Autobiography

1. *Topic and perspective of the paper*

Your evolving literacy is the topic of your paper, but you will need to focus on some aspect of your development. Are you interested in how your love for television has influenced your reading habits? Do you want to remember the key people who have motivated you to read and write? How did moving seven times during grade school influence your reliance on books as friends? State the main point and perspective of your paper.

2. *Purpose of the paper*

Although you have already considered some purposes for literacy autobiographies, your professor or you may have a different idea. Include the suggested purpose or another one appropriate for what you plan to write.

3. *Audience for the paper*

An audience of your peers is a real audience because they can use the information from your paper to be better readers of your future writing in this class. If you are writing for a different purpose, identify the appropriate audience for your paper.

4. *Evidence for the paper*

Make a list of the main people and events that you envision including in your paper. Beside each item on the list write a reason for its importance in your literacy story.

5. *Probable challenges and ways to meet them*

Writers need to think about such issues as availability of sources, length constraints, and timetables as they begin writing projects. For example, if you choose to interview your parents and grandparents about their influence on your reading habits, you will need to contact them in time to generate the material you need for your first draft. If your literacy autobiography is assigned to be no more than three pages, you will need to focus narrowly, a difficult process that may take some dialogue journal entries to figure out. Identify the particular challenges of your topic and perspective and ways that you can meet those challenges.

Because Justin's writing appears throughout this book and his Course Portfolio is included in the last chapter, you will want to pay close attention to the first introduction to his work so that you, like his classmates, can be an effective reader of his writing. What do you learn about Justin's role as a writer and as a learner from the proposal?

Justin's Proposal for Paper 1, Literacy Autobiography

1. Topic and perspective: I want to show how my dad's leaving our family when I was very young influenced my developing literacy in important ways. At this stage in my life I want to get over being angry with him.
2. Purpose: I am planning to write chronologically in order to show that I have reacted in different ways to my dad's leaving. My purpose is to show readers how I have gotten to where I am today.
3. Audience: The other members of my class will be reading my papers all term. My professor will even read their reactions to my writing. I want them to understand why I choose some of the topics I do and that I really want to learn something in this class.
4. Evidence: I'll have to remember certain events that symbolize the stages of my development.
   a. My mother used to read to me. I liked to know that my mom would be home every day and would read to me each day. She encouraged me to buy books and to use the library, habits I still have.

```
   b. A contest that I won for a free camera introduced
      me to photography, which I love. I understand
      myself and other people through the camera.
   c. I think that music is a form of literacy. I play
      the saxophone. Playing the saxophone is a way of
      expressing feelings.
   d. I read in chapter 1 about roles. I'm in many roles
      myself, but I'm entering a new role now. I'm a
      college student, and I'd better learn something new
      here.
5. Probable challenges and ways to meet them:
   a. There are so many events that I could use. I'm
      going to have to choose only a few events or this
      paper will get out of hand. Anyway, I have only
      eight days to write the first draft.
   b. I've always felt funny about writing about myself.
      I can see, though, how knowing about the other
      people in this class will help me understand their
      writing better.
   c. Last year my teacher complained that I got off
      track after I started with a subject. I hope this
      proposal helps focus me on the topic. I will ask my
      girlfriend to read my draft to see if I include
      only points about my main topic.
```

Justin's proposal was read by several of his classmates. They encouraged him to have a positive attitude about writing about himself: they all felt reluctant also, so they were empathic. One peer suggested being more specific about his purpose. "How I have gotten to where I am today" seemed too broad, although relating to his dad's influence would help focus. One responder warned Justin that complaining about his dad's absence would put the emphasis on his dad, not on Justin.

After Justin got responses from his classmates about his proposal, he decided to be sure that the tone of his paper was not whiny or complaining. He felt encouraged that peers understood his reluctance to write about himself, so much so that he began his writing immediately because he felt less apprehensive about dealing with issues of his own life.

Justin wrote a draft of his literacy autobiography. He used his dialogue journal entries and responses, ideas from classmates, and his proposal as guides to the paper. He wrote his draft over several days, allowing the evening before the draft was due in class for writing another document for readers of his draft. This document, called a Writer's Statement, focuses the attention of a writer on questions about his own draft. It also helps readers understand what the writer is trying to accomplish in the draft.

USING WRITER'S STATEMENTS TO COMMUNICATE WITH READERS

In addition to dialogue journal entries, brainstorming lists, and proposals which you have already done, you can use Writer's Statements during your writing process and in your Working Portfolio. Writer's Statements enable you to communicate with your readers so that they can be better readers of your work.

When I went to high school, I would be given an assignment, write it at home, and turn it into the teacher; then I would wait to see what the teacher would say about my writing. Usually the paper came back with only a grade on it although occasionally the teacher would cross out some words and substitute "more precise language" or would tell me that I should have referred to a particular example. Every once in a while the teacher would tell me to rewrite the paper with the more logical order she had stipulated on my paper. Never was I able to explain the circumstances in which I wrote the paper or to ask the questions I had about parts on which I'd worked particularly hard or about which I was concerned.

In this writing class, however, you have the opportunity to communicate with your readers so that you can become a better writer and so that they can be better readers of your work. By generating a Writer's Statement for each draft of your paper, you can (1) explain the context of the draft or paper, (2) ask questions about your paper, and (3) reflect on the production of the paper.

1. Explain the context of your draft or paper.

Sometimes you will make statements about matters that you think the reader should know about. One issue for any writer, for instance, is time management. Although you try to allot enough time for writing or even take all the time that you have, inevitably you have more that you would do with a paper "if only I had another day."

In a Writer's Statement for a draft I was reading, Jack commented about the conclusion of one of his papers: "If I had more time, I would definitely research the last paragraph of my work. I believe that the idea of being afraid of amounting to nothing can be worked into a full paper in itself. If I had more time, my focus and topic probably would have changed altogether." Jack wrote here about a draft that served him as a discovery draft; that is, he discovered his main point through writing the first version of the paper. Because Jack already knew that he had come up with his true subject only at the end of his paper, I as a reader could simply agree with him, knowing that he knew how to proceed as he dramatically revised the piece for his Course Portfolio.

Your instructor may supply guiding questions to help you focus in Writer's Statements on areas you are currently studying in class. For example, at the beginning of a term, I ask students to start the practice of reflecting on their writing process and themselves as writers. For Paper 1 in an introductory composition course, I asked students in their Writer's Statement to answer the following question about their individual writing processes: "What have I learned about myself as a writer through the process of putting this paper together?" Jacqueline wrote, "I have learned that I need to try to take my time and think about what I am writing, do more proofreading ALOUD and listen to what I am saying. I also learned that when I am dividing my paper into sections, I tend to choose whatever the hardest part for me is in the paper and make it first so I can get it out of the way and go to simpler things."

For the Writer's Statement for Paper 2, I asked Jacqueline and her fellow writers to answer another question that emphasizes applying what writers learn from one assignment to the next: "What did I learn from doing my first essay that I applied in writing my second essay?" Jacqueline responded, "I learned to be specific about what my point is in every paragraph. I have stated my point and then explained it." Your instructor, too, may ask questions like this one that relate to the context of your course.

2. Ask questions about your paper.

Your questions are a central part of your Writer's Statement. You can ask about those areas that you know need revision or that you are focusing on in a particular paper. If you have had difficulty in the past with a certain aspect of your writing, you may want to check out your skill with it in the current draft. Writers have diverse reasons for asking questions in their Writer's Statements.

When Jack finished a draft of a paper on the effect of European greed on the Lakota Indians, he gave it to Wendie with the following questions.

Jack's Writer's Statement Questions

1. How is my voice present in this piece?
2. What is the central controlling statement?
3. What is my organizational pattern? How do you know?
4. Do I have one clear purpose for the paper?
5. Do I spend too much time away from the purpose?

Wendie provided answers for each question.

Wendie's Responses

1. I think instead of your "I" being present IN this piece, your "I" is looking in on the paper along with your reader.
2. "Greed in the world has run rampant since the beginning of man" is your controlling idea.
3. I'm not sure if I consider myself qualified to identify your organizational pattern, but I believe that you organized your paragraphs by describing various illustrations to support your first sentence which I believe is your thesis statement.
4. I don't think so. Upon a second reading of your paper, I come to the impression that the oppression the Indians felt is the purpose of this paper, rather than the greed of mankind, although mankind's greed certainly plays a central role in that oppression. I enjoy your comparison and contrast. Specifically, "Custer's Last Stand" appears to pale in contrast to the last stand so to speak of the Lakota Indian tribe.
5. A suggestion I have with reference to your paper is that you give some thought to writing an essay based on your personal thoughts about greed and your observations on not only how it has affected man in history but now. Your excellent descriptions of the oppression of the Lakota could be incorporated therein.

Julie wrote a different set of questions for readers of her first draft of a paper.

Julie's Writer's Statement Questions

1. Is the ending too abrupt and ambiguous? Should I go further?
2. Is the last part of Paragraph #3 corny?
3. Is the second sentence of the second paragraph too long?

Maureen answered each of these specific questions.

Maureen's Responses

1. The ending was not abrupt, but perhaps you could include what you expect to happen in the future.
2. In paragraph three I was indeed impressed that you had heard of Van Halen and Bon Jovi--I don't believe using them is corny. It shows that you are keenly aware of the important things in the lives of your children--even if you see no importance in them.
3. The second sentence of paragraph two is lengthy, but it flows well. I had no trouble reading or understanding the point you were making. (By the way, your description of the toddler is magnificent.) If you're bothered with long sentences, then maybe you should divide it into two, but personally I think it's a challenge to make the fit as nicely as you've done.

Your instructor or you may well have questions that form the basis for all or part of a Writer's Statement designed to gather information about your writing process and about the progress and success of your paper.

3. Reflect on the production of your paper.

After writing her paper with five different readers reading her drafts, Julie reflected on the paper. Notice as you read her Writer's Statement that she feels satisfied that she has reached the goal in her proposal of writing with conviction. Because she was concerned with oversubjectivity, she also comments on readers' responses to her piece.

Julie's Writer's Statement

The most important accomplishment for me in writing this paper has been learning the value of seeking responses from others. I found it difficult to do this since my writing has always seemed a private endeavor. However, an awareness of similar feelings of some classmates allowed me to be more open to this sharing experience. Many of the responses I received were a factor in the final outcome of my papers. I do not feel confident in my response to others' writing, however, but

I presume that with practice I will be able to effectively impart honest and objective criticism.

My decision to write a personal story "from the heart" probably affected the tone of the paper. It was a challenge to try to put into words the intensity of emotions and thinking that led up to this point in my life, and I feel I did the best that I could without becoming too maudlin or repetitive.

My choice to use my husband as a responder to my writing, although I vacillated at first, was enormously helpful to me. I decided on a theme for the paper based on one of his comments in my dialogue journal, and he has continued to give me constructive input throughout the writing process.

I had originally finished the paper with the second to last paragraph, feeling that it was an appropriate ending for the story. However, after one classmate's comment and a re-thinking of the theme, which is about learning throughout life, I decided to project into the future, and I feel that it will create greater reader interest.

I would like to be able to be more focused when I am writing. My mind often wanders from one thought about the paper to another. It is difficult for me to organize my thoughts clearly, and concentrate on one aspect at a time. I think that with experience I will be able to control this problem. Somehow, I managed to put it all together for this paper, and I am satisfied with the outcome at this time. I feel that with practice in the process of writing, my apprehension will lessen and I may become more focused.

This paper is very similar in theme to a poem I wrote about middle age last year. Again, the intensity of my experiences begs for expression, and I have enjoyed writing about them. My letters to relatives and friends are similar in tone to this paper, but of course are less formal. I do have a propensity toward the dramatic!

Notice the cues that Julie gives herself about how to write and read her next paper. She has some specific writing tasks in mind for herself: she wants to express certain emotions strongly, and she wants to stay focused. When she writes and reads a draft of her next paper, she can look especially at emotional intensity and focus.

You may think that considering Writer's Statements before you write a draft is getting things out of order. Knowing about Writer's Statements before you compose a draft, however, can be reassuring because you know from the start that you will have the opportunity to converse with your readers about the process of writing the paper and about the paper itself.

One objective of portfolio learning is studying the effect of the process of your writing on your drafts and papers. Writer's Statements help you as you write to get ideas for revision. Later, when you put together your Course Portfolio, Writer's Statements can help you reflect on and understand the choices you made, the problems you had, and the ways that readers helped you revise.

PREPARING A WRITER'S STATEMENT

Justin wrote a Writer's Statement to express his questions and comments on his draft. Although some issues in the draft reflect Justin's points in his proposal, some new issues emerged as he wrote. Notice similarities and differences between what Justin foresaw for the writing of his draft and what happened during his writing.

Justin's Writer's Statement for Paper 1, Literacy Autobiography

Diving Away from the Wreck

1. This writing about myself is hard. I have so many memories. I'm not sure which ones I should use. Is the part about soccer and going to eat really about my topic? It includes something about my dad, but I'm not sure it has much to do with my literacy.
2. The audience for this paper is supposed to be the other people in our class. Is this paper interesting to you so far? I want to read other people's papers in my writing group so I can see what they thought would be interesting.
3. I like the specific examples I used in the paragraph about photography. Do you think I need more specific examples anywhere else in the paper?

4. The frame (a term I learned recently that means a way to structure the beginning and end of a paper--I like the term because it is just like photography) for my paper is about dealing with my dad. I think that that is pertinent to what I am doing with my life, but does talking about my dad get me off the topic of my literacy autobiography? I hope not cause I'd have to start over basically.
5. My girlfriend, who read this draft, thinks I need to talk more about writing. Do you think so? I do write pretty well usually. I even won an essay contest in high school. I could write about that and about how I'm doing in other classes with my writing. This paper could get out of hand, though, with too much in it.
6. Do you have any other suggestions about what I should revise?

As you read Justin's draft, think about his proposal and his Writer's Statement to help you understand what he is trying to accomplish and what he accomplishes in the draft.

Justin's Paper 1, Draft 1, Literacy Autobiography

Diving Away from the Wreck

My girlfriend likes poetry. When she read some poems to me from a book by Adrienne Rich called *Diving Into the Wreck,* I began thinking about how my life has been the opposite. I've been avoiding a wreck, using language like Rich but other things, too. Now, however, I'm ready to move toward something, hopefully through my college education.

When I was three my dad left my mom, my younger sister, and me to try to find a better job. The trouble was that he never let us know if he found one. My father had dropped out of school when he was sixteen. My mom says that he never really learned to read well, so that he ran into a dead end at each job when his inability kept him from advancing. Although I understand his frustration now I spent most of my younger years mad at my dad for deserting us. My mom has pointed out to me that I tried to be everything he was not: I read everything I could, I did well in school, I was as responsible as could be expected to my mother and sister, and I refused to speak about my father.

My mother supported me in every way. Since I was really little she read to me every day. I liked animal stories, so she read the entire Black Stallion series and books like *Bambi* when I was little and *The Red Pony* when I grew older. She had a deal that she would pay for half of any book that I wanted to buy. We used the library most of the time, but if I wanted a book, I had to save only half the price from my allowance or paper delivery money. I remember that the first book I bought was *Lassie Comes Home*, which I found in the children's section at our local bookstore, Fine Print.

In third grade the Polaroid Company sponsored a contest that led to another way in which I could document my life. I took the free camera given by Polaroid and took pictures of my house, my neighborhood, my mom, my sister, and events in our family. Later I received a Kodak 16 millimeter of my own. I have albums with pictures of Uncle Jims fortieth birthday party, of my sisters room with all the posters of Hootie and the Blowfish, and of the roses that my mom cultivated each year. I have pictures of my Boy Scout troops trip to Gatlinburg, Tennessee, my sixth grade classes production of *You're a Good Man, Charlie Brown*, and my junior prom. I also liked to take pictures in our town, of people shopping, of homeless people asking for money, and of sidewalk vendors.

I like music, too. I've really enjoyed playing the saxophone. I liked being part of an improvisational jazz group, although I never got very good. I find that the sax expresses my sadness in a way that I can't with words or any other form of expression. Sometimes I wonder if other people feel the deep sadness that I feel sometimes. Not that I'm usually sad, but occasionally I feel really sad for reasons that I'm not sure about. I don't think that this feeling is related just to my dads leaving, but I don't know how else to explain it.

Just so you don't think I'm a morbid person, you should know that I like athletics. My mom says that my dad liked football. She has a high school picture of him in his uniform. I played soccer. Since the goalie seemed to have ultimate responsibility for stopping the other team I decided to be a goalie. By the time I wanted to play, my mom had graduated from college in accounting, so she had a good enough job to pay for the special equipment a goalie needs. When other guys dads came to every game I used to feel cheated, but my mom and sister were always there. My sister didn't understand anything about the game, but she yelled for me anyway. After we'd win we'd stop at Taco Bell for ten soft tacos to go. When we'd lose my mom would insist that we stop anyway, but I'd order something different. I got good in soccer, but I'm not going to play in college because I didn't get a scholarship and I need to work part-time.

I'm now nineteen, and I am a student, a bookstore employee, a roommate, a boyfriend, and still a son and brother. I find it hard to balance my commitments, and I realize that I'm understanding more and more about my dads life. He was only twenty-two when he left us. Probably he just couldn't take all the responsibility when he knew things wouldn't get any better. I hope that I don't cave in under the stress of supporting myself and going to school. It may not seem like much, but I realize that I have to discipline myself now to work toward something. Instead of fighting my memory of my dad, I want to build my own memory for myself and for my family in the future. I want to study how people operate in society, so I'm going to study sociology. My literacy history is already different from my dads and I intend my future to be different, too. I'll let go of being concerned with his decisions and make good ones of my own. I'll use learning toward that goal, so here I come college.

ANALYZING JUSTIN'S DRAFT

In your dialogue journal, answer the following questions.

1. Did Justin's draft fulfill the anticipated goals of the proposal? At what points did the draft take a different direction? Might Justin return to the proposal for any more help in writing this paper?
2. Write a brief answer to each of the major questions in Justin's Writer's Statement. Did you find yourself thinking about the questions as you read? Can you cite evidence from the draft to support your answers?
3. Compare your answers to Justin's Writer's Statement questions with a classmate's. How are your answers similar, and how are they different? What do the different answers indicate about having multiple readers of a draft?

DRAFTING YOUR PAPER

You have read a literacy autobiography by a professional writer and by a student writer. If your assignment is a literacy autobiography, now you are ready to draft your own literacy autobiography. If your assignment is a different one, you will follow the same process of writing a proposal, discussing the proposal with your classmates, drafting the paper, writing a Writer's Statement, and anticipating responses.

1. Write a proposal. Use the proposal sections suggested in this chapter or others suggested by your teacher or your own purposes.
2. Discuss your proposal with your peers. Consider their responses as you begin your draft.
3. Draft your paper. Follow guidelines supplied by your instructor.
4. Write a Writer's Statement to submit with your proposal and draft to your classmates and to your instructor for response.
5. Anticipate helpful responses that will guide you as you continue to develop your paper. Write a dialogue journal entry that forecasts reader responses and then compare it with the actual responses of your readers. Use these responses to see how you and others are similar and different readers of your writing.

WORKING PORTFOLIO UPDATE

Putting all your preliminary writing, including brainstorming and other exercises, in your Working Portfolio enables you to save ideas that you may want to use at other points during the term. Although all preliminary writing may not go into your Course Portfolio, you may want to provide an example of the process that led to the finished piece of writing. For example, Justin might include his dialogue journal entries and brainstorming in his Course Portfolio to demonstrate his careful planning for his literacy autobiography.

Your Working Portfolio will grow as you include the multiple kinds of writing that support the development of a paper. From chapters 1 and 2, you have dialogue journal entries, practice exercises, a paper proposal, a draft, and a Writer's Statement. As you continue to work, you will use other kinds of writing to generate new ideas, more evidence, and fuller development of your paper. Chapter 3 introduces you to more ways to generate material for your papers.

CHAPTER 3 Narrowing the Lens

"Once upon a time" is an appropriate beginning for a fairy tale. Although the phrase sets the scene in a vague long ago, the phrase does contain the word *once,* so a single story can be told. Sometimes student essays begin with the phrases "since the beginning of civilization" or "in this world today," two inappropriate phrases. The phrases signal an impossibly broad scope for even the most extensively researched papers. The writer of such phrases has insufficient focus. A more appropriate setting of the lens ensures sufficient narrowing of a topic so that the writer can say something significant.

USING QUESTIONS AND RESPONSES TO ASSESS FOCUS

When two classmates answered Writer's Statement questions on Justin's first paper, the questions you read in chapter 2, Justin learned that lack of focus was one problem on which he could work in his next draft. Notice as you read Stacey's and Stephen's responses that they identify getting off the topic as a recurring issue in Justin's draft.

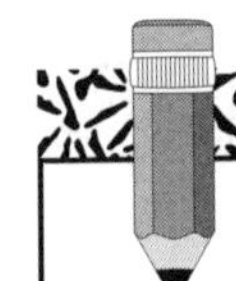

Justin's Writer's Statement Questions for Paper 1, Literacy Autobiography

1. Is the part about soccer and going to eat pertinent to my literacy story?
2. Is this paper interesting to you as a class member?
3. Do I need more specific examples in the paper?
4. Does talking about my dad get me off the subject of my literacy development?
5. Should I talk more about writing? Can I do so without this paper getting out of hand?
6. Do you have any other suggestions?

Stacey's Responses

1. You're right to ask this question. I play soccer, so I was interested that you do, too. I never played goalie, though. Anyway, the soccer bit shows great support by your mom and sister. It doesn't tell me anything about your literacy, though. Unless you want to say that it took time away from your school work and you didn't do as well in school or something.
2. Yeah, it's interesting. My paper talks about my favorite books from when I was little until now. I try to show how each book says something different about me as a learner. I get writing in by quoting from my diary and from papers I wrote in high school about certain books. My paper may be the opposite of yours. Mine may be too limited. Oh, well, I guess we'll both find out.
3. I like the examples of the first books you read and were read to you. I was surprised that the photography paragraph did seem to belong in your paper. I was convinced by it that the pictures you take are a form of literacy because you tell stories of people's lives by them. You seem to use pictures like some other people use words. If you take out the

soccer stuff, you might put in another point with some examples of papers you've written in the past. Are any of them about your dad? That would fit with what you call your frame (yeah, a good term!).

4. I don't think you have to start over even if you take out the soccer and rewrite the last paragraph, which I want to talk about now. Your dad is important, I know, but you need to emphasize yourself more. The lens of your camera needs to be on yourself. Pretty good use of language, huh!?
5. If you're worried about bragging, don't. Knowing about the essay contest would be helpful. Was your essay published anywhere? What other kinds of writing have you done? Also, I'd be interested if you write music. Is that like writing papers at all?
6. What is your major? Do you know what you want to be when you grow up?! I'm thinking that I should talk about my major in my paper, too, because it will involve lots of reading (I want to be a book critic for a newspaper) and ties to my "book history."

Stephen's Responses

1. Cut the soccer. It just doesn't add to the purpose of this paper.
2. I do like your paper because you seem to be really honest in it. It isn't a lot of BS to fill the assignment. You seem to be working out something in this paper. Sometimes I think you are concentrating on your dad too much. You've already moved beyond your dad in many ways. You can talk about yourself a lot in an autobiography.
3. Do you have any pictures of you writing or reading or something? I'd like to read a description of a picture of you as an example.
4. I hate to revise, so I hesitate to tell you this. But I think you can talk about your dad without making him so important. You can still use your "frame" but you can make yourself the center of the picture.
5. What else do you have to say about writing? I guess one question I've been asking myself is, "What shows I'm literate?" If more about writing shows you are literate, especially when you talk more about yourself, good.

6. I like examples. If you decide to write more about writing, use examples. The photographs you mentioned are good examples of what you're interested in and what you try to do with photography. Maybe you could do the same thing with some of your examples of writing. Hey, I know what you mean about things getting out of hand. Guess you'll have to decide when to stop.

Justin received some concrete suggestions from classmates when they responded to his Writer's Statement questions. In class he learned another way to improve the focus of his paper as he approached his first revision of his literacy autobiography. This technique is called freewriting.

FREEWRITING TO FOCUS AND DEVELOP IDEAS

Justin learned how to use freewriting to focus on his topic; however, freewriting is useful for many purposes. You will learn here some ways to do and use freewriting, read some examples, and then see how Justin used freewriting to focus the next draft of his paper.

Guidelines for Open Freewriting

1. Keep your hand or fingers moving, continuing to generate words, phrases, or sentences, without stopping to think logically, correct a spelling error, or scratch your head. You don't need to write fast, but you need to keep writing.
2. Look through your freewriting, underlining ideas that could provide topics for further writing if that is your goal in the freewriting.
3. Write in your dialogue journal about the various possibilities for topics. What would your purpose be in writing about each of the topics that surfaced in your freewriting? Who would want to read about the topic? What do you already know about the topic that you could use in the paper?
4. Ask a member of your class or writing group to read your freewriting and your dialogue journal entry about it. Does your reader see other potential topics? Which of the topics would she like to read about? Why?

Freewriting is a thinking strategy that frees you to put ideas on paper or on the computer without worrying about the constraints of formal writing. You cover the page or screen with lines of writing but without stopping to edit. You don't have to worry about writing complete sentences, making transitions, or punctuating or spelling correctly: you simply write anything that comes to mind. Often writers set a time limit of five or ten minutes to write anything, logical or not, that occurs to them in order to get out some ideas to work with.

If you are looking for a topic, for example, you may discover one or more possible topics as you do an open freewriting.

When you already have a topic, a *directed* freewriting may be more useful than open freewriting. Doing a directed freewriting takes more concentration and discipline than doing an open freewriting.

Guidelines for Directed Freewriting

1. Write a topic or a question you want to answer at the top of the page or screen. Focus your thinking on that topic and follow the guidelines for open freewriting: write for a predetermined amount of time; keep writing; and do not stop to correct spelling, punctuation, or sentence structure.
2. If you find yourself straying, get back on the topic by stopping the train of thought that leads elsewhere, drawing a line and starting anew, or acknowledging your drift by writing "Oh, no, I'm off the track" and by heading back into your subject.
3. When you have finished the directed freewriting, look at those places where you adjusted your writing to see whether you were really off track or whether you were starting to pursue an idea worth exploration that may prove to be related to your topic after all. Give your mind the benefit of the doubt: examine your side trips.
4. Write in your dialogue journal about what you discovered in your directed freewriting. For instance, if you were looking for more examples, list the examples that came out of your directed freewriting.
5. Ask a classmate to read your directed freewriting and your dialogue journal analysis of it. See if he agrees with your analysis or if he can find other useful information in the freewriting or journal entry.

Julie's English course combined reading and writing. One assignment in that course was to read and respond to Scott Russell Sanders's "The Singular First Person," the essay you read in chapter 1. Because the instructor in Julie's course was interested in students' defining the essay as a form, he made the following paper assignment: Discuss Sanders's characterizations of the essay in relation to your own experiences as a reader and writer of essays.

Julie's first task was to break down the assignment. It had two elements, one that asked Julie to identify and discuss Sanders's ideas about what an essay is and a second that asked Julie to relate her own experiences as a reader and writer of essays to Sanders's ideas about that particular form of writing. In fact, the assignment emphasized that Sanders's ideas about the essay should be discussed directly as they related to Julie's experience, not as separate, abstract ideas.

In preparing for this assignment, Julie decided to do a directed freewriting. First, she looked at Sanders's ideas about the essays, and then she spoke from her own experience. She chose to number her various ideas because she recorded them as she thought of them and they weren't necessarily related.

Julie's Directed Freewriting #1

Question to answer: What are Sanders's ideas about the essay form, and how does he express them?

1. Interesting introduction, grabs attention with humor and vivid language. Can visualize the scene through eyes of the writer as he becomes aware of the courage of the orator who speaks so openly--perhaps Sanders's first glimpse into the mind of the essayist (who he compares to orator.) Both open selves up to the audience, completely vulnerable--his thoughts open to scrutiny. Risky.
2. Is soapbox orator an egoist? Is essayist? Or do they want to share their thoughts and experiences with others for their benefit? Sanders dwells on the ego of essay writers--why do so many want to expose themselves to the world? He contrasts them to poets and fiction writers who hide behind imaginary characters and abstract ideas. How do essayists have the nerve to share their thoughts unless they have a strong sense of self?
3. Love his metaphors, even the "corny" ones. A good essayist uses language to clarify, gives particulars, avoids abstractions.

4. Sanders shows pleasure at breaking taboo against using I in composition. Says use of I is what keeps the readers attention.
5. Love the term "opinionated monologue."
6. The most important character in the essay is the singular first person--the author of the essay. The writers Sanders talks about are eclectic, writing about geology and other aspects of nature, including in this century and before. Montaigne was the first: I didn't know that. Sanders defends the individual essayists idiosyncrasies: he says that enables the essay to "command attention."
7. The center of the essay begins when Sanders celebrates his abdication of the old taboos against using "I". Up to this point, he exemplifies qualities of the essay by using examples of essayists. After this point, he continues his defense by quoting other essayists.
8. Don't know Sanders's background. He plainly enjoys the essay form of writing. He talks about the importance of writing from a region "close to the heart." I presume Sanders is an established literary figure since his advice to writers to distinguish themselves in another form first in order to speak with a voice of authority lends credibility to an "opinionated monologue."
9. Writing an essay on the essay is a clever method of teaching this genre. We not only learn its characteristics but get a perfect example of how it is accomplished in his own essay.
10. Sanders must have a solid literary background to use the authors he does. Uses the reinforcement of the various essayists whose words support his own. That's a skill.
11. I hope Sanders writes more. He has a wealth of knowledge and experiences, admirable writing skills, and a hint of self absorption that lend themselves to endless number of essays to be shared with readers.
12. I measure Sanders's success in writing this piece by my positive reaction to it. I will never read an essay in the same way again. My agreement or disagreement with the subject matter of essays will be outweighed by my new-found respect for the author who dares to share a piece of herself with the world.

In Julie's directed freewriting, you can see that she stays on her topic of exploring Sanders's ideas. She discusses Sanders's characterization of the essayist; his contrasts between poets, fiction writers, and essayists; and other important points. She addresses Sanders's use of metaphor and offers her own response to this language: "I love the term 'opinionated monologue.'" Julie has taken the first step toward fulfilling the assignment by including many of Sanders's main points in this directed freewriting.

The second step is for Julie to relate Sanders's points about the essay to her own experiences reading and writing essays. In a second directed freewriting, her focus is on her own experiences.

Julie's Directed Freewriting #2

Question to answer: How does your own experience relate to the points in Sanders's essay?

1. Description of early English instructor resembles mine! I'll never forget Sister Hilda's diligent efforts to limit the number of "I's" in a paper, certainly never beginning a paragraph with one, and rarely a sentence! I never thought about it much until now, reading Sanders's essay, the meaning behind the word "I." It carries more weight than I realized: it puts a writer on the line, exposes her.

   Maybe that's why essays are not easy for me. I am addicted to the abstract. I'm guilty of the "babble" in conversation that Sanders points out perfectly. Although I enjoy opinions, etc. of others, I can't imagine why anyone would want to read about me. But I am improving with experience and positive feedback. Since most of my essay-writing exercises are done in college courses, a safe haven for "opinionated monologue," I am happily getting both.
2. I don't know many of the writers in Sanders's essay. Bet I'd get something out of reading more essays by different writers.
3. My earliest memories of essay writing are from junior and senior high school when they usually had a negative connotation since they usually dealt with homework or test taking. Most essay writing since those early days has been connected with college courses. I don't usually read books of essays, but I read and enjoy an essay in magazines, such as in *Time*.

```
4. My father's frequent letters to the editor, although
   not classified as essay, gave me insight into the
   "opinionated monologue"!
5. Not being an expert in the essay, I have no
   disagreement with Sanders. I welcome any attempt such
   as that of Sanders to avoid some of the old strict
   rules of writing that I was taught. My proclivity for
   technical perfection often inhibits a free flow of
   thoughts and ideas and wastes time. His essay has
   awakened me to the fact that I have a tendency to
   hide behind the words "seem" and "appears," perhaps
   an attempt to lower the risk of appearing arrogant! I
   am improving with experience and time.
```

When Julie was finished with the directed freewriting, she wrote in her journal: "The directed freewriting exercise, one that I don't often use, was very helpful to me in preparing for the writing assignment. Highlighting Sanders's characteristics of the essay in the first exercise and comparing them to my own experiences as essay reader and writer in the second gave me some valuable ideas for the paper. . . . Sanders's essay and my freewriting on essay characteristics reveal that I wasn't completely aware of the essay form, that I've had some distorted beliefs about my own writing (that I am not allowed to 'seem' arrogant!), and that I can fully enjoy the essay outside academia for its content, sincerity, and rich language."

She explores further Sanders's discussion of the taboo on "I" and its effect on her own ideas about essays: "This awareness gave me insight into my reluctance to comfortably write essays which by Sanders's characterizations require a strong ego. It also suggests why I may be attracted to poetry and other more abstract forms of expression. I have been programmed from an early age and didn't even know it! The exercise also made me wonder: If I am open to others' writing and opinions, wouldn't others be open to mine? Perhaps I have been avoiding the 'I' for too long."

Julie clearly believes that the directed freewriting helped her formulate some important ideas that will be helpful in fulfilling the assignment. It allowed her to think on paper, yet encouraged her to direct her thinking to the elements of the assignment, making the exercise highly efficient. Most writers responding to an assignment of any sort have little time to waste. A directed freewriting offers both latitude and some boundaries to that latitude.

PRACTICE WITH DIRECTED FREEWRITING

1. Choose a text to which you wish to respond. You might select the Sanders essay, an editorial, a poem, a magazine article, or a selection from any

textbook in which you have been assigned some reading you hope to make sense of or to use as the basis for some writing.

2. Do a directed freewriting responding to the text. Write your topic or focus at the top of the paper. Write for at least ten minutes, or keep writing until you have put down as many ideas as the text elicits.
3. Read your directed freewriting. Underline ideas that seem useful or interesting. You may want to practice underlining the important points in Julie's first and second directed freewritings before you work with your own materials.
4. In another journal entry, discuss the practice of directed freewriting. You might consider some of the following questions as you reflect: What ideas did you generate that you would like to pursue? How was doing directed freewriting different from other ways that you have used to get started writing? If you were to continue with your writing about this topic, what would you do next?
5. Ask someone who has also done directed freewriting to read your directed freewriting and your discussion of it. Your reader might consider some of the following questions about the directed freewriting itself: What idea or ideas are interesting to you? What more would you like to know about them? Does the freewriting spark interest in the original text? Did the directed freewriting deal specifically with the text read? How do you know? Your reader might consider these other questions about the discussion of the directed freewriting: What did the writer get out of the freewriting? Was the writer's experience with directed freewriting similar to or different from your own? Do you see any ideas in the freewriting that the writer may have missed? Do you have any suggestions for further thinking or writing?

LOOPING TO GENERATE IDEAS

A combination of open freewriting and directed freewriting is another way to generate ideas: the combination is called looping. Looping encourages a writer to move deeper and deeper into a topic.

Guidelines for Looping

1. Begin with an open freewriting. When it is finished, choose from that freewriting one topic or idea that you want to explore further.
2. Write that idea at the top of your paper or computer screen. Use that idea to do a directed freewriting in which you generate only ideas related to that specific topic. If needed, do a second directed freewriting.

Bethany made a list of topics that emerged from an open freewriting in which she was trying to find a subject for an open topic assignment. Her list included waiting tables, being a student, her university campus, shoes, restaurants, being a new student, and walking. When her instructor asked her to analyze the list in her journal, she wrote, "I would be especially interested in writing about waiting tables as it would be a good chance to discuss personal experiences." From her open freewriting she picked the topic of her experiences with waiting tables to use for her directed freewriting.

The Directed Freewriting Part of Bethany's Looping

I worked at Swensons in Indianapolis for a year and learned that waiting tables is lots of work but very enjoyable too. I got to put my theatrical skills into practice. I had regular customers who got to know me but sometimes with strangers I used my Jersey accent and sometimes I was just perky--difficult acting for me! I could decide how to be when I saw who my customers were. I really liked the kitchen staff too. The cooks were my friends, young Black guys mostly who played great music on their radio back there while goldie oldies filled the dining room. They would make me dinner when I was tired --whatever I wanted. I found out that the kitchen staff can make your job as a waitress easy or very hard. It's important to have a good relationship with them.

From this directed freewriting, Bethany decided to write about the importance of waitresses developing a good relationship with kitchen staff. She could have done another directed freewriting on that topic to continue her looping. She had narrowed from her open freewriting on possible topics to a focus on waiting tables in her directed writing and, finally, could have done another directed freewriting on the importance of a waitress having good relationships with the kitchen staff.

You can follow the same process or part of it to prepare for a piece of writing when you choose the topic. You might even extend the exercise as Bethany could have, pulling an idea out of the second freewriting, looping down into yet another directed freewriting. The more times you loop and focus, the narrower the topic becomes and the more specifics will emerge for your paper.

PRACTICE WITH LOOPING

1. Do a looping. Begin with a new open freewriting or return to an open freewriting you have already done. Write or enter a topic from the open freewriting at the top of your page or screen. Follow the guidelines on page

53 for a directed freewriting. If you find yourself straying, look at the top of the page or the first screen, literally refocusing your attention.

2. In your journal, write about the material in the looping. Did your ideas become more specific? Underline material that you might use in further writing. List the possible topics for further writing. What material would you choose to ignore? Why? Who would want to read about those topics? Why?
3. Exchange journals with a classmate. Respond to her choices. What other potential topics do you see? Which of those topics would you want to read about? Why?

Because Justin knew that he needed to focus more in the next draft of his literacy autobiography, he decided to use looping. He did three looping exercises concerning examples of papers he had written in the past, his contest-winning essay, and photos he had taken that might say something about his literacy development.

For the first looping exercise, Justin typed at the top of his screen "Papers I Have Written" and gave himself five minutes to write. This directed freewriting resulted in the identification of four pieces of writing not mentioned in his draft.

Justin's Looping for Paper 1, Literacy Autobiography

I wish I was at home where I have some papers in a box in my closet, but I'll do the best I can from memory. I remember writing a poem in elementary school. It was supposed to be about my family, but I lied. I wrote a poem about a dad, mom, girl, and boy who led the American apple pie sort of life. The teacher really liked it. I never mentioned my dad was gone. I wrote a short story in junior high. I really remember that one. I didn't know we'd have to let other people in class read it. I wrote about being a big stud who had all the girlfriends I wanted. I was so lucky to get Becky Jenkins as a reader. She was too nice to make fun of me, at least to my face. I avoided her like crazy after that though. My best research paper ever was on Alfred Stieglitz, the photographer. He really inspired me. I actually used many sources without copying from any of them. I didn't need to copy because I actually had

```
something to say about him. I talked about the way his
ideas about framing pictures came from his purposes in
taking the pictures. No one that I read had said what I
said before. I'm running out of time. In high school I
wrote a poem about learning from other people,
especially my music teacher.
```

When Justin read this directed freewriting, he circled the sentences about the junior high experience and about the research paper. For his looping, he decided to write more about the Stieglitz paper.

```
    I remember reading that Stieglitz wrote to Georgia
O'Keeffe once about framing her pictures. She had asked
why they had to be framed. He had said that paintings
might lose some freedom in frames--but there was no
other way to protect them for viewers. I remember he
wrote to her "Life again!" I like that. Even if life
does not have frames around parts of it, art has to.
    S. also answered questions about his own photos. He
talked about how a single item in the center of a photo
could call for a certain kind of frame around it. I
wonder why I liked that answer. I think I liked it
because I had the same feeling when I took pictures
sometimes. I remember one picture of my uncle fishing
that needed the big lake and distant trees around it to
show that one reason he liked fishing was that he felt a
small part of larger nature. I had to use a wide lens to
get it all in.
```

Justin then did one more directed freewriting in the looping process. He decided that his realization about one basic difference between life and art might be useful in his paper, so he wrote "Frames in life and in art" at the top of his screen. His resulting entry revealed to him a way to show how life without his father had influenced his uses of art to make sense of his life.

The trouble with life is that you can't choose your frames. In photography you can so you can decide what you want to say about something. You can control things. Being literate means that. You can understand something by seeing it in relation to other things. When you read you compare stuff to your own life. When you write you pick out only certain stuff to tell. What's important about being literate? You need many ways to understand and control life even if life is really uncontrollable.

Notice that Justin is struggling here toward ideas about the uses of literacy and the relationship of literacy to living one's life. From a specific example of an idea within a paper, he moves to a higher level of abstraction. Although the original response to his draft asked for more specific examples of papers he has written, he has generated not only an example of a specific paper, the research paper on Stieglitz, but also an important conceptual idea that could influence his entire literacy autobiography.

Next Justin did a looping about the essay in the contest. He wrote the name of the essay at the top of a sheet of paper and did a directed freewriting. Then, for a second directed freewriting in his looping, he chose one point from that freewriting, that winning an essay contest helped him know that he had good ideas.

It's hard to know if you really have anything to say that's worth it. My friend Lucia writes poems that she never shows to anyone because she's sure no one else will like them. I used to be that way about my writing before I was required to enter the essay contest and won it. That's the way with music too. I can play all I want in my basement. But, when people applaud when our band plays I feel it in my bones. I know that my music is being understood. Are you literate if you don't know if anyone else understands you?

Finally, Justin did a looping about pictures he had taken. After an initial directed freewriting, he made a list of the photos he remembered that seemed pertinent to this essay.

my mom reading to my sister when she was little
our band
my uncle fishing
the Tomb of the Unknown Soldier at Arlington
my grandma baking cookies
the sign in front of the library that announces story hours
Maria from Sesame Street when she visited our mall
Melissa Etheridge when we saw her in concert

He then did a directed freewriting about the Maria picture.

I grew up watching Sesame Street. Maria was as familiar to me as my relatives. In this picture I tried to get Maria surrounded by the kids who had come to see her but also by the stuff for sale in the store window that she was standing in front of. I thought that she was trying to show the kids an alternative to the store's stuff. Learning about letters and numbers would allow them a way past the stuff. They could go beyond the commercial junk to understand something more important. I'm amazed that I thought of that. Did I think of it then or only now?

Justin has developed during these looping exercises some more rich material to mine as he returns to his draft. He can be more focused on his own literacy development rather than on the influence of his father, who rarely turns up in these looping exercises. His instructor, however, suggested that he try another technique that would also help him focus his piece.

CLUSTERING TO VISUALIZE IDEAS

Do you understand things better when you can visualize them? Some people are visual learners; that is, they process information through seeing visual representations. This next way to learn can help anyone, but particularly visual learners like Justin who learns through photography. When you try clustering, you will find out if this way of generating information, linking ideas, and focusing on ideas suits your way of learning.

In clustering, you create a spatial relationship among ideas. When you cluster, instead of listing ideas, you work outward from the topic or central focus, creating clusters or groups of ideas that are somehow connected.

Guidelines for Clustering

1. In the center of a page, write a single word or idea. Draw a circle around the word or idea.
2. Write a related idea beyond the circle. Draw a circle around that idea and a line to connect it to the original circle.
3. Write your next idea. Circle it and draw a line from it to the idea with which it is connected.
4. Continue to write down ideas until you have exhausted the topic. Then read the words you have written and draw more lines between any circled ideas that are connected in some way.
5. At the bottom of the page, write words to complete the following sentence: "If I were to write on this topic, I would _______."

Because people think differently, employ this strategy at different stages of their work, and have varying levels of knowledge about their topics, no two clusters look alike. The samples you see here take different shapes and employ different approaches yet still accomplish the general purposes of the cluster.

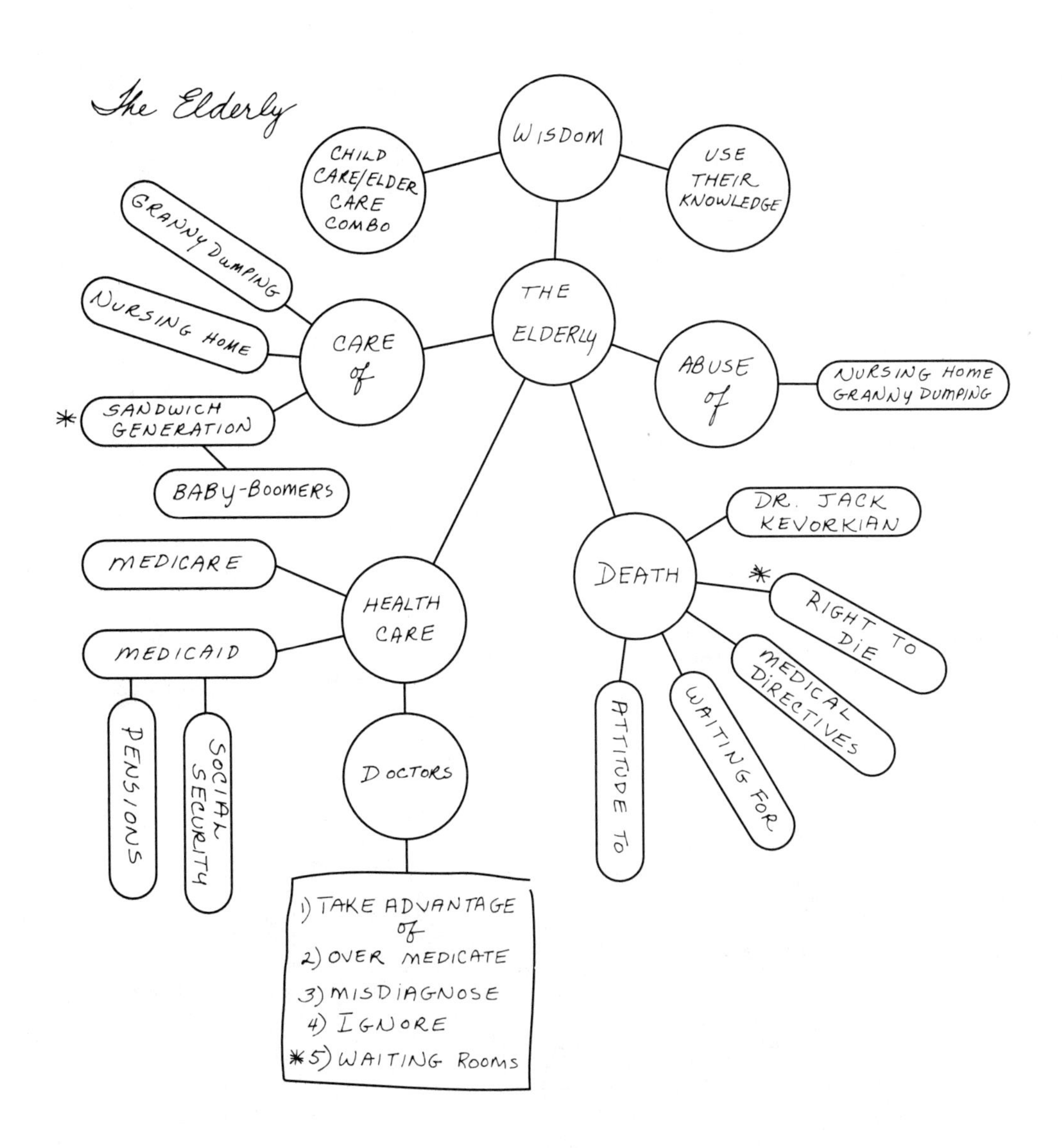
The Elderly
WISDOM
CHILD CARE/ELDER CARE COMBO
USE THEIR KNOWLEDGE
THE ELDERLY
CARE of
GRANNY DUMPING
NURSING HOME
* SANDWICH GENERATION
BABY-BOOMERS
ABUSE of
NURSING HOME GRANNY DUMPING
HEALTH CARE
MEDICARE
MEDICAID
PENSIONS
SOCIAL SECURITY
DOCTORS
1) TAKE ADVANTAGE of
2) OVER MEDICATE
3) MISDIAGNOSE
4) IGNORE
*5) WAITING ROOMS
DEATH
DR. JACK KEVORKIAN
* RIGHT TO DIE
MEDICAL DIRECTIVES
WAITING FOR
ATTITUDE TO

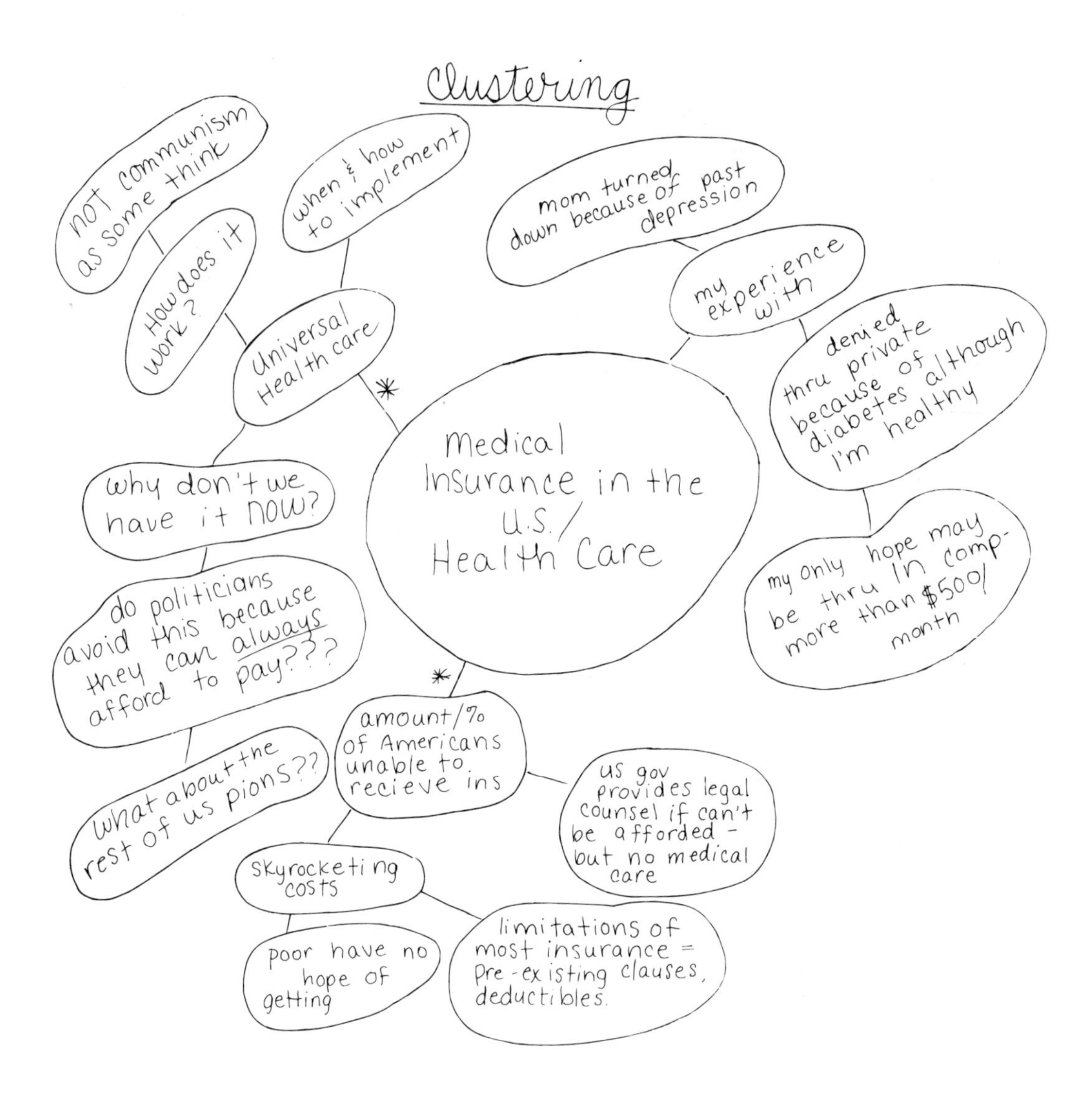
Clustering
Medical Insurance in the U.S./ Health Care
Universal Health care
How does it work?
not communism as some think
when & how to implement
why don't we have it now?
do politicians avoid this because they can always afford to pay???
what about the rest of us pions??
my experience with
mom turned down because of past depression
denied thru private because of diabetes although I'm healthy
my only hope may be thru In comp- more than $500/ month
amount/% of Americans unable to recieve ins
US gov provides legal counsel if can't be afforded - but no medical care
skyrocketing costs
poor have no hope of getting
limitations of most insurance = pre-existing clauses, deductibles.

JIM GARRISON

CLAY SHAW DAVID FERRE

- WHY WERE HIS OFFICERS BUGGED?
- WERE THEY BUGGED?
- WHY DID HE HAVE SO MUCH TROUBLE W/HIS SUBPOENAS OF ITEMS RELATING TO THE ASSASSINATION?

JACK RUBY

- HOW DID HE GET INTO THE BASEMENT OF DALLAS CITY JAIL?
- HOW DID HE GET IN W/ A GUN
- WHY WAS HE JAILED W/OUT BAIL?
- WHY WAS HE QUESTIONED W/OUT AN ATTORNEY?
- HAD HE ACTUALLY MET OSWALD?

LEE HARVEY OSWALD

- IF HE WAS SUCH A POOR SHOT, BORN OUT BY HIS MARKSMAN'S RECORD IN THE MARINE CORPS, HOW DID HE THEN ASSASSINATE PRES. KENNEDY – AND WITH A RIFLE OF NOTABLY POOR MANUFACTURE?

- HOW DID HE GET FROM THE SIXTH FLOOR TO THE SECOND FLOOR SNACKROOM, BUY A COKE, OPEN IT UP, BE TAKING A SIP, ALL UNDER SEVENTY SECONDS, WHEN A POLICEMAN BURST IN THE ROOM, AND, NOT BE OUT OF BREATH?

- HOW IN THE HECK DID HE DEFECT TO RUSSIA, MARRY THE DAUGHTER OF A HIGH-RANKING RUSSIAN SOLDIER, AND THEN BE ALLOWED BACK IN THE U.S., WITH HIS WIFE, AND FUNDED BY A CHECK FROM THE STATE DEPT.?

- WHY WAS OSWALD QUESTIONED BY THE CHIEF OF THE DALLAS P.D., W/OUT A LAWYER AND W/OUT A TAPE RECORDER – IMMEDIATELY AFTER HIS ARREST?

WHO DID IT?

WHO STOOD TO GAIN?

THE ASSASSINATION OF PRES. JOHN KENNEDY

- WHY WAS THE AUTOPSY INTERRUPTED IN DALLAS, THEN THE BODY TAKEN BACK TO D.C., AGAINST TEXAS LAW AND PERFORMED BY SOLDIERS WHO WERE DOCTORS, BUT UNTRAINED A PATHOLOGISTS?

FBI

- WHY WAS THE PARADE ROUTE CHANGED THE LAST DAY?
- WHY WERE SECURITY PRECAUTIONS SO LAX?
- HOW WERE PEOPLE ABLE TO WATCH FROM OPEN WINDOWS, WITH CLEAR SHOT(S) AT JFK?
- IF OSWALD MADE THE SHOTS, WHY COULD NONE OF THE FBI'S BEST MARKSMAN DUPLICATE HIS FEAT?
- WHY WAS THE MOTORCADS ALLOWED TO SLOW DOWN TO 11 MPH ON THE TURN ONTO ELM (?), INSTEAD OF MAINTAINING A SPEED OF 44 MPH – PER FBI REGULATION?

THE WARREN COMMISSION

GERALD FORD / EARL WARREN

- MAGIC BULLET THEORY
- LONE ASSASSIN
- WHY DID SO MANY WITNESSES REPORT THAT THEIR TESTIMONY HAD BEEN ALTERED?
- WHY DID THEY REJECT THE TESTIMONIES WHICH GAVE REPORTS OF SEEING SMOKE COMING FROM DIRECTIONS OTHER THAN THE BOOK DEPOSITORY?

THE MOB

- WERE THEY INVOLVED?
- PISSED OFF BECAUSE OF THE BAY OF PIGS?
- DID THEY CONTRIBUTE TO THE ASSASSINATION?
- COULD THEY HAVE ANYTHING TO GAIN?

The first cluster, on the elderly, is done entirely in words and phrases. The second, on medical insurance, combines phrases, questions, and sentences. The form, however, is not important: the ideas themselves and what you learn about the ideas from seeing them grouped in the cluster are the point of the clustering.

The writer of the first cluster can see that her ideas about doctors and the elderly are more specific than her ideas about death. In the second cluster, the writer asks some important questions about American health care as well as considering her personal connection to the topic.

Another student generated a cluster that looks very different from the first two examples but which achieves a similar purpose of focusing. An English major with an interest in recent American history, David was preparing to write in response to the following assignment: Write a paper about a significant event in America in the last fifty years. From his work as a tutor in the University Writing Center, David knew that this assignment was extremely broad. Even when he decided on the assassination of John F. Kennedy as his topic, he wrote in his journal, "What a broad topic!" As an experienced writer, he knew that he could not possibly discuss in a single paper what had already been examined in thousands of books, reports, articles, and movies. To narrow his focus, he did a cluster on the topic of the Kennedy assassination. In his clustering, David separated the material into subtopics that could provide the narrower focus he was looking for, but he also broke those subtopics down even further and began to make connections among the subtopics.

David's cluster clearly divides the assassination into a number of its aspects: people involved, groups involved, and important questions. As you look at the parts of the cluster, you can see the further narrowing that he describes in his journal: "Clustering offered me a chance to let my mind drift onto one facet of the assassination at a time. I could see how I could narrow the topic." Originally, David believed that the volume of material he had generated about Oswald pointed to the accused assassin as the narrowed topic for the paper: "It was easy to see that pursuing Oswald's involvement was the way to go." But later he remarked, "I could also see how I could narrow the topic further, perhaps to his rifleman's record or how he was able to defect and then return. This also showed me how far I could move from that broad topic in the middle but still investigate a piece of it."

PRACTICE WITH CLUSTERING

1. Think of a topic to explore, one from a current assignment, a directed freewriting, a journal entry, or some reading you have done. In the center of a large sheet of paper, write your topic with a circle around it. Then write down everything that the topic evokes from you. Write ideas that seem related close together in circles around the central circle. When you start on

a new tangent, move to another space near the center circle. Write until you run out of ideas.

2. Read your cluster. Draw lines between entries that seem related. Put asterisks beside parts of the cluster that intrigue you. Explain your cluster to another person, including more about those parts that most interest you. At the bottom of your page, finish the following sentence: "If I were to write on this topic, I would _____."
3. In your journal, write about clustering. How did it work for you? How does it compare with other ways of generating ideas on which to focus? What would you do next if you followed the leads you got from clustering?
4. Exchange clusters and journals with a classmate. Read your partner's cluster and respond to his journal reflections on clustering. What similarities and differences are there in the ways you and the writer responded to the cluster? Do you see anything else the writer might want to consider? If the writer were to pursue the topic or perspective derived from his cluster, would you be interested in reading about it? Why or why not? Were your partner's and your experiences with clustering as a way to learn about your topic similar or different? In what ways?

Using Clustering to Relate Ideas

Justin decided to do a cluster around the saxophone: he was still unsure how to relate his musical side to literacy. Although he hadn't asked the question in his Writer's Statement because he was at that time more worried about other parts of his draft, he later wondered about the emphasis on feelings in the paragraph on music. Justin's cluster revealed that understanding feelings is a part of his sense of the uses of literacy.

Notice that some items on the cluster labeled feelings. Justin was not surprised that the word *sad* appeared, but he was surprised at the word *joy.* Also, Justin read *way of expressing my feelings* as an indication that like other kinds of literacy that help us make sense of the world, his saxophone playing served him as a mechanism for understanding life. Justin wrote about the cluster: "I need to think about the definition of literacy as including the ability to express oneself, whether in words or musical notes or whatever. Also I want to change the paragraph on the sax to show that my music helps me express and understand good things too." Justin decided in his revision to focus more on the ways that playing the saxophone helped him understand himself and the world through music.

At this point Justin was ready to write another draft of his paper, based partly on what he had learned from his looping and clustering.

Justin's Clustering for Paper 1, Draft 2
Literacy Autobiography

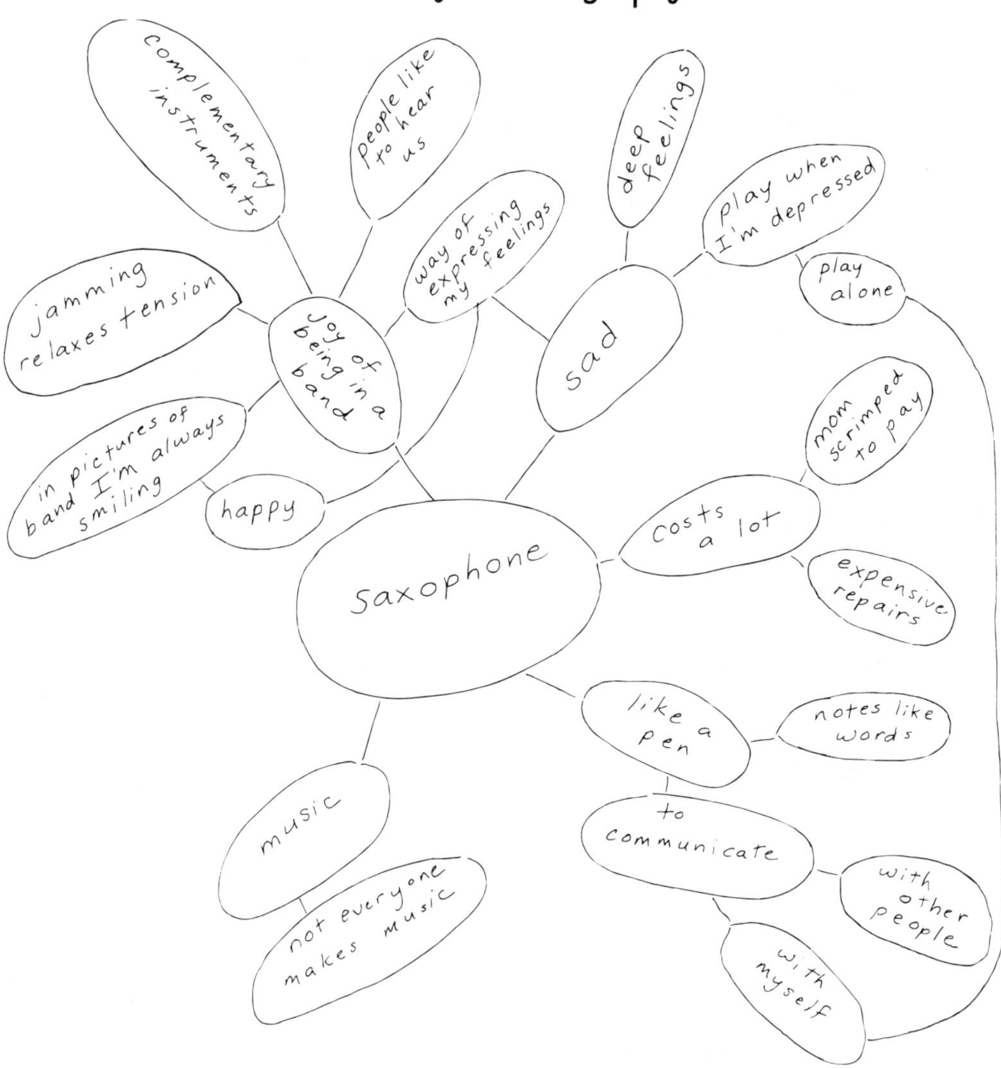

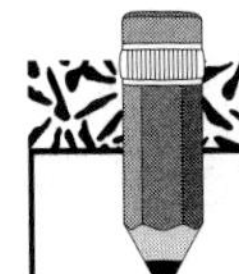

Justin's Paper 1, Draft 2, Literacy Autobiography

Diving Away from the Wreck

My girlfriend likes poetry. When she read some poems to me from a book by Adrienne Rich called *Diving Into the Wreck* I began thinking about how my life has been the opposite. I've been avoiding a wreck, using language like Rich and also pictures and sounds. Now, however, I'm ready to move toward a new stage in my life, hopefully through my college education.

Although my dad left our family when I was three partly because he couldn't advance on his jobs with his lack of reading ability my mom supported me in every way. The most important way was in promoting reading. When I was little she read to me every day. I liked animal stories, so she read the entire Black Stallion series and books like *Bambi*. We had a deal that she would pay for half of any book that I wanted to buy. We used the library most of the time, but if I wanted a book I had to save only half the price from my allowance or paper delivery money. The first book I bought was *Lassie Comes Home*. One thing I liked about stories was that they had a beginning, middle, and end. Even if not everything turned out the way you wanted you could understand from the story why the ending was as it was.

Two experiences with photography taught me that pictures are another way of understanding the world, the goal of all kinds of literacies. In third grade the Polaroid Company sponsored a contest in which I won a free camera. I took pictures of my house, my neighborhood, my mom, my sister, and events in our family. Later I received a Kodak 16 millimeter of my own. I have albums with pictures of Uncle Jim's fortieth birthday party, of my sister's room with all the posters of Hootie and the Blowfish, and of the roses that my mom cultivated each year. I have pictures of my Boy Scout troops trip to Gatlinburg, Tennessee, my sixth grade class production of *You're a Good Man, Charlie Brown,* and my junior prom. I also liked to take pictures of people shopping, of homeless people asking for money, and of sidewalk vendors. When I took many of these pictures I didn't understand why I felt satisfaction taking them. Writing a research paper on Alfred Stieglitz helped me understand.

In this most original research paper I have written to date I wrote about the way that Stieglitz talked about framing. He wrote to Georgia O'Keeffe once about framing her pictures. She had asked why they had to be framed. He had said that paintings might lose some freedom in frames--but there was no other way to protect them for viewers. I remember he wrote to her "Life again!" I interpreted that to mean that even if life does not have frames around parts of it art has to be understandable and enduring. Stieglitz also talked about his own photographs within each picture was an item that called for a certain kind of frame around it. I understood what he meant. I remember using a wide lens to get a picture of my uncle fishing that needed the big lake and distant trees around it to show that one reason he liked fishing was that he felt a small part of larger nature. In life you can't choose your frames like I couldn't choose that my dad left me, but in photography you can control what you want to frame. You can understand something by seeing it in relation to other things. Being literate includes comparing what you read to your own life, picking out something particular from your whole life to write about, and taking pictures that mean something. We each need many ways to understand and control life even if life is really uncontrollable.

Another way that I am literate is through music. Playing the saxophone helps me express my feelings that are part of my life. Better than writing for expressing sad feelings is playing the sax, especially playing jazz. But, I can also express happiness with music. Sometimes the sadness and happiness are mixed, just like words can have two meanings at the same time. I try to understand life through music as well as through words and pictures. It's the greatest when other people understand what I'm trying to say through my playing. When people applaud our band I know that I am being understood. Part of being literate is being able to express yourself so somebody else understands.

I'm now nineteen, and I am a student, a bookstore employee, a roommate, a boyfriend, and still a son and brother. I'm not a father yet, but I have the advantage of reading and writing and having other ways of expressing myself and understanding the world that my father did not. My literacy history is already different from my dad's and I intend my future to be different too. I am moving in a positive direction in college as I continue living my literacy.

ANALYZING JUSTIN'S DRAFT

After you have read and reread Justin's current draft, answer each of his Writer's Statement questions below. Although Justin will be moving on to another paper, he will have the opportunity later to revise again before he decides whether to include this piece in his Course Portfolio. He will rely on answers to his questions from other readers to help him decide on revising.

Justin's Writer's Statement for Paper 1, Draft 2, Literacy Autobiography

1. I tried to focus more on me than on my dad in this draft. Is the paper more focused on me? Does it say enough about me to give a full picture or to qualify as a literacy autobiography?
2. I left out the soccer stuff and the last part about my dad. I'm not sure I added enough examples like Stephen wanted. I almost think I need to talk to someone about that because I can't remember enough.
3. I like the part about Stieglitz. I have a lot more I could say about what I learned from that paper. But I'm afraid I'd get that part out of balance. It might seem more important than something else.
4. I realize that I haven't talked about the essay contest. It would fit the idea of having other people understand you. But I think I have enough in the

essay already. What do you think? Should I include the essay contest stuff?

5. When I read Jackie's draft in class today, I liked the way that she used dialogue. She had actual quotes from people. Do you think that I should use some quotes in my paper? Why?

REVISING YOUR PAPER

You have read the ways in which other writers have prepared themselves to revise their drafts. You may have already used some strategies to generate more material, reorganize your ideas, or concentrate on another aspect of your writing that you want to improve in a next draft. To improve focus, you may now want to use questions and responses, open and directed freewriting, looping, and clustering. As you work on Paper 1, Draft 2, use your own resources and those of others to help you revise.

1. In your dialogue journal write about your revision objectives. Use this entry to remind you as you revise of the areas within the piece that you want to improve.
2. Write Draft 2 of Paper 1. Follow guidelines supplied by your instructor.
3. Create a Writer's Statement so that your peers and your instructor can respond to those areas on which you want to focus.

WORKING PORTFOLIO UPDATE

To add to your Working Portfolio, you now have a series of exercises with freewriting, looping, and clustering, and another draft of your paper. You also will want to keep all the responses that you have from readers of your exercises and drafts. These responses will provide evidence for your analysis of your term's work when you write the introduction to your Course Portfolio.

In the next chapter your repertoire of ways to answer questions in Writer's Statements will expand to include multiple other ways to respond to the writing of another person and to your own writing. Because the meaning of a piece of writing is complete only when it is understood and interpreted by readers, responding to writing is an important part of the writing process.

CHAPTER 4 Responding to Writing

I remember the first time that I handed a piece of my writing to another student in graduate school. I shuddered from what is called the impostor syndrome: I was sure that the other student knew more about my subject than I did, was a better writer, and would discover that I didn't belong in the graduate program. To my pleasant surprise, the more experienced student not only thought I had a promising idea but also had some suggestions about where to find more material and how to reorganize one part of my paper.

With little practice in assessing my own writing and in asking for response from other writers, I had been deprived of the benefits of having a reader. I wasn't a very good reader of my own writing and knew little about how to ask questions of my classmates. I saw my instructors only as overwhelmingly intelligent scholars who certainly did not need my questions to lead them to the parts of my papers that needed improvement. Patti, a student in an introductory writing class, had apprehensions similar to mine. For her first finished product, Patti consciously kept the paper short. When she was asked if length were a serious concern for her, she replied, "You know, I've had favorable comments so far on my writing, but I know the day's going to come when somebody's going to say, 'This is junk, this is no good.' And so I feel real nervous about putting it out there, because what I think is okay and what I think I wanted to say, somebody else might wonder why I'm even in here. And I feel kind of like I'm . . . vulnerable, I guess. So I decided to limit the length, hoping to limit . . . the criticism, I guess. At least it would be over fast."

Getting it over with fast or not sharing work at all is the wish of some writers who have had bad experiences with readers of their work or who simply don't know what the experience will be like. If you are apprehensive as Patti and I were when we first shared our work, this chapter will provide you with ways to read your own writing and ways to be a helpful reader for other writers. Up to this point, you have read and made responses to Writer's Statements, one type of exchange between reader and writer. You have also seen how Justin used his peers' responses to his Writer's Statement on his literacy autobiography. Other response methods, however, can be similarly beneficial as you compose and revise your papers.

Because writing is a social act, a piece of writing needs to be written *and* to be read to have a completed meaning. When you read your writing or someone else's, you are helping to create the meaning of the piece of writing.

Sometimes you will be the reader of your own writing. In a portfolio process you have time to distance yourself from early drafts so that you gain perspective on your writing. In this chapter you will learn how to be a better reader of your own writing through tracing your writing process, responding to your proposal, and revisiting goals through writing on the response side of your dialogue journal about earlier entries. You will also continue to compose Writer's Statements that reflect your concerns about your writing and that help other readers understand how they might help you as readers.

Sometimes other people will be the readers. They bring a different perspective to that role, offering you a more objective, and perhaps longer, view of your work. Reading a draft of a paper later in the term, classmates may suggest that you use a technique from that draft as you revise an earlier piece for your Course Portfolio. In this chapter you will learn about ways that readers can respond to writing through computer conferences, descriptive analyses, and identification of powerful words.

RESPONDING TO YOUR OWN WORK

Three ways to respond to your own work are tracing your writing process, responding to your proposal, and revisiting goals. Each of these methods enables you to serve as an effective reader of your own work.

Tracing the Process

Although most people think of reading their papers as the only way to read their own writing, reading your own writing process can also be productive. Keeping a record of how you produced a paper enables you to see productive and nonproductive patterns. For example, Jack, who wanted to write on the value of contemplation, traced the evolution of his second draft of a paper. As he thought about the work he had done between two weekly class meetings, he wrote the following dialogue journal entry.

Jack's Dialogue Journal Entry

Today, Tuesday, February 9, we must explain how our papers got to their present forms from the messes of last week. Personally, my paper had some major changes from one week to the next. When Melanie read my paper aloud, I understood why we were doing this protocol stuff. I immediately saw that my paper was very boring and filled with nothing but experiences of others. She didn't even have to give her opinion for me to know that.

Wednesday saw me going about my business of rewriting my paper. I took almost all of the quotes out and told my own feelings. I then went to bed.

Thursday, I looked over my lines and liked it a little better. One concern I have is my disrespect for any topic. I usually try to stay away from the normal way and have a distinctive paper. This would of course be all right if I had a motive and better way to write, but I only do it to stay away from others.

Friday, I shaped it up a little and put quotes in to try and back up my stance. I then got a puppy from the humane society.

Saturday and Sunday were domestic days with said puppy.

Monday I edited my paper and wrote a bibliography.

Notice all that Jack has learned and can learn from "reading" his own process. He noticed the value of hearing his writing read aloud by someone else, the importance of using other authorities not to build an argument but to buttress his own argument, and his problem with motivation as he approaches topics. Analyzing this chronological scan of his writing week, he can note that he worked on his writing five of seven days, left editing appropriately to the end of the process, and felt differently about the piece when he could look at the revision after a night's sleep. Describing and analyzing the process of writing can help Jack as he composes and revises his next piece.

Responding to Your Proposal

You can focus on your own work in another way by responding to your proposal. In chapter 1 you read Julie's proposal for a paper on her return to school as an adult. You looked also at the cues that Julie gave herself about how to read her next paper.

Julie has contributed toward her Course Portfolio because she has a record from her dialogue journal entries, proposal, readers' written responses on drafts, drafts, paper, Writer's Statement, and journal reflection. When she describes and evaluates her work over the term, she will be able to track her progress. Notice that she already is looking ahead to feeling less apprehensive about putting together a paper. At the end of the term, she will be able to analyze the reasons that she is or is not more at ease with producing a paper.

Revisiting Goals

When you set goals at the beginning of this term, you had areas on which you wanted to concentrate as you began your learning and writing. Rereading those goals is another way to make you a better reader of your own writing. When I read a book on theology, I have a purpose: right now I am reading Carol Newsom and Sharon Ringe's *The Women's Bible Commentary* in my feminist theology discussion group to discover the newest scholarship about the authentic place of women in the *Bible.* When I read *Redbook,* I have the goal of entertaining myself with short articles and attractive pictures. When I read a draft of a student paper, I read to learn from new ideas and to answer questions on the Writer's Statement.

As you read your latest draft, you may do so in terms of the goals that you set for yourself. If one of your goals is writing complete sentences, you can watch for fragments or run-on sentences. If one of your goals is using figurative language, you can look for metaphors. If you are trying to diversify your sources of evidence, you can note the variety of periodicals, the number of authorities, or the ethnic makeup of your interviewees.

Your goals can supply a perspective from which to read your work that ties the reading to other writing from the term and over time. For example, if a class goal is that each class member will try several genres during the term, you may note that so far narratives dominate your pieces of writing. Even if not expressly assigned by your instructor, you may, therefore, determine to write an analytical piece in order to practice expository prose. In reading your own draft you would ask yourself if the piece fulfills its analytical purpose. The goal of genre diversity pushes you beyond the reading of only one piece to consideration of the body of work in your Working Portfolio. From that body of work you will later choose pieces for your Course Portfolio that exemplify progress toward your goals.

PRACTICE WITH YOUR ROLE AS A READER OF YOUR OWN PROCESS AND PRODUCTS

1. For the next week, record in your dialogue journal your writing activities every day. If you are trying to learn what your patterns of writing are in general, you might record every type of writing that you do, including

making grocery lists, writing Grandma, answering a survey, filling out health forms, and writing an academic paper. If you are more interested in how you produce your papers for your writing class, you might record all activities that contributed to the writing, including thinking about a topic while commuting, talking with a friend about her perspective, conducting a phone interview with an authority, jotting notes during a boring lecture in history, doing a cluster, making a journal entry, and writing a first draft.

a. Bring your dialogue journal entries to class. Ask a classmate to respond in your journal, answering questions that you pose about the entries or responding to the processes that the reader sees. Discuss your process with classmates. Compare and contrast their processes with your own. What from their experiences is useful to you?

b. Then, if you have been writing a draft during this week, look at your draft. Can you identify certain features of your draft that have been directly affected by your process? For example, your procrastination in setting an interview with a vital source of information may account for the scanty evidence for one of your main points. The acquisition of a spellcheck for your computer may mean that you have all words correctly spelled, even in a draft, for the first time in your life. Or you may see how getting a reader response from a friend early in the week enabled you to make important changes in organization before bringing your first draft to class.

c. Next, write in your dialogue journal about changes you will make in your process during the upcoming week(s).

d. Repeat this recording and analyzing for at least three weeks to become conscious of your process and to enable you to read your writing process productively. This information will be very useful to you when you write your portfolio introduction.

2. Write a proposal for the next paper that you want to write. Answer the following questions in the proposal.

   a. What is the purpose of this paper for you? What is the purpose of this paper for your reader(s)?

   b. Who is the audience for this paper? In other words, who do you think might want or need to read it?

   c. Why are you a good person to write this paper? Do you have a particular interest in the topic? Do you have a novel perspective on the topic? Do you have prior knowledge on which to build the paper?

   d. What perspective are you taking on the topic? Why?

   e. What other important considerations are you making as you approach the writing of this paper?

Once you have finished a draft of the paper, return to your proposal. Read your draft in terms of your original intentions. Because we discover ideas and perspectives as we write, you may have changed intentions as you wrote; however, the proposal provides one way to read insightfully what you have actually written. In your dialogue journal, record what you have learned from looking back at a proposal after writing a paper.

PRACTICE IN ASSESSING PROGRESS TOWARD GOALS

Reread the goals for this writing course. In your dialogue journal write about those goals toward which you have made progress. For each goal toward which you claim progress, supply some evidence of your achievement. You may choose to refer to other dialogue journal entries, either your entry or another's response; your use of a strategy such as clustering; your methods of gathering information; instructor responses to your writing; or other sources that show your progress. Are there goals toward which you or your classmates have not made progress? If so, how do you account for the lack of progress? Has one goal been replaced by another one? Do you need to make the change on your list of goals so that you will assess yourself against a functional list of goals? Or how can you change your own work or the work of the class to ensure more progress toward the goal(s)?

RESPONDING TO THE PROCESS AND PRODUCTS OF OTHER WRITERS

You can also learn about your own writing from responding to the writing of others by yourself or within a group. Useful methods are conversations on computer, dialogue journal responses to drafts, descriptive analyses, and identification of powerful words. Other methods for response groups include real-time conferences on computer, read alouds, peer-group discussions about Writer's Statements, playing the opposition, and upping the ante.

Jack and Julie both mention having conversations with readers about writing in progress. Talking about writing is part of the process of writing; however, unless a writer takes extensive notes, some of the richness of the conversation can be lost. Conversing on the computer is one way to solve that problem. Some computer systems enable real-time conversations: a writing group can write simultaneous responses to a draft and to one another's responses. With a hard copy of the conversation session, the writing group has a record of the interchange to learn from as writers and as readers.

On-Line Conversation

The following conversation followed Tami's reading aloud her draft of a paper on modeling. Tami had just participated in a model search, which is a gathering of potential models hoping to be picked by a modeling agency. She had collected photographs, traveled to another city, undergone an emotionally draining modeling session, and returned with new questions and insights about her proposed profession. The first draft of her paper contained a great deal of information about the modeling world and some description of her recent experience. Tami, her classmates, and her two teachers conversed on-line about possibilities for Tami's paper.

Barbara: I learned something about modeling from this piece, especially the *what* of the Manhattan Model Search. But, I'm not sure what you want a reader to get out of this piece. Some of it seems to be straight reporting, but I read glimmers of a perspective: you state or imply that because perceptions of beauty change, don't get discouraged; believe in yourself; and try different kinds of opportunities.

Did you come up with these ideas from the search only? Your references to sources make me think that you know more than is reflected so far in this piece. I guess I'm looking as a reader for more of your perspective and learning from your experiences and reading.

Tami: OK. It's not my greatest work. When I explained to classmates what I wanted to write, I was telling a story instead of reporting. When I started writing, it became less and less helpful to use my sources because I was trying to shift to analysis. I got too bland trying to make it an article more than a story, which I think would have done the piece more justice.

Patti: Tami, I think this will turn out to be a very interesting piece because few people have any idea of what goes into becoming a model. I am particularly interested in what you say about the different types of people who show up at these open calls. For example, it would never occur to me in a million years that fat middle-aged people would have a shot at something like this. Don't they just want "the bold and the beautiful"? What happens to all the young hopefuls who never make it but are unwilling to give it up for something more realistic?

Steve: I agree with Barbara. I would like to see a little more of you in the piece. As it is, it comes across as sort of a newspaper story. I would prefer to see something a little more in depth, something that gets inside the models' heads--their needs, motivations, frustrations, etc. Go into a little greater detail; it will make the whole experience come alive for the reader.

Barbara: Tami, have you thought how to de-bland the piece?

Barbara: Steve and Tami, I'm interested that Steve is interested in the perspective of the models and candidates for models. Tami, your sources in the piece were on the other side of the aisle, the people choosing. Do you have some models as sources?

Steve: Patti has an interesting point here. None of the models I see on television or in print look anything like me. I am not tall, thin and beautiful. I would like to know more about what drives people who do not fit the conventional standards of beauty. Again, this relates back to getting inside the models' heads and finding out their stories.

Tami: The ideas of not getting discouraged, believing in yourself, etc. did not come from the model search alone, but were reinforced by the model search because I was one of the many that didn't get called back. It just becomes so personal--How do I separate?

Anne: One of my questions about the piece is "Who is the expert here?" While you are clearly informed about this search, your lack of first person leaves me unsure of who is giving this information. You cite some sources, to give some authoritative information, I assume, but your own authority is not capitalized upon.

Patti: Tami, I have had similar difficulty getting into a piece. I overcame this by getting on the computer and doing lots of freewriting. When I printed out, the first page or two was virtually useless; however, I could clearly see where all that superfluous stuff ended and the "real" writing began. (I didn't throw away the beginning stuff and it actually fitted into another part of the piece that I didn't initially recognize.)

Barbara: I'm struck by the fact that each of us has a different set of questions about this model search process but that we all want to know your perspective, Tami. You have obviously sparked interest on our part in your piece.

Why are you worried about getting personal? You, as Anne says, are an authority because YOU, not us or your intended readers, have the information and experience about and with this matter.

Anne: De-blanding the piece is an intriguing--and important--issue. I frequently think of a piece of work as a balancing act. How much is in the piece to give background information, how much to establish credibility, how much to pique the reader's interest, give him/her concretes to connect to?

Steve: In the closing paragraph, you seem to change subject matter part way through. More importantly, you wind up with a basketful of clichés. The notion that a person should "believe in yourself and go for it if you really want it" is so hackneyed. Also, the paragraph goes into a little cheerleading phase that would be better off if left out. I am not faulting the point that you are trying to make, quite the opposite, really, just the manner in which you expressed it.

Barbara: Tami, Anne uses the term "balancing act," which speaks to your sense of not wanting to be too personal but also not wanting to be too reportorial (does such a word exist?!). I hear us saying that the personal currently doesn't get enough weight to hold up its end of the see-saw.

Tami: I never really thought of it that way--It's like, I don't even have to include major details about the search itself, but maybe more about the models themselves. I just wish that I could find some models that attended this thing. Manhattan Model Search is monumentally busy, as I tried calling them. Everyone seems so reluctant to talk. Oh, well, I'll have to try. Thanks!

Anne: Patti's suggestion about freewriting is a good one. And I would suggest also doing some quick visual things, strong images from that experience. By doing little thumbnail pieces of description, you can develop some strong concretes that may serve as indications of important elements of your experience.

Tami: Barbara, the only way I'll be able to de-bland this piece involves this class, the input from all of the people in it. I've already picked up a couple of new twists!

Steve: Patti has a good point here. Quite often when I write a piece, especially nonfiction, I have little or no clue as to where it is going. Sometimes I think I know, but often I am proven wrong. However, the more I write and revise, the more the piece comes into focus. I think of writing as similar to walking into a darkened room. At first, I can't see anything and am literally in the dark. But after a while, details become noticeable and eventually I can make out what is before me and deal with it.

Lessons from Analyses

Although engaging in a computer conversation helps as you revise a draft, you can also glean general advice from analyzing a computer printout. Reading this conversation many months after its occurrence, I drew four conclusions about responding to my own writing processes and products and to another person's writing. These generalizations may be useful to you, too.

1. The author's perspective interests readers.

Several readers wished for Tami's voice in her writing. For example, Steve said, "I would like to see a little more of you in the piece." One reader after another asked questions in order to solicit from Tami her reactions to the model search, her point of view on the modeling profession, and her conclusions from her experience. When a piece emerges from the personal experience of an author whose readers know little about the topic, readers seem to crave knowing what the author has learned.

When I read my own writing, I need to ask myself, "Have I established a clear perspective? Do my readers know how I feel about this topic?"

2. Getting started is difficult for many writers.

After Patti's advice about freewriting one's way into a paper, Anne responds with another technique about visualization. Steve's reassuring analogy about the darkened room strikes home with Patti. Steve notes that as he writes and revises, his piece comes more and more into focus, just as after a time in a darkened room, he begins to see the details with which he must deal. Anne reinforces this idea, suggesting that a writer stay with a piece, however much stamina is needed.

I learn from this interchange that particularly on a well-developed first draft a reader might comment on how effectively the author has moved through the writing process. Even on a draft that reveals a struggle on the writer's part, the reader might acknowledge how difficult beginning can be. Also, in my own writing I can feel free to grumble in a Writer's Statement about my problems with beginning: many readers will understand and perhaps be able to give me suggestions.

3. Engaging in conversation awakens new thoughts.

Notice how often people build on one another's responses in this interchange. Steve says, "I agree with Barbara." Anne notes, "Patti's suggestion about freewriting is a good one." What one person says encourages another to amplify the idea or to remember something else to tell the writer.

Tami has an ah-ha experience after reading several parts of the conversation: "I never really thought of it that way—it's like, I don't even have to include major details about the search itself, but maybe more about the models themselves." One reason that people like to talk about their ideas is that they can discover new approaches to the topic.

4. Conversing on the computer can be easier than conversing face-to-face.

Early in the term Steve and Patti had argued so vehemently about Steve's response to one of her drafts that both of them had considered leaving the class. The interchange about Tami's piece, therefore, becomes doubly significant, providing Patti an opportunity to compliment Steve in another computer exchange several days later. She wrote, "Steve, I liked your analogy of walking into a darkened room and staying until your vision clears. This is a great analogy which applies to the writing process as well as to human relations. I'm glad we both stayed long enough for this to happen. I've benefitted greatly from your presence in this class, and I've learned a lot from you and your perspectives."

Dialogue Journal Responses to a Draft

We are all readers, but we all react differently to writing based on our background, knowledge base, interest in a topic, relationship to the writer, and many other factors. A writer benefits from knowing how various readers begin to make meaning from the text. Spoken or written first responses to a piece of writing help the author know how some readers are making sense of her words.

After Anne wrote a short piece about apples in her dialogue journal, Steve and Patti wrote in the response section of the journal their thoughts as they read the piece for the first time. Patti's descriptive phrases and comments appear in the right column opposite Anne's piece.

Anne's Essay in Her Dialogue Journal and a Reader Response

It is that singular annual day when something brings Rocky Mountain air to Indiana. Judy and I have been to the orchard where we stood knee deep in flowers and tasseled grass to pluck dappled burgundy apples from gnarled limbs. Our baskets filled too fast: we wanted to pick forever.	Sets up pleasurable experience.

Now, however, they stand on her blue-painted and slightly rickety kitchen table, a lone yellowjacket drifting lazily from apple to apple. Tomorrow our friend Andy will be here to haul his cider press--"I told her it was the only thing I wanted when we split"--out of storage in Judy and Chip's garage, and a swarm of people will vie with the bees for the glowing, amber juice.

Who is Andy?

How does this quote fit in? I'm confused.

Great use of the word "swarm" for people and bees.

Tonight Judy and I will sit cross-legged before the fire, big earthen bowls in our laps, sweater sleeves shoved up, and peel apples for the cobblers we will serve tomorrow's guests. Outside the air is crisping. Coffee steams in blue mugs.

Choppy.

I can hardly wait to touch once more those slightly dusty apples, their matte surfaces so different from the glistening waxy fruit of the supermarket. I want to see the dull green of a leaf against red, to carefully slip my knife blade under the skin at the top of the globe and glide it, round and round, creating a long striped curlicue while

This sentence unfurls just like the apple peel.

the white meat appears and the sweet juice drips down my hand, wetting my wrist.

We will gossip, drink wine, and listen to guitar until we have mounds of crisp crescents, ready to be sugared and spiced and stowed away until tomorrow morning.

Describes the pleasure and bond it creates.

I have just rolled two perfect white apples into my bowl when Kate comes prancing into the room. Her silky black tail beats my back as she gazes up at Chip who is standing there, big and ruddy in his flannel shirt. "Look what I found in the basement," he says. He holds out a gray and red metal gadget. "Just let me fasten it to the table here." He grunts as he bends down to fumble with levers and a handle. "Watch this." He reaches for an apple, inserts it into the machine, and turns a crank. In an instant the peel unfurls to the floor and the core has plunked out. One movement more and the fruit itself has been sliced into another long crisp spiral. He is delighted, reaches for another, repeats the act, then generously steps aside.

Men love gadgets: mechanization. Their pleasure finds expression in different ways.

"Now you try it." He is motioning to me.I look at Judy in dismay. But I love Chip. So I do it. I surrender my apple to the jaws of the machine. And zap. The work is done. And done, and done. And then we are done. Chip takes the bowls into the kitchen. "Let me bring you some wine," he says. "I'll heat up some soup. You two just sit there and talk."

So Chip really does understand how special this time is for you and Judy.

So Judy and I pull chairs up to the fire. We sit, sipping wine and talking quietly while a guitar plays and Chip makes homey noises in the kitchen. My sweater sleeves are in place; my wrists are dry. My hands are in my lap.

It's okay, but not the same. The pleasure and mood diminish.

Patti then summarizes her version of the main point of the piece: "You gave up something which gave you pleasure out of love and respect for someone else. Now you don't know what to do with yourself."

After Anne read this description and also Steve's remarks, she took the important step of responding to the reader responses. She asked herself questions that she wanted to come back to during her revising. She became a writer reading and reacting to the written responses of other readers.

Anne's Response to Readers' Responses

In revising the apple piece, I need to set up the relationships among the characters more clearly. Who is Andy: Is he important; do I even need to mention him? And what is the relationship between Chip and Judy and me? I need to clarify that, probably just through appositives early in the piece, expanding those into paragraphs a bit.

```
    Chip, the way I present him, is a major problem in
this piece. I don't want to align him--the only male in
the piece--with insensitivity to the pleasures of the
apple flesh. I don't want to set up gender conflict or
even contrast. I want to be careful about associating
men with machines/women with sensual pleasure. I need,
according to Steve's advice, to expand the section at
the end, somehow emphasizing who Chip is, that he is
not just an insensitive clod who came in and spoiled
our pleasure without even knowing it. That is not who
he is, does not accurately reflect the situation. But
right now, I am not sure how to approach that. It may
appear to be trying to make amends, or trying to make
up for a wrong. So, maybe earlier in the piece, I
need to establish Chip, not only his relationship to
Judy but who he is. I need to characterize, let the
reader know who he is, that he too takes pleasure in
beauty--he is, after all, a photographer--another
machine, how do I get away from this--show something
about him?  What, I do not know. I am interested in
Patti's point about the machine tie with Andy as well.
What do I do about this?
```

Anne finds Patti's and Steve's remarks thought provoking. By reading their initial reactions to her piece, she can now make a revision plan.

Descriptive Analysis

Conversation on the computer or in a dialogue journal can provide helpful response for a writer. Other more structured techniques, however, can also contribute to progress in writing. You can provide a writer with information about her piece by describing what you see in each paragraph. You can tell first what the paragraph *says* by identifying its main idea. Then you can tell what each paragraph *does* by identifying its function in the whole paper.

In responding to the apple-peeling piece, Patti instinctively described what some paragraphs said. For a complete descriptive analysis she would expand her descriptions for each paragraph and then decide the purpose of each paragraph in the piece. A descriptive analysis of the apple-peeling piece might read like this:

Paragraph 1:

```
Says:  Judy and the author relish apple picking in
       fall in Indiana.
```

Does: Introduces the invigorating nature of apple picking.

Paragraph 2:

Says: The apples will be processed so many people can enjoy the fruit.

Does: Widens the reason for joy in picking to fixing for others' enjoyment.

Paragraph 3:

Says: The process of peeling is communal.

Does: Establishes importance of connectedness as central to the author's pleasure in the experience.

Paragraph 4:

Says: These apples and the author's reaction to them are different from apples bought in store.

Does: Details the physical pleasure of peeling apples and being one with nature.

Paragraph 5:

Says: Judy and the author will prepare apples for tomorrow.

Does: Continues to establish the sensual pleasure of the process.

Paragraph 6:

Says: An apple coring machine is efficient.

Does: Contrasts the efficacy of the mechanical peeler with the pleasure of the human peeler.

Paragraph 7:

Says: The work of peeling is done quickly.

Does: Reinforces the loss of physical and psychological joy felt earlier.

Paragraph 8:

Says: Being inactive signals resignation.

Does: Establishes distance between original vital experience and current, passive one.

If Anne were also to make a descriptive analysis of her own piece before reading her responder's version, she could learn if the reader's sense of the meaning and purpose of each paragraph were similar to hers.

Notice that the descriptive analysis does not enable us as readers to comment on the lushness of the language in the first four paragraphs, the matching of the sentence lengths in paragraphs four and seven to the extended pleasure and the choppy efficiency of the two peelers, or the gender implications of the episode. In other words, the descriptive analysis primarily addresses central ideas and main functions. You will want to use the descriptive analysis along with other methods of response, though, to alert the writer to all that you note in her piece.

Identification of Powerful Words

As I read the apple-peeling piece, I have a physical reaction to some of the words: *Rocky Mountain* air helps me feel the brisk, invigorating chill of fall in Indiana; *sweet juice drips down my hand, wetting my wrist* evokes the feel of crushed grapes that we picked each year from our neighbor's trellis; and *sugared and spiced* makes my mouth water for the blueberry crisp my mother made.

To other words I have an emotional response. *Blue-painted and slightly rickety kitchen table* reminds me of my grandmother's blue willow dishes and, in contrast to this rickety one, her solid kitchen table at which I picture her peeling potatoes as we arrived for our yearly summer visit. *I surrender my apple to the jaws of the machine* saddens me as I recall the times that I have silently sacrificed personal pleasure. *A swarm of people will vie with the bees for the glowing, amber juice* sustains my sense of identity with other creatures of the earth.

When you identify for an author the effect of certain words on you, the author learns the suitability of her word choice. Maybe, for instance, Anne does not want her readers to be sentimental when reading paragraph two. Maybe *rickety* was chosen to signal instability. Would another word do that job more surely? If Anne were to hear several responses to her language choices, she could know the connotative value of the words for her readers. She would learn what meanings the readers bring to the words and derive from the words in their current contexts.

PRACTICE WITH YOUR ROLE AS A READER FOR OTHER WRITERS

1. If you have access to a networked computer, write your responses to a classmate's draft. The draft may be on-line, or you may use a hard copy. Other classmates and even the author may be present while you are responding, as with Tami's paper, or you may simply type in your responses. Other classmates may respond later to the paper and to your comments. The author may enter questions about your responses, so you may want to log in a

second time to see what help you can provide. Use the full range of your computer's capabilities as you respond to your classmates' work.

2. In the author's dialogue journal, write responses to parts of the draft that warrant comment during your reading of the draft. Remember that the more specific you are, the more honest you are, and the more thorough you are, the better for the author trying to revise. When you get dialogue journal responses in your own journal, you may want to analyze the responses. What changes will you make in your writing based on what you have read in the response section of your dialogue journal? Do you want to talk with the reader about certain of his responses or to ask questions about what you could do to revise a certain portion of your paper? If you write down your reactions to the reader's responses, you will have a record of what you want to do when you revise and a record for your portfolio introduction as you complete your Course Portfolio.
3. Do a descriptive analysis of a draft of a paper you are writing. Then ask a reader to do a descriptive analysis of the same paper. Next, compare the two descriptive analyses, if possible talking with the reader about similarities and differences. For example, if you and the reader disagree about the purpose of a certain paragraph, ask the reader what cued him about that purpose: What words were significant? Was the tone the one you had intended? Did a certain anecdote imply that you had a purpose different from the one you intended? Finally, list changes you would make in your draft based on the comparison of the two descriptive analyses.

   If you are writing a descriptive analysis of a lengthy paper, you may want to break the paper into sections rather than writing about each paragraph. Decide what will benefit you most in the time available as you ask your reader to do this descriptive analysis for you.
4. If you have hard copy of a draft on which to write, underline or circle powerful words. In the margin or at the bottom of the page, identify their effect on you as a reader. If you are reading on the computer, boldface those words that affect you particularly. In brackets you can explain your responses: the writer can then read and delete your responses after she has learned from them. The writer may also want to print out a copy of the draft with your responses to show how she has benefited from your reader response.

Although each of these exercises has indicated a single reader, multiple responses are, of course, beneficial in understanding the variety of responses different readers have to a piece of writing. For example, the positive connotations of the kitchen table in Anne's piece for me might be negative for a person who grew up in poverty and wants to be as far from his rickety kitchen table as possible. If Anne received opposite responses to highly connotative words or images, she would need to decide if she wants to guide her readers more directly to the response she hopes for by changing vocabulary or adding description. Because receiving multiple responses is often helpful, let's look at some ways of responding in a group to one another's work.

RESPONDING IN GROUPS TO ONE ANOTHER'S WORK

Many writing classes depend on peer groups for major contributions to the revising process of writers in the class. One advantage of working in a group is that a writer can receive multiple responses to a piece of writing at one time. Also, the readers and writer add to one another's reactions to a piece of writing in a way that produces more understanding than any one reader can offer. As you develop your ability to ask for the kind of analysis and response that you want, you will be able to take full advantage of peer group work.

Real-Time Conferences on Computer

The earlier example in which readers conversed with Tami illustrates the benefits of one kind of group responding. Although the example appeared earlier as an instance of networked stored responses allowing readers to work individually, real-time conferences also offer writers multiple perspectives simultaneously.

When Steve reacted to his first experiences with real-time computer conferences, he wrote, "I liked it. After my initial trepidation, I found it to be an effective way to generate a discussion. Using Interchange allowed more reflection and contemplation than would normally be found in a verbal discussion. Plus, it was nice to be able to go back over previous entries to reread and comment on them. Having a physical record of the discussion is valuable, too. Two thumbs up!" Through computer-mediated responding, Steve could offer ideas after having time to think about a useful comment.

Just as an often silent class member found a voice that helped classmates, other class members who dominate conversations find that they are not the only voices on computer. If one person disregards other entries, his or her responses are blatantly and visibly not part of the interactive conversation. Also, a writer can ask a classmate for a response without having to interrupt a dominant talker. Susan commented after one real-time conference session, "I never knew that Janice had so much to offer. She never speaks up in our peer group meetings. I'm glad to know what I can now ask her about in the future: she is particularly attuned to nuances of language. I guess that's because she's a poet, something else I didn't know about her before."

Read Alouds

Hearing someone else read his work aloud can help a writer catch awkward expressions, appreciate well-told anecdotes, and realize paucity of evidence for a certain argument. Remember when Jack wrote, "When Melanie read my paper aloud, I understood why we were doing this protocol stuff. I immediately saw that my paper was very boring and filled with nothing but experiences of others"? Jack was an astute listener who then revised his paper to feature his own ideas.

Sometimes, however, it is more difficult to hear all the features of the paper that might need reworking. Having other peers who can also express their reactions to the reading adds to the pool of information for the writer.

Steve wrote the following first draft of an essay. One of his peer group members read it aloud as each group member took notes.

Steve's Draft 1

It was the pictures that made me suspicious. The women, they were naked, all of them. What was the point of that? What kind of place was she taking me to? It looked normal from the outside.

Inside was an arrow shaped stage. It had a brass pole on each end that stretched upwards for ten feet. Chairs lined the stage, and farther back, away from the bright lights were high legged tables. A small bar sat tucked into a corner.

We slipped through pools of light into the surrounding blanket of darkness and sat down at a table. The girl on stage looked like she was an ex-cheerleader in need of some extra cash. She strolled from end to end, pausing occasionally to gyrate politely in front of an outstretched dollar bill. The owner of said bill was then treated to a sisterly peck on the cheek and a light drubbing with her breasts.

I drank my beer in small sips and concentrated on looking bored. As we sat there, Jennifer treated me to a running commentary on the various qualities of the dancers that graced the stage that evening: that one was too clumsy, that one wasn't energetic enough. She was a good dancer. I liked her routine and so on. I learned a lot about what it takes to be an effective topless dancer. I learned how to shake my moneymaker to its best advantage and how to pick up dollar bills without using my hands. She gave me some pointers on how to deal with obnoxious drunks, always valuable knowledge in any line of work, and I could have taught a seminar on the proper ways to use the brass poles. Clearly, much more effort was involved here than I would ever have imagined.

I watched the dancers cycle across the stage in succession, some were good but most were not. The featured dancer was Swedish import with expensive breasts and a habit of berating her audience. I was getting one hell of an education.

Once again I had underestimated her. Never, not once, even under a full blue moon would I ever have brought myself here on my own. The thought would just never occur to me. I don't even own a raincoat. But still, here I was.

"I figured you should go," she said later and blew smoke in my face, laughing.

I could not help but be impressed.

We met in writing class. We spoke little during the semester, although I had been aware of her from the very beginning. She sat over by the windows, and I opposite under a chalkboard. Her work was quite good, her poetry among the best in the class. She wrote in a beatnik style that roared off the page in a rush of images, words tumbling into one another like a waterfall. Traditional punctuation was discarded in favor of feeling, as if the very notion of a sentence could not contain her message.

I was definitely a sucker for a lady who has a way with words. So in a sense, that first day of class was the start of a chain reaction that led in its own serpentine way to my spending an evening in the Red Garter. What will come next, I do not know; she has an extremely active imagination. I am curious to find out, however, and more importantly, I want to see if I can turn this thing around and top her.

We shall see.

After hearing his work read aloud, Steve decided to make some wording changes in this piece. He noticed some unnecessary or dissonant wording: he decided to leave out "always valuable knowledge in any line of work" as an unnecessary sarcastic aside, "in succession" after "cycle across the stage" as redundant, and "beatnik" as an antiquated term. The sound of the words spoken aloud helped Steve realize their contribution or lack of contribution to his meaning.

Yet other listeners added more considerations for revision. Patti commented on "right-on words": "*Serpentine* is so perfect because it implies seduction into evil by the snake in the Garden of Eden," and "*top her* at the end is appropriate to the topless bar experience and to possible developments in your relationship with Jennifer." Patti also, however, questioned that purpose of the piece. She asked Steve, "Are you wanting to focus on your developing friendship with Jennifer or on the disrupting of stereotypes that you had of topless dancers? You seem to have known that Jennifer was unconventional, so why are you surprised that she would take you to a topless bar?" Anne, too, was interested in the connection between Steve's attempt to understand his attraction to Jennifer and its relationship to the trip to the bar: "Is the example of going to the bar an extended example of Jennifer's 'extremely active imagination'? You mention that you are 'a sucker for a lady who has a way with words,' but I don't see how taking you to the bar supports Jennifer's ability with language."

Steve listened to others' responses to the read aloud and revised several more times. In the Writer's Statement of the third draft, he wrote that "the intent of the piece is to show my reaction and impressions of my trip to a strip joint, my first. This serves as an elongated introduction to the real point of the piece, my new insight into the person who brought me there in the first place. I wanted to show my new found respect for the women who dance in such establishments and my amazement that my date would want to take me to one." When Steve heard his third draft read aloud, however, he decided that the elongated example drew so much attention to itself that it did not serve to illuminate his impressions of Jennifer. His own attention as a listener was focused on the details of the dancers' performances. Steve decided to shift the emphasis of the piece on to what he learned about the dancers and, as a result, about himself. His final draft, therefore, contains a title that is the name of the bar, new details about the setting, and more reflection on his own learning. Notice that the question at the end of the first paragraph sets up the answer he will provide in the paper.

Steve's Draft 4

The Red Garter

The pictures made me wonder. It looked normal from the outside: red brick, low roof sporting a lone neon sign that blinked sporadically. It was your basic joint, nothing special. Inside, pictures of women, all of them naked to one degree or another, plastered one wall near the entrance. What kind of place was Jennifer taking me to?

Further inside was an arrow-shaped stage. It had a brass pole on each end that stretched upwards for ten feet. Chairs lined the stage, and nearer the back, away from the bright lights were high-legged tables. A small bar sat tucked into the corner.

I counted around twenty revelers scattered throughout the joint. Empty chairs outnumbered patrons by two to one, with most of the occupied chairs right up at the edge of the stage. We slipped through pools of light into the surrounding comfort of darkness and sat down at a table.

The girl on stage looked freshly scrubbed and affable, a cheerleader type. She strolled from end to end, pausing occasionally to gyrate politely in front of an outstretched dollar bill. The owner of said bill was then treated to a sisterly peck on the cheek and a light pummeling with her breasts.

I drank my beer in small sips and concentrated on looking bored. I felt vaguely nervous, as if I should have asked permission before entering. Strip bars had always seemed somewhat otherworldly, places one read about but never actually saw in person, like Africa or the moon. It felt odd to finally be in such a place.

Jennifer treated me to a running commentary on the pluses and minuses of the various dancers that graced the stage that evening. Some were attractive but lousy dancers, and it was one of the more shopworn performers who put on the best show. Clearly, skill and imagination won out over simple good looks with the present crowd.

I learned a lot about what it takes to be an effective topless dancer. I learned how to shake a moneymaker to its best advantage and how to pick up dollar bills without using the hands. Jennifer made me aware of the importance of making use of all of the parts of the stage; I could have taught a seminar on the proper ways to use the brass poles. Amazingly, more effort was involved here than I would ever have imagined.

There was more to being an exotic dancer than just stripping down and highstepping around for the length of a song. A good dancer would carefully plan out a routine and make the most of what she had to work with. This meant using not only her body but also any props that would encourage the audience members to part with their hard-earned dollars. For example, several metal bars were attached to the ceiling around the stage. Few dancers bothered to pay them much attention, but those who did were suitably rewarded with a flurry of dollars.

As the evening progressed, I began to watch the performers with a critical and appreciative eye. Some were good, but most were merely average. The featured dancer was a Swedish import with expensive breasts and a curious habit of berating her audience. Her routine was first rate, and it was clear that she put in a lot of time rehearsing.

My whole concept of strip joints and the women who danced in them had been totally turned on its head. I realized that what I had seen was essentially a group of women earning a living. I admit that it is probably not the most glamorous job around, but there is still a certain amount of respect due people who are able to support themselves. I came to see them as more than just strippers, nameless and trashy. They were earning their keep, and I can respect that.

It was a weird experience, the Red Garter, but I am glad I went. Once I got over my initial shock, I ended up having some fun. I came to see the performers as people, not just abstractions in g-strings and pasties. What is dirty and obscene to one person is a steady paycheck to another. It was quite a learning experience.

I still haven't told my parents, though.

Steve's refocusing of his piece highlights a broader perspective on stereotyping that his readers might apply to their own thinking, no matter what their view about topless bars. The added details about the place and the dancers provide a knowledge base for understanding Steve's new awareness. His willingness to rethink a previous notion about people builds credibility and encourages readers not to stereotype Steve for visiting a topless bar. Patti's and Anne's questions about his main purpose in his first draft and another read aloud of his third draft prompted Steve to decide that his change in perspective about a stereotype was a more significant topic than his evolving relationship with a girlfriend. Steve was willing to make major revisions in his piece based on his decision about focus and purpose.

Hearing his piece read aloud and hearing the responses of other listeners made a significant difference in the final draft of Steve's piece. As you listen to your writing read aloud, take notes and ask your peers to take notes so that you can discuss your reactions. You will have food for thought as you continue the revision process.

Peer Group Conversations about Writer's Statements

Earlier you learned about Writer's Statements, which contain an author's questions and observations about her draft. Writer's Statements can direct a peer group discussion as readers refute, supplement, or add new ideas to the responses of classmates. As a peer group member responds to a Writer's Statement, the author can write or type notes.

Shelley asked in her Writer's Statement about the amount of evidence that she had supplied to support her argument that workers should have written job appraisals, even if they are part-time employees. She had given an example of her own experience as a part-time clothing salesperson, comments from an interview with her neighbor who managed a grocery, and statistics about how many times people can expect to change jobs during their lifetimes. These responses to her question occurred during a peer group conversation.

`Randy:` Although you interviewed a grocery manager, I think that you need more evidence that managers would have time to do what you want. For instance, so many people work at the McDonald's when I do and there is so much turnover, I can't imagine that the manager would have time. I'm also not convinced that a future employer of mine would pay any attention to how well I flipped hamburgers.

`Mohammed:` I agree that you need more evidence, but I disagree that Randy's future employer wouldn't care about how good an employee he was, even if the job was low skill and part time. Coming to work on time. Not cussing at customers. All that stuff is significant.

`Mary:` Maybe it's up to the employee to ask for an appraisal. Some employees might not care. Your example of yourself is interesting, but how many other people want this kind of thing?

`Leslie:` I haven't had a job yet, but I know that I'm scared about applying. If I had a positive appraisal of a past job, I'd feel better. But what if the appraisal was bad?! Would I have to use it? Having a job appraisal might work against me if I hadn't done well. Have you thought of that?

`Tyrone:` Hey, I had a write-up when I loaded trucks at a lumber yard. The guy who supervised me checked off a list about my work. I remember he liked the way that I worked hard, but he carped about my being late. He didn't care that my bus was usually late, and I didn't have a choice. I wouldn't have been late if I had a car.

`Kevin:` You don't do much with the benefits of having appraisals. Mary's right that you need to know how many part-time employees really want them.

Shelley decided on the basis of her peers' responses to her Writer's Statement and to one another that she would take a poll of all her classmates who worked part-time to see if they would want appraisals, that she would look for information about companies that conduct appraisals of all their employees and why, and that she would expand the section of her paper on the benefits of appraisals. Her final draft was more persuasive because she learned early from readers about their opinions on her evidence and argument.

Playing the Opposition

A technique for testing points of view in a paper is playing the opposition. One member of the peer group speaks positively about a point in the paper—a specific argument, the choice of a word, or the effectiveness of a piece of evidence. Then another member of the peer group takes the opposite stance about the same point. The writer listens, learning in the process the range of possible reactions to the same point in the paper. Peers can have fun taking stances that they do not necessarily hold but can imagine others taking. Being as concrete and persuasive as possible, peers represent the ends of the continuum of reaction.

The first one-sentence paragraph of Jacqueline's paper titled "Then and Now" read, "There is a vast difference between the way I was raised and the environment I was raised in, and the way my brother is being raised and his environment." Focusing on this introduction, Shawn anticipated a paper that would portray the differences in various home environments. He foresaw that Jacqueline could emphasize the positive benefits of a stable household.

Taking the opposite point of view, Andrea worried that the paper would not interest readers. She asked, "Why will readers care about how you and your brother were brought up?" Andrea wondered why Jacqueline would write about this topic for anyone but her own family.

Unfortunately, Jacqueline did not hear Andrea's warning: her paper was indeed a simple accounting of the ways in which her brother received more family support than she had as a child. Part of the assignment had been to use outside sources to support personal experience; however, Jacqueline relied only on her personal experience. In addition, Jacqueline did not make clear what she expected readers to learn from her own experiences. Although Shawn had signaled that he as reader would have been interested in the positive benefits of a stable household, Jacqueline chose only to complain about the inadequacies of her mother's early parenting.

For any response technique to work, the author needs to consider seriously what her classmates say. Certainly, the author may reject or modify advice or reactions, but peers represent potential readers, so the author needs to use the valuable comments of peers to modify her writing. When Jacqueline submitted her paper without revising in response to her classmates' responses, Jacqueline's instructor noted that it focused only on her interests as the writer. The instructor asked, "Could you think of ways to make it reader-based, that is, meeting needs of potential readers?" Had Jacqueline really heard the remarks of her oppositional readers, she could have shifted from writer-based to reader-based writing before submitting the paper for evaluation by the instructor.

Upping the Ante

Have you thought at one time or another what most of us have as writers: if I only had more time, I would have done thus and so? We may be well aware of the possibilities of our papers but simply do not have or do not take the time or energy to improve them.

On the other hand, all of us have limited imaginations and knowledge bases. Peer groups offer the opportunity to draw on the thinking and experience of colleagues. A group discussion in which peers offer additional sources for a writer's paper can be invaluable. Talking aloud together can inspire a reader to think of ideas that he would not have reading alone. A sample of upping the ante demonstrates how each member of the peer group tries to add to a comment of the person before. Anthony's peer group responded to his paper on student evaluations of teaching.

Leonard: Anthony, you're a freshman, but you talk about the effects of teaching evaluations as if you knew a whole lot. My brother, who's a senior, could tell you how teaching evaluations are ignored by most professors he's had.

Betsy: I'm a political science major. In mydepartment the teaching evaluations are published. If a professor doesn't pay attention, everyone knows. You should talk to professors in my department in addition to students like Leonard's brother.

Ricardo: Did you read the student newspaper two weeks ago? You don't mention it. That article reported how student evaluations are used in deciding which professors get tenure. Tenure is their job security, so it's important.

Damon: Oh, yeah, I remember that article, and I remember that it refers to some study that was done here last year. Some administrator wanted to know if students took filling out the evaluation forms seriously. He found out that most students just blow it off.

From this discussion Anthony gains knowledge about four resources: the perspective of a senior who has filled out many evaluation forms, the perspective of professors for whom student evaluations are made public, information from the student newspaper, and the results of an administrative survey. Notice that Betsy refers to Leonard's remarks, and Damon builds on Ricardo's memory. Upping the ante requires readers to stretch their thinking in the service of the writer.

PRACTICE WITH YOUR ROLE AS A MEMBER OF A PEER RESPONSE GROUP

1. If you have access to real-time conference capability, conduct a session with your peer group in which you read and write together for a designated amount of time about the work of each writer in your group. You could also use such a conference to explore possibilities for fulfilling a certain assignment, to suggest resources for one writer on his chosen topic, or to focus on an area of weakness from a previous paper that the writer hopes to improve in this one. Be sure that each writer in your group gets responses on his paper. If possible, print out your conference. Then you can analyze the effectiveness of your responses by asking each writer what kinds of comments were most useful as he revised.
2. In your group take turns reading papers aloud for one another. Listeners, including the author, should take notes to share aloud or submit to the writer after the reading. Be sure to allot enough time so that each writer gets a turn. This activity can be done during a peer group meeting outside of class as well as in class.
3. If possible, exchange drafts and Writer's Statements before the peer group meeting so that you will have a chance to read each of the papers and Writer's Statements. If you do not have the luxury of reading ahead, allot time for reading before you begin talking about the pieces. As you respond aloud to each Writer's Statement, be careful not to repeat what another reader has already said but to build on that person's comments by refuting, agreeing, or adding to. Your group can set its own guidelines about taking turns or accepting interruptions. Authors need to take notes.
4. For playing the opposition, you might draw a long line across a sheet of paper so that the author can make notes along the line showing the opposing points of view. If the group decides to discuss the two points of view, the author can then note modifications on the perspectives wherever the modifications would logically appear on the continuum. Or another member of the group could perform that task so that the author can question readers as they express their points of view.
5. For each person in the group, play upping the ante. Challenge each reader or listener to add to the questions or information of the previous responder. The purpose is to add something new to the resource base of the writer, so even a source that seems tangential is worth mentioning to stretch the possibilities for the writer. Again, the writer may take notes or someone might be recorder for the writer so that she can pay close attention and ask questions as suggestions are made.

6. Be sure to add all these interchanges to your Working Portfolio. When you write your portfolio introduction, you can quote from or draw from what you and others have said and written.

RESPONDING TO THE COMMENTS OF OTHER READERS

Family and Friends

Although we have been considering practices that use ourselves as writers and readers and our classmates as readers, you have other possible sources to aid you during the revising process. Julie mentioned earlier the help of her husband as she revised a piece of writing. Sometimes we forget that our family members and friends outside of class might be excellent readers for us. If we are dealing with nontechnical material or if we are writing for a lay audience, family members and friends may contribute to our thinking if we ask them the right questions. Simply saying "Will you tell me what you think of this paper?" is usually not enough. Just as Writer's Statements help classmates know what you want to know about the paper, a specific question or set of questions for other readers can evoke useful comments. For example, if you are worried that a certain statistic might be regarded as out of date, ask specifically, "Did you notice the date of the data about drunk driving? If so, did the date of the statistic affect how much you were persuaded about the need for more stringent penalties for drunk driving?"

Knowing how much time and interest a certain person is likely to have, you can include an appropriate number of questions. Also, knowing the knowledge level and attitudes of that person, you can ask more or less probing and more or less volatile questions.

Writing Center Tutors

Many colleges and universities have Writing Centers with students and faculty trained in responding to student writing. Such centers are usually for all writers, those who are accomplished and realize how helpful responses from readers are during any revising process and those who are less accomplished and perhaps more reluctant to ask for help. Remember that people who work in Writing Centers are sympathetic to writers, know how to help them proceed as they revise, and want them to do well.

If you bring a piece of writing with specific questions about it to the Writing Center tutoring session, you will get more out of the session than you will if you simply place a draft in front of the tutor. Just as you are now accustomed to using Writer's Statements with your peers and instructor, you can facilitate a productive tutoring session in the Writing Center by being prepared with some questions.

Be willing to go to the Writing Center multiple times. Even the best of writers can benefit from response on each piece of writing. The Writing Center is not a quick fix but a reliable resource for making progress over time.

External Readers

You might consider soliciting an appropriate reader outside your class or outside the university. For example, if your paper's purpose is to convince the school board that classes in your child's school are too large, you would benefit from a reader's response from a school board member. If your paper explores availability of birth control information to teen-agers, you might ask a Planned Parenthood employee to respond to your work. In other words, seek response from a member of the audience to whom your paper is directed or a person who has specific expertise on your topic or perspective. Although soliciting a response takes effort on your part and allowance of enough time for a busy person to answer your questions, you are practicing excellent revision strategies by enlisting responses from the actual audience for your writing.

You may feel better about asking for external readers if you are willing to be an external reader for others. For example, if you work for the welfare department, you might be an appropriate reader for a paper on caseloads of welfare workers. If you are a parent who participated in a home birth, you are a valuable reader for a paper advocating or deploring home births. Other writers will appreciate your making yourself available through formal means, such as a list of resource readers in the Writing Center, or through informal means, such as letting your classmates know your areas of experience or interest so that they can tell friends.

In grade school I perfected the art of covering my paper with one hand as I wrote with the other. I had been taught that what I wrote was my work. Having help from others was a form of cheating because I could not claim that the writing was exclusively mine. My teachers then did not have the advantage of knowing all that we do today about the ways in which knowlege is constructed and the ways in which composing and revising are social acts.

I no longer have to cover my paper or hide a computer screen as I write. I'm flattered when peers ask to read what I'm writing and immediately ask them a question I'd like answered: "Does my introduction encourage you to read on?" "Is the example in the third paragraph clearly supportive of my point in that paragraph?" or "Do you know any sources about my topic?" And I also invite others to respond to my drafts by asking, "What technique for responding shall we use?" This chapter has explored some of those techniques; you probably know others. Giving and receiving responses to writing during the writing process contributes significantly to the quality of the experience and the product.

Justin and his classmates discussed and practiced many of these ways of responding so that as he began his second paper, he had confidence that he would have ways of improving his writing with the help of others. In this next assignment he drew on the ideas that he found in the writing of another person as well as the ideas of his own readers as he revised.

WORKING PORTFOLIO UPDATE

Your Working Portfolio is growing because you now have many examples of ways to respond to writing, both your own and that of others. When you get ready to respond to writing throughout this term, you can refer to tracing the process, conversations on computer, analyses of conversations, dialogue journal responses to drafts, descriptive analyses, identifications of powerful words, real-time conferences on computer, read alouds, conversations about Writer's Statements, playing the opposition, and upping the ante.

Even at this point in the term, you might want to select examples of the methods that have worked best for you or that seem most amenable to the way that you learn. For example, you can mark dialogue journal entries where reader responses resulted in actual revisions in your draft. Or you can underline sections of a real-time computer conference that caused you to add certain examples as evidence. In other words, you can prepare for making a convincing argument in your Course Portfolio that you have improved your writing process during the term.

CHAPTER 5 Learning Across Drafts

In many writing classes, each paper has a separate and finite life span, born as an assignment and buried as a final draft never to be exhumed. In such classes, a new paper is born only after the life cycle of the preceding one is complete.

In a portfolio class, however, the life span of a paper is much longer. As you produce the drafts from which you will choose materials for the Course Portfolio, you collect all your writing in a Working Portfolio. Because those drafts and their accompanying documents, such as proposals, responses, and Writer's Statements, are considered works-in-progress and are easily accessible, they remain a viable part of the classwork, offering you many opportunities to extend your learning, illustrating the essence of portfolio learning.

In this chapter you will see Justin using his drafts in just this way as he finds guidance for a new paper in the response he received on another paper he had previously drafted. You will also see that portfolio learning is not linear. It does not progress in a straight line but rather doubles back, snaking around in what may sometimes appear to be a disorganized fashion. But this nonlinear process allows you to make use of earlier work as a basis for improvement.

BEGINNING WITH ONE ASSIGNMENT

Justin discovered this aspect of a portfolio class during his work with the second paper. That paper began well with an assignment he decided to use for his sociology class as well as his composition class.

> Assignment: In your journal, you have been recording your response, twice a week, to a text you are reading—an article, a chapter in a textbook

for another class, a novel, even instructions for a new computer. Choose one of those texts as the basis for Paper 2. In the paper, respond to an important idea presented in the text and explain the reasons for your response. Do you agree or disagree with the author? Why? What basis do you have for your response? Include an identification of the author and a summary of the article in your paper.

Justin decided to write about an essay from a collection of readings for his sociology class, one that he had already written about in a journal entry. The essay, written by Ishmael Reed, is titled "America: The Multicultural Society." Justin was pleased to be able to use his work for two assignments and believed his choice would provide double motivation to work on the paper. "I feel very efficient," he wrote. "I've got an essay to write about, I've already done the work in analyzing it in my journal, so I feel like I'm really ahead on two papers, the one for this class and the one for sociology."

He was right: his early work on the paper went very well. But as you will see, when Justin finished the draft of Paper 2, the responses of his classmates and his teacher confirmed his own fears about it. His difficulties had a bright side, however, because they led him to take advantage of the nature of portfolio learning. He found that his teacher's and classmates' responses to his first paper provided guidance that helped him revise this second piece of writing in time to make his deadline.

America: The Multicultural Society

by Ishmael Reed

> At the annual Lower East Side Jewish Festival yesterday, a Chinese woman ate a pizza slice in front of Ty Thuan Duc's Vietnamese grocery store. Beside her a Spanish-speaking family patronized a cart with two signs: "Italian Ices" and "Kosher by Rabbi Alper." And after the pastrami ran out, everybody ate knishes.
>
> *New York Times,* June 23, 1983

On the day before Memorial Day, 1983, a poet called me to describe a city he had just visited. He said that one section included mosques, built by the Islamic people who dwelled there. Attending his reading, he said, were large numbers of Hispanic people, forty thousand of whom lived in the same city. He was not talking about a fabled city located in some mysterious region of the world. The city he'd visited was Detroit.

©1994 by Ishmael Reed, "America: The Multinational Society" from *Writin' Is Fightin': Forty-Three Years of Boxing on Paper* (Atheneum).

A few months before, as I was leaving Houston, Texas, I heard it announced on the radio that Texas's largest minority was Mexican-American, and though a foundation recently issued a report critical of bilingual education, the taped voice used to guide the passengers on the air trams connecting terminals in Dallas Airport is in both Spanish and English. If the trend continues, a day will come when it will be difficult to travel through some sections of the country without hearing commands in both English and Spanish; after all, for some western states, Spanish was the first written language and the Spanish style lives on in the western way of life.

Shortly after my Texas trip, I sat in an auditorium located on the campus of the University of Wisconsin at Milwaukee as a Yale professor—whose original work on the influence of African cultures upon those of the Americas has led to his ostracism from some monocultural intellectual circles—walked up and down the aisle, like an old-time southern evangelist, dancing and drumming the top of the lectern, illustrating his points before some serious Afro-American intellectuals and artists who cheered and applauded his performance and his mastery of information. The professor was "white." After his lecture, he joined a group of Milwaukeeans in a conversation. All of the participants spoke Yoruban, though only the professor had ever traveled to Africa.

One of the artists told me that his paintings, which included African and Afro-American mythological symbols and imagery, were hanging in the local McDonald's restaurant. The next day I went to McDonald's and snapped pictures of smiling youngsters eating hamburgers below paintings that could grace the walls of any of the country's leading museums. The manager of the local McDonald's said, "I don't know what you boys are doing, but I like it," as he commissioned the local painters to exhibit in his restaurant.

Such blurring of cultural styles occurs in everyday life in the United States to a greater extent than anyone can imagine and is probably more prevalent than the sensational conflict between people of different backgrounds that is played up and often encouraged by the media. The result is what the Yale Professor, Robert Thompson, referred to as a cultural bouillabaisse, yet members of the nation's present educational and cultural Elect still cling to the notion that the United States belongs to some vaguely defined entity they refer to as "Western civilization," by which they mean, presumably, a civilization created by the people of Europe, as if Europe can be viewed in monolithic terms. Is Beethoven's Ninth Symphony, which includes Turkish marches, a part of Western civilization, or the late nineteenth- and twentieth-century French paintings, whose creators were influenced by Japanese art? And what of the cubists, through whom the influence of African art changed modern painting, or the surrealists, who were so impressed with the art of the Pacific Northwest Indians that, in their map of North America, Alaska dwarfs the lower forty-eight in size?

Are the Russians, who are often criticized for their adoption of "Western" ways by Tsarist dissidents in exile, members of Western civilization? And what of the millions of Europeans who have black African and Asian ancestry, black Africans having occupied several countries for hundreds of years? Are these "Europeans" members of Western civilization, or the Hungarians, who originated across the Urals in a place called Greater Hungary, or the Irish, who came from the Iberian Peninsula?

Even the notion that North America is part of Western civilization because our "system of government" is derived from Europe is being challenged by Native American historians who say that the founding fathers, Benjamin Franklin especially, were actually influenced by the system of government that had been adopted by the Iroquois hundreds of years prior to the arrival of large numbers of Europeans.

Western civilization, then, becomes another confusing category like Third World, or Judeo-Christian culture, as man attempts to impose his small-screen view of political and cultural reality upon a complex world. Our most publicized novelist recently said that Western civilization was the greatest achievement of mankind, an attitude that flourishes on the street level as scribbles in public restrooms: "White Power," "Niggers and Spics Suck," or "Hitler was a prophet," the latter being the most telling, for wasn't Adolph Hitler the archetypal monoculturalist who, in his pigheaded arrogance, believed that one way and one blood was so pure that it had to be protected from alien strains at all costs? Where did such an attitude, which has caused so much misery and depression in our national life, which has tainted even our noblest achievements, begin? An attitude that caused the incarceration of Japanese-American citizens during World War II, the persecution of Chicanos and Chinese-Americans, the near-extermination of the Indians, and the murder and lynchings of thousands of Afro-Americans.

Virtuous, hardworking, pious, even though they occasionally would wander off after some fancy clothes, or rendezvous in the woods with the town prostitute, the Puritans are idealized in our schoolbooks as "a hardy band" of no-nonsense patriarchs whose discipline razed the forest and brought order to the New World (a term that annoys Native American historians). Industrious, responsible, it was their "Yankee ingenuity" and practicality that created the work ethic. They were simple folk who produced a number of good poets, and they set the tone for the American writing style, of lean and spare lines, long before Hemingway. They worshipped in churches whose colors blended in with the New England snow, churches with simple structures and ornate lecterns.

The Puritans were a daring lot, but they had a mean streak. They hated the theater and banned Christmas. They punished people in a cruel and inhuman manner. They killed children who disobeyed their parents. When they came in contact with those whom they considered heathens or aliens, they behaved in such a bizarre and irrational manner that this chapter in the American history comes down to us as a late-movie horror film. They exterminated the Indians, who taught them how to survive in a world unknown to them, and their encounter with the calypso culture of Barbados resulted in what the tourist guide in Salem's Witches' House refers to as the Witchcraft Hysteria.

The Puritan legacy of hard work and meticulous accounting led to the establishment of a great industrial society; it is no wonder that the American industrial revolution began in Lowell, Massachusetts, but there was the other side, the strange and paranoid attitudes toward those different from the Elect.

The cultural attitudes of that early Elect continue to be voiced in everyday life in the United States: the president of a distinguished university, writing a letter to the *Times,* belittling the study of African civilizations; the television network that promoted its show on the Vatican art with the boast that this art represented "the finest achievements of the human spirit." A modern up-tempo state of complex rhythms that depends upon contacts with an international community can no longer behave as if it dwelled in a "Zion Wilderness" surrounded by beasts and pagans.

When I heard a schoolteacher warn the other night about the invasion of the American educational system by foreign curriculums, I wanted to yell at the television set, "Lady, they're already here." It has already begun because the world is here. The world has been arriving at these shores for at least ten thousand years from Europe, Africa, and Asia. In the late nineteenth and early twentieth centuries, large numbers of Europeans arrived, adding their cultures to those of the European, African, and Asian settlers who were already here, and recently millions have been entering the country from South America and the Caribbean, making Yale professor Bob Thompson's bouillabaisse richer and thicker.

One of our most visionary politicians said that he envisioned a time when the United States could become the brain of the world, by which he meant the repository of all of the latest advanced information systems. I thought of that remark when an enterprising poet friend of mine called to say that he had just sold a poem to a computer magazine and that the editors were delighted to get it because they didn't carry fiction or poetry. Is that the kind of world we desire? A humdrum homogeneous world of all brains and no heart, no fiction, no poetry; a world of robots with human atttendants bereft of imagination, of culture? Or does North America deserve a more exciting destiny? To become a place where the cultures of the world crisscross. This is possible because the United States is unique in the world: The world is here.

SUMMARIZING AND ANALYZING A READING

In a journal response to Reed's article, Justin used an approach he had learned in high school to analyze it. He included a summary as well as an identification of several elements of the article.

Justin's Dialogue Journal Entry on "America: The Multicultural Society"

When I read the article by Ishmael Reed, I remembered some things about how to read, I mean how to sort of attack a piece of writing. The idea in this piece is not hard to figure out, but he uses a lot of examples that I'm not familiar with, and some of the words are not totally familiar either.

When I took a reading skills class in high school, they taught us to summarize the main idea of the article. The main idea of this one is: America has a sort of two-sided history, a history of new people coming here to mix with those already here and a history of groups of those people trying to be in power within the democratic system. The author thinks that the mixing is very important to making America great.

They also taught us in our reading class to look for the main ways that the author makes his points and supports his main idea in the paragraphs that make up the rest of the article. He makes his point by offering lots of examples. The Puritans are a major example of people who had a major influence, both good and bad, on the way we still are today. He also uses lots of examples that support the idea that "Western Civilization" was not a thing all on its own. It was influenced in lots of ways from countries and people from other places.

Another thing that we did in that class was look up new words. I made a list of words in this article to look up:

bouillabaisse--one definition said fish soup, but that didn't make sense to me, so I looked in another place and found out it's a soup made of several kinds of fish and shellfish. That makes more sense.

monolithic--a large block of stone or a large organization that acts as one powerful unit

Tsarist--variation on czar, like the Czar of Russia

There were other words I didn't look up, like "Yoruban," because I could tell that it was an African language, even though I don't know exactly where it comes from.

Another thing we did was to try to identify the questions being addressed in the article. In this article, the author is asking and trying to answer whether or not the US is really a part of "western civilization" and even whether western civilization was as "European" as we often think. He is also asking where we got the idea that certain groups are more "elect" than others. He is also asking whether the US is a crossroads of cultures. And, I guess, whether that's good or bad.

I agree that the US is a crossroads and that's a good thing. I have friends from other cultures and backgrounds, and I like different things about them that are interesting. My best friends in high school were guys from other backgrounds. But, I have also seen lots of problems that are the result of all the mixing of different groups and races. So, I guess I have mixed feelings about it all.

PRACTICE RESPONDING TO READING

1. Choose a piece of writing—a classmate's text, an article you have read recently, a text from another class, or one your teacher suggests—to summarize as the following guidelines suggest. You may work alone and share your summary with a classmate, or you may work together to create a summary paragraph.
2. Using Justin's journal entry as a model and following the guidelines given, add to the summary paragraph you wrote in step 1 by analyzing language and purpose and by reacting to the author's points. You may

Guidelines for Responding to Reading

SUMMARIZE: Find and underline twice the main point presented in the piece. Most often, though not always, the main point, or thesis, is presented near the beginning and sometimes again near the end. If you're unsure of the main point, the title may offer clues. Next, in each paragraph, underline the main point, which often appears early in the paragraph. The main point of the piece plus main points from the paragraphs should be the most important ideas in the piece. Following the order in which they appear in the original piece, combine these ideas into a summary paragraph.

ANALYZE SUPPORT: How does the author support or attempt to prove those main points? Does he offer examples, statistics, testimony from experts?

ANALYZE LANGUAGE: What sort of language does the author use? Is it colorful; does it show a strong bias; is it technical or elevated to appeal to a particular audience? Identify and define unfamiliar words.

ANALYZE PURPOSE: Identify the questions being addressed in the text; what questions does the author try to answer for the reader?

REACT: State your own reaction to the author's points. Do you agree or disagree with the author? Why? What experiences, reading, or other sources of information support your reaction to the author's points?

also want to continue to practice this approach to reading as you respond to classmates' papers, to assigned reading in this or other classes, or to your own papers.

USING JOURNALISTIC QUESTIONS

Justin's teacher foregrounded the assignment for the second paper by asking students to respond to reading in journal entries. She also asked her students to choose a strategy that could help them generate additional ideas about their chosen texts. Justin decided on journalistic questions, which, as he said in his journal, "seemed to really dig into the subject."

Guidelines for Journalistic Questions

"Who," "what," "when," "where," "why," and "how" make up the traditional journalistic questions. Tailoring them, as they are below, to be readily applicable to your topic makes them easier to use.

Who is important? Who is an expert? Who is affected by this topic?

What is significant in this topic? What are the details? What has happened, is happening, is likely or unlikely to happen?

When did it or will it happen? When else has it already happened? When will we know the results?

Where did it happen? Where else has it happened?

Why did it happen? Why did it happen to that person at that time and place?

How did it happen? How could it have been prevented? How did it come to light?

Following are Justin's answers to the journalistic questions regarding Reed's essay. You can see these questions used in a different way as Justin prepares for Paper 3 on page 126.

Justin's Journalistic Questions

Purpose: I am answering these questions to help me understand what Reed says in his essay.

Who: This article is mostly about the people who have made up the bouillabaisse that is America. It is also about people now who have different ideas about what is important.

What: Different cultures adding to America; the debate over what is western civilization; what is happening in America today and is it new are all significant parts of the Reed essay. Also, what will happen--America will continue to evolve, to take in other people who will change the American culture.

When: It has been happening as long as 10,000 years, according to Reed, though that sounds extreme to me. It will keep happening even if some of the people wanting to strengthen immigration laws have their way.

Where: America--all over.

Why: Why are some people upset--because they think that America has a definable culture, a European one. Why is there debate--because those people are probably wrong, because America is a "crisscrossing" of cultures and nobody can really even define "European" culture.

How: How did America become this "fish soup"? By taking in all the people who came to its shores for centuries. It isn't preventable and its not a good idea. It will keep happening. How does Reed convince me of his point? By offering lots of examples, like the different cultures obvious in Detroit, by showing how hard it is to separate out different influences in music like Beethoven's 9th Symphony, for instance, and by saying that the Iroquois may have influenced our system of government.

PRACTICE WITH JOURNALISTIC QUESTIONS

1. With classmates, create a list of journalistic questions about a text you have all read. You could use chapter 1 of this book, a selection from a class reader, a magazine article on the topic of your next writing assignment, or another text that you all know.
2. Write answers to each of the journalistic questions that you prepared above. Exchange journals with a classmate. Put an asterisk beside your classmate's answer that is most interesting to you as a reader. Take back your own journal. Put two asterisks beside your own answer about which you would like to write more.
3. Choose one of your answers to one of the journalistic questions, noting the marked selections as likely choices. Now describe briefly in your dialogue journal a paper that might result from focusing on that aspect of the text.
4. Share with a classmate or a group the variety of possibilities for topics and perspectives evoked by each of the journalistic questions.

5. Reflect on the process of working with journalistic questions. In a dialogue journal entry, explain what you learned from the collaborative activity above and from your own creation and answering of questions. Did this strategy work for you? Why or why not? Did certain questions elicit more thorough answers than others? Why or why not? Under what circumstances would you consider using this strategy again? Why?
6. Exchange journals with a classmate and respond to each other's reflection. Did you have similar experiences? Different ones? What can you learn from the other writer's experience that you can apply next time you use journalistic questions?

DEVELOPING A PAPER THAT RESPONDS TO READING

When Justin had explored Ishmael Reed's essay in his journal and through the journalistic questions, he was ready to propose a more formal response to the essay to meet the assignment for Paper 2. Within his proposal, you can see how he plans to use material generated in preparation for this paper and how positive he feels about the paper's potential success. As you read the paper, keep Justin's proposal in mind. Does he fulfill his plans for the essay?

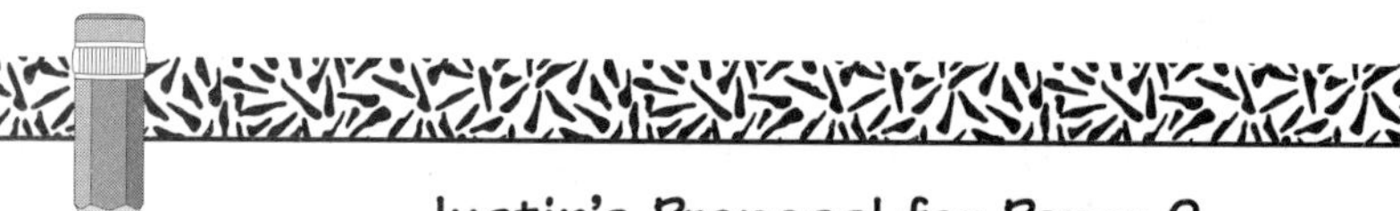

Justin's Proposal for Paper 2, Response to Reading

The assignment is to write a paper that responds to a text I have recently read. I will write about Ishmael Reed's essay "America: The Multicultural Society," which I had to read for my sociology class. I think that my experiences with friendships with people from different backgrounds can be interesting and helpful in showing a reader how different groups of people come together in our society. That makes my point that true assimilation is not very easy and may take a long time.

My audience for the paper will be my sociology teacher and the others in my class because we have been talking about this essay and because they will already understand the concept of assimilation and I won't have to explain it.

I have already summarized the essay in my journal and I have defined some of his vocabulary. I will rework that summary as one part of my response and also add examples from Reed to explain the essay, and I will use personal examples of my friends and me. I want to say that I agree with Reed about the need for diversity and to also talk about his point about the way some people persecute others. One more point is that while I've been working on this paper, I keep thinking about Rodney King asking if we can just get along. Those should be all my major points. I want to remember to quote the essay. I think this will make a good paper.

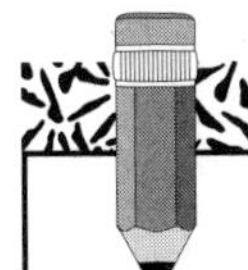

Justin's Paper 2, Draft 1, A Response to Reading

Crisscrossed World

In the article, "America: The Multicultural Society" Ishmael Reed tells his readers that the America of today, in fact historical America, is a society made up of many cultures. The article focuses on the combining of cultures in cities like Detroit and the impossibility of identifying a set of beliefs, or a culture or a human activity such as the arts, that are not a mix of cultural influences. He identifies the Puritans as the foremost influence on this country's tendency to selectively persecute members of various groups in various times in our history. He asks what kind of world we want.

I agree with Reed that our world and our country today is a mixture of all kinds of cultural elements. In his introduction he recalls a phone call from a poet who has visited Detroit, which he says has both mosques and a substantial Hispanic population. Reed tells us that the largest minority in Texas is Mexican-American and then he relates an experience with a white Yale professor in Milwaukee who was there to speak to African Americans about his study of the African cultures. This leads to a description of the United States as a bouillabaisse, a soup that includes several kinds of fish and seafood.

In my experience I have come to know and adopt some habits from people of other cultures. In fact it is hard to think of their cultures as "other," since they live near to me, I have gone to school with them, and we share so many things in common. My high school was not a melting pot, but it did have its share of minority students. I entered it already friends, for many years, with Darnell, an African American guy I had known since third grade. He has been to my house so many times that he calls my mother "Mom" sometimes. One year he spent Thanksgiving with us, and when he calls on the phone other members of my family walk by and put in comments, like, "Tell Darnell this or that." He tried to show me how to do my hair in dreads--it's frizzed. His mother gave my mom a recipe for sweet potato pie. But those just seem like the differences any friend would bring. I know that when he goes to Tennessee with his family they have other rituals, different food, maybe because of the place, maybe because of their different racial heritage.

My other friend, Rajesh, is Indian. I learned to eat some strange foods at his house. He is not Christian, so Christmas was kind of new to him when he came here and we taught him Christmas carols. He works in his family's store, and works very hard at school too, and doesn't always get to have much fun. I taught him to play ice hockey and he loves Blues Traveler. Once he gave my mother a scarf his mother painted.

When we were all seniors we boycotted the prom together. We were all having girlfriend problems or didn't have them or any money, so we had an all-night marathon basketball game.

I like knowing people from other experiences. But I know that Reed is right about the tendency some people have to persecute others or to take excessive pride in their own cultures. In fact as well as the "majority" view some minority groups take that kind of pride in their own ways. Rajesh's family is very strict because they come from wealthy, educated people in India. They think most Americans are sort of unsophisticated compared to their family and friends at home in India.

It's views like that, the differences that come not just with race and culture but with backgrounds, that will keep everyone who comes here from being assimilated anytime soon. Assimilation means actually becoming part of the dominant culture. I think that will take a long time because it means moving beyond our family backgrounds and that takes generations. It would be a loss to the richness of our culture. I liked hearing Darnell's mother tell us about the slaves in her family background. I like the way that Rajesh's house smells like incense.

Reed asks what kind of world we want. "A humdrum homogeneous world of all brains and no heart, no fiction, no poetry; a world of robots with human attendants bereft of imagination, of culture? Or does North America deserve a more exciting destiny? To become a place where the cultures of the world crisscross?" I want a crisscrossed world and I'm glad I met it through my friends.

Justin's Writer's Statement for Paper 2, Response to Reading

Purpose: My purpose, according to the assignment, is to respond to the article by Reed in a 2-3 page paper, identifying a main idea in his article and including a summary of the article. I took the position that I agree with Reed basically. Crossing cultures is a positive thing. But I do not believe that true assimilation of all the cultures is likely, and I don't even think it is desirable.

Audience: My sociology teacher and other people in my class, but I think lots of people would be interested in this topic.

Rationale: I chose this article because I can use it for my writing class and my sociology class where every week we have to read an essay or article related to the class. The discussion of assimilation is one we are having in that class now.

Strengths and Weaknesses: I like the details I used about my friends. That is a strength. And I like the way those details relate to Reed's essay. But I think my weakness might be the same thing. I may have too much about my friends and not enough about the issue of assimilation and the "elect". It needs more for a sociology paper. In fact, I think my literacy autobiography has the same kind of problem. My other problem is that for this class the paper is 2-3 pages but my sociology teacher will only read up to 2 pages, so I will have to take some out for that class.

Questions for Response:

1. What can I take out to make the paper shorter?
2. Is the paper too personal?
3. Do I need more about assimilation?

Suellen, a member of Justin's class, responded to his questions in the Writer's Statement.

Readers' Responses to Justin's Paper 2, Response to Reading

After reading your draft, I want you to know that I really agree with you that we should keep the variety of cultures and influences we have in this country instead of having them all merge. But you have some problems accomplishing your purpose for your audience. I think that your sociology teacher would want a lot more about assimilation. You actually only talk about assimilation in one paragraph. I agree with your Writer's Statement that you have lots to say about your own experiences, but you need to discuss assimilation more and to show how it is connected to the rest of the paper including the part about your friends. Maybe you need to be more clear about what you think about assimilation and WHY. I did not get a very clear idea of what the article was all about, though your audience may not need that. So, I think yes, you need more about assimilation, yes, I think too much of the paper is personal experience not tied to your purpose, and yes, some of that could be taken out.

Monica agreed with Suellen in her response but offered an additional perspective since she had recently come to the United States from Romania.

I was very interested in your essay's topic since I am an ESL (English as a Second Language) student myself. I agree with you that United States is a sort of bouillabaisse. I got the impression that the concept of assimilation is very significant, yet you assume everyone in your class will understand it. I suggest you tie in the assimilation concept with your personal experiences. You could make your conclusion stronger and longer by telling your audience how you feel to the answers some of those questions provide. Also, you could expand your Indian friend example, because if you compare it to the African American friend, it doesn't have as much detail. Think about "strange" foods. You use a single point of view there. You consider them strange but Rajesh might consider Christmas strange. I like the details you wrote about your friends. I hope my comments will help you in your essay's revision.

Justin's teacher suggested taking a different approach:

Go back into your Working Portfolio, Justin, and pull out the responses to your autobiography. Then put them up against Suellen's and Monica's responses to Paper 2. What do you see? Please write in your dialogue journal about what these responses tell you. Then we'll talk.

In his journal, Justin quoted Stephen's, Stacey's, Suellen's, and Monica's responses to his first two papers and then drew conclusions from them.

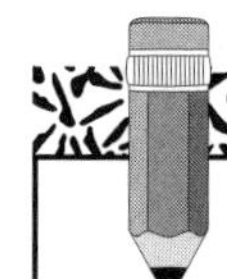

Justin Considers the Responses

Stephen: Cut the soccer. It just doesn't add to this paper. You're concentrating on your dad too much. What else do you have to say about writing. I've been asking myself, "What shows I'm literate?"

Stacey: The soccer doesn't tell me about literacy. Your dad is important but you need to emphasize yourself more. The lens of your camera needs to be on yourself.

Suellen: You have some problems accomplishing your purpose. Your sociology teacher would want more about assimilation. You address it in only one paragraph. Too much of the paper is personal experience.

Monica: You assume everyone in your class will understand assimilation. Make your conclusion stronger and longer by telling how you feel to the answers some of those questions provide. Also expand your Indian friend example. You use a single point of view.

I can see here that all these people are saying that both papers have too much stuff that doesn't help accomplish my purpose and not enough of what the papers are supposed to be about. I actually did know that. I guess I just figured I'd fix it later. But now I have to get the Reed one done so I can hand it in to my sociology teacher, either that or write another paper for that class. I also want to think about Monica saying that I have a single point of view. She's right.

As Justin was returning to earlier work to try to identify the problems in Paper 2 and to profit from the insights they could offer him about his writing, the class was also moving forward. The next assignment had been made, so Justin found himself working on two papers at once. You may encounter that same situation as you go back to material in your Working Portfolio, looking for information to help you improve your work. Although you may find it confusing at first, you may also be surprised at the knowledge about yourself as a writer that you gain from the experience. Keep thinking of all your papers as works in progress, papers you can return to at any time as you continue to work and grow as a writer.

As you work with the following assignment or another assignment your teacher supplies, consider how these activities could be applied to other pieces of writing whether in this class, at work, or in another class. While you look forward to your next draft, look backward also, reminding yourself of your successes, your weaknesses, and the resulting learning that can be applied to this next paper and other writing as well.

DRAFTING YOUR PAPER

1. Develop a set of journalistic questions for a text you have read recently. Answer them in your dialogue journal.
2. What is the main idea you would like to communicate about this text? Write that idea in a statement at the top of a journal page and then below it write everything that comes to mind about that idea. Write for at least five minutes. Refer to your journalistic questions and answers if necessary.
3. Within the text, mark with asterisks any significant points that will help you explain or support your main idea.
4. Write a proposal for this paper. Include those main points in the order you think you will use them.
5. Draft your paper and write a Writer's Statement to accompany it.

TURNING TO THE NEXT ASSIGNMENT

In his writing so far, Justin has used his own experience as the basis of one paper and the text and ideas of another writer as a springboard into the second paper. Now the assignment for a third paper introduces a new source of information. Justin and his classmates must conduct an observation in preparation for this paper.

> Assignment: Develop a question about events and interactions in the public areas of your campus, such as classrooms, canteens, or sports facilities. To help you answer the question, plan and conduct an observation, recording what you observed. Write a paper that uses your observation and any other information sources you choose in answering your original question.

Guidelines for Planning and Conducting an Observation

Planning

1. Develop a research question for investigation. Observations function best to answer questions such as what happened, who was involved, how long did it take, or how are relationships conducted or tasks performed.
2. Choose a situation that will help answer the question.
3. Make arrangements to conduct the observation and obtain the necessary permissions.

Observing and Notetaking

1. Identify your purpose in conducting the investigation. What will you be watching for?
2. Devise a format for recording your observations: a chart, a set of questions, or a chronological log of events you observe.

Interpreting Data

1. Draw conclusions supported by your data. Observation can rarely support a conclusion about WHY something happened.
2. Make reasonable generalities. An observation in your football stadium may support a generality about football fans on your campus but not about college football fans in general.

DEVELOPING A PAPER THAT USES OBSERVATION AS AN INFORMATION SOURCE

As the work for the observation began, Justin was still engaged in the Reed paper, so he decided to extend his investigation of assimilation to this third paper. "I don't think I can start thinking about a whole new topic right now," he wrote in his journal. "I have gotten pretty interested in how people of different backgrounds relate—I liked all the stuff about my friends in the Reed paper. But that's not assimilation. I've got to take all that out of Paper 2 so maybe I can find a way to use some of it and learn more about inter-group relations."

Another journal entry shows Justin's brainstorming a list of questions that might serve as the basis for his observation.

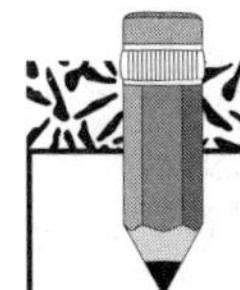

Justin's Brainstorming

How do college students choose friends?

How do college students meet people from other backgrounds?

How assimilated are international students on our campus?

What do people like about friends from different backgrounds?

Do students on our campus interact with people from different backgrounds?

How common are friendships between students from different backgrounds?

Justin's proposal shows that these questions were a starting point for the ideas he developed in his proposal and for the journalistic questions that helped him develop the specifics of his observation plan.

Justin's Proposal for Paper 3, Observation

The assignment is to write a paper that addresses a social issue we have read about and that is related to the public life on our campus. The paper must include findings from an observation. I am going to write about assimilation, which I began working with in another paper after reading Ishmael Reed's article, "America: The Multicultural Society." In my last paper I talked about my friendships with people from other races or backgrounds. It reminded me of Rodney King and his question about "getting along" after the L.A. riots. I think that people in my generation do have friends from other backgrounds, but I don't know how much assimilation is really taking place. I also wonder whether or not that is really a good thing, to assimilate. Reed seems to think that we're better off with a mix of differences, but maybe the question is whether we can "get along" when we're so different. Tolerance for the difference might be the issue. But I'm interested in friendships between people of different races and cultures and I think that can be not only about tolerance but appreciation of differences too. I want to remember what Monica said, about not looking at it just from my own perspective. That's important to be a friend. So I want to explore friendships between people from different cultures and races in my next paper. I want to look at that issue specifically on our campus.

As I do all this, I have to remember to stay on the real topic and not go off the track like I did in the other papers. Stephen says he kept asking himself how he knows he's literate, maybe I'll find a question like that to ask.

The nature of portfolio learning has emerged here. Not only is Justin referring to earlier documents to try to solve present problems, but now he is also reaching ahead, expanding the thinking about multicultural issues that he began in Paper 2. And, in choosing a strategy for Paper 3, he returns to journalistic questions: "I'm just not up to something new," he explains. This time he seems more comfortable with these questions, adapting them more easily to the task in this second practice with them.

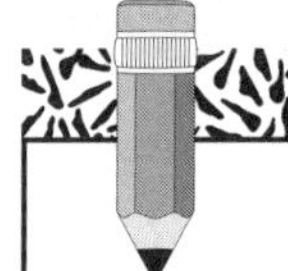

Justin's Journalistic Questions for Paper 3, Observation

I am going to use the journalistic questions to help me decide about this paper, my planning for the observation.

Who will I observe? I will observe students who are in groups in the student union. I will look at both large and small groups.

What do I want to try to find out? I want to see how people of different backgrounds interact. Do they often spend time together?

When will I do my observations? I will do them at lunchtime and in the late afternoons when students have free time to spend with friends.

Where will I do my observations? In the Student Union.

Why did I make these choices? I chose to watch groups of students because I want to try to watch people from different backgrounds interacting; I chose the union because lots of international students go there. Also, lots of people gather there to watch sports on the big screen TV. I chose the times because that's when people have free time. I didn't choose the library because lots of people study together who aren't really friends, and I want to know about people who choose to be together.

How . . . I don't know how to do this question.

Justin used the journalistic questions not directly about his topic but about the project of observing people to help answer his question. The answers gave him confidence that he could move ahead with the observation.

Justin's Notes on His Observation

I went to the Union at 4 pm on Thursday, February 4. I sat in a booth and watched several groups of students all of them seeming to be alike, for instance, one group of three white girls, another group of four white guys. A black couple came in and sat down. Later three students who were Oriental and one white guy came in a group. When it started to get busy, I decided to make a chart that showed how many at a table and what racial or cultural group they seemed to be from. It was obvious right away that I could only identify those groups who have something that identifies them. Skin color or dress as with many Indian or Muslim women or some other characteristic. That will limit my project.

Thursday night there was an NBA game on, so I went to see who was in the union. Immediately I noticed that the large groups were often exclusively black or white. One table had about ten people, both men and women, all white. The other biggest group was eight black students, again, mixed gender. These and other groups of up to six people were watching the game. Two of these groups included people who seemed to be from another background than the majority, for instance one Oriental student with three white students, and two black students in a group with five white students. None of the rest of the groups were mixed. There were, however, people in booths who didn't seem to be paying attention to the game. I saw more mixes there. There was one set of two made up of one black person, one white. There was one black/Indian set, one white/oriental set, and lots of same-look sets or groups of three.

I'm afraid I'm not being correct in the way I'm identifying these different groups of people, I just don't know how else to put it.

I went back to the Union on Monday at lunchtime to see if I could find any patterns in what I saw. It was pretty much the same. Large groups of people, like when they pulled tables together, almost always appeared to be a group of people from the same racial or cultural background. Small groups were either the same or mixed. More sets of two were mixed than any other kind of group, and that was true for sets of same and different genders.

I can see that it's a good thing I'm not trying to see if people are being assimilated, I don't even know what the dominant culture is, basketball? jeans? hamburgers? But I can tell who probably chooses to spend time together. I also wonder if college students are more open to people of other backgrounds than other people. I think I'm trying to do way too much here.

Justin's sense that he cannot make sweeping conclusions about assimilation, or anything else, is correct. When you read his draft and Writer's Statement below, be aware of the conclusions he is drawing. Do his observations support them? What other kinds of information does he use to help make his point?

Justin's Paper 3, Draft 1, Observation

In our society today, relationships between members of different racial or cultural groups is a big issue. It's on the front page or on the news every day. The big question seems to be the one that Rodney King asked after the LA riots. "Can't we just get along?" On my campus, the answer seems to be that we can to a certain degree. Watching groups of people in the student union, you can see that there are friendships and maybe romantic relationships between members of different groups. But that seems to be more on a one to one basis than a free mixing in all kinds of situations.

An observation in our student union showed that at most times of the day, students come in various sizes of groups. You can almost always find big groups of people. In nearly every case during a three day observation those groups were made up of people who appeared to be from the same racial group. Gender was mixed, race or obvious cultural background was not usually. Smaller groups were more likely to have people of two different backgrounds in them but I never saw a group with three obviously different people. And they all seemed to get along.

The mixing of backgrounds happened most often with pairs of people, when the genders were the same or different. When people sat at small tables or booths in twos, all kinds of mixes showed up but same group pairs were the most common.

If Rodney King wants to know if we can get along, I think the answer is yes but on a more personal level. We make friends with individual people and we enjoy our time with them, but when we join a small group of people different from ourselves, maybe because one of our friends introduces us, we probably don't feel comfortable joining a large group where we are the minority.

This makes sense to me because that was my experience in high school. My friends were from different backgrounds than mine. From third grade, Darnell was my best friend. He was an African American guy who even now when he's at another college is the person who knows me best. When we were growing up together, we were in and out of each others' houses and went lots of places together. He even spent this Thanksgiving with us when he came home from college and his family wanted to go to Tennessee. But I was not best friends with any other Black guys or any other white guys. As we grew older, Darnell and I developed separate groups of friends that were not part of our friendship. So we did not widen our group of friends out of a pool of each others' friends the way we did by meeting friends through other people. I didn't learn to get along with people from other races or cultures because I had one friend from a different group than my own.

One friend Darnell and I did have together was Rajesh, an Indian guy who had come to our high school as a freshman. We were all in the same math class, and it took them both to get me through. Darnell and I got to know Rajesh because he sat next to me and tried to help me, which was Darnell's lifelong roll in math class. So they joined up to help me and we all became friends. We may be unusual, because I did not see any groups in my union observation of people from three different groups.

In an essay by Ishmael Reed, he talks about the mixing of cultures in America and whether or not assimilation or "crossing" of cultures is best. He says that America is like bouillabaisse, a rich fish soup made up of all kinds of ingredients. That kind of mixture certainly makes for a more interesting situation. And it's not just in America or where two countries' borders come together. When mother was in London, she was surprised to find lots of Indian curry restaurants and lots of Jamaicans as well. Those cultures are very different from the English and she said they add a lot to the atmosphere of London. That kind of mix can only make a place better, I think, if--and its an important if--they can get along.

The answer to that seems to me to get to know people as individuals, to take advantage of situations like classes or organizations or work that bring people of different backgrounds together. That way you have something in common to start with to help make up for the differences. Then the differences can turn into a plus. And then maybe we can start to get along.

Justin's Writer's Statement for Paper 3, Observation

Purpose: (Assignment) To write a paper using an observation and talking about a social situation we have read about and that we want to know about on our campus. (My purpose) To show that people of different groups get along when they can relate to each other on a one to one basis.

Audience: I'm not sure. I think it should be other college students who are concerned about relationships between groups in this country and on campus.

Thesis: That people tend to make friends with people from other groups on a one to one basis rather than mixing with a lot of other people from a different group.

Process: I began by choosing a topic from an essay I had already written about. I was interested in the issue of cross-cultural or racial friendships. The assignment included conducting an observation and choosing a thinking strategy. I used journalistic questions to help me decide how to do the observation. I conducted it to help me see in our student union if I could see any behavior patterns related to my topic. When I wrote out my observations I could see that the pattern was that small groups and pairs were more likely to contain mixes. When I thought about my own friendships, I realized that was my pattern too. Then I thought about what would go into my paper, starting with the Rodney King statement. I like to start with a quote. And then I reported what I observed, then I tried to lengthen the paper and go on with the discussion by talking about my friends and about the essay I read by Reed. I tried to stay on the focus of inter-group friendships and I think I did stay on focus and accomplished my purpose better than I did in the first two papers. I also took Stephen's idea of asking a question and decided in this paper to try to stay focused on King's question. I tried to address it in every paragraph. Working on this paper while I'm trying to get my paper on the Reed essay finished has kept my attention on sticking to the topic in this one. I don't want to have to do it over! I feel pretty good about this paper and want to see what other people say about it.

Questions:

1. Did I use my observations the way I was supposed to? I thought they should be more important in the paper but I didn't know what else to say about them.
2. Should I have given more information about the Reed essay?
3. How did my personal experiences work in the paper?
4. How did the references to "getting along" work to keep me on the topic?
5. Do you think I would offend anyone with this paper? I am not sure how to refer to people from other groups.

ANALYZING JUSTIN'S DRAFT

1. Write your responses to Justin's Writer's Statement questions about Paper 3. Exchange responses with classmates and discuss the issues Justin raises in his Writer's Statement. What application do those issues have to your drafts or the drafts of others in the group?
2. Analyze Justin's draft for evidence that he has indeed stayed more firmly focused on his stated topic and purpose. Do you agree with his assessment that this paper is more successful in that regard than were Papers 1 and 2? Why or why not?

PRACTICE WITH OBSERVATION

1. With a classmate or on your own, identify a question you would like to answer about activities in public areas of your campus. For instance, you may want to find out what student interactions take place in computer labs

or among the smokers who congregate outside smoke-free buildings, or you may want to know how many cars in the faculty lot are illegally parked.

2. Formulate your question and plan your observation. What will you observe? Where? When? Why did you make these choices? Do you need to obtain permission?
3. Plan your notetaking. Will you simply take notes, answer a standard list of questions about each person or group observed, or construct a chart?
4. Conduct the observation.
5. In your dialogue journal, report the results of the observation by describing the situation and what took place as you observed.
6. Draw appropriate conclusions. How does your data support your conclusions? How reasonable are any generalities you have drawn?
7. Exchange journals with another student or observation team. In the response side of the journal, address these questions: which details best help you to understand the setting and the participants of the activity observed? How was the observation limited? How appropriate are the conclusions?
8. In your journal, discuss your experience with observation. How would you improve upon the observation itself and the reporting of the experience if you were to repeat it?

DRAFTING YOUR PAPER

1. In your journal, write a proposal for a piece of writing that addresses the question you posed for your observation. You may keep the original question as the central focus, or you may go back to one of the strategies presented in chapter 3, such as looping or clustering, to find a different way to approach your topic. For instance, you might compare the interaction among smokers outside an academic building and in another location. Or you might analyze the data you recorded for gender or age or some other factor, allowing you, for instance, to conclude that more women than men are in the smoker group or that more young women than older women are smokers.
2. Include both purpose and audience in your proposal. What purposes can you serve for them? Who is your audience for such a piece? Why would your audience want to know the answer to your question? What do they already know? What else would they have to know? What background information is necessary? What information about the observation is needed? How would you synthesize that information into your draft? If you have trouble answering these questions, you may want to brainstorm possible purposes and audiences before beginning your draft.

3. Add to the end of your proposal questions about your proposal and the piece of writing it projects. If you worked with a partner, exchange proposals with your partner. Respond to his questions, and then add a statement about how your proposed draft will differ from or be similar to his.
4. Draft your own paper answering the question you posed earlier and incorporating the information you collected from your observation. Use responses to your proposal from your teacher and your peers.

RETURNING TO A PRECEDING ASSIGNMENT

Justin's work to clarify his focus and better accomplish his purpose for Paper 2 was interrupted by the urgency of the new assignment for Paper 3. As he was conducting his observation and drafting the resulting paper about intergroup friendships, he still had to finish the response to Reed's essay for his sociology class. So he returned to the responses he received from his classmates and to his teacher's suggestions.

After reading the responses of his classmates, Justin had agreed that both Paper 1 and 2 did stray from their original purposes. In a conference, his teacher suggested that to clarify his focus he try a thinking strategy called cubing. Cubing approaches a topic from six of many possible perspectives. "Think of your topic as sitting inside a cube with each side representing a different angle or perspective by which to view it," his teacher told him. "Then do a series of brainstormings directed by the various perspectives."

Guidelines for Cubing

Investigate your topic by choosing six of the following perspectives.

1. Describe your topic.

What is its color, shape, size, texture, smell, taste, or sound?

2. Analyze your topic for elements.

What are the parts, important elements, or characteristics of your topic? What categories does it break into?

3. Analyze your topic for cause-effect relationships.

What conditions or people caused it? What motivates the people involved with it? What are its results or effects? Who is affected?

4. Exemplify your topic.

In what specific instances have you or an acquaintance had experience with this topic? What examples of it have you encountered in your reading or in other media?

5. Compare or contrast your topic.

How is it like other things? How is it different?

6. Apply your topic.

How is it used? What is its purpose?

7. Associate your topic.

What does this topic make you think of? For example, what books, songs, paintings, or movies are related to it?

8. Argue for or against your topic.

What are its positive and negative aspects? For whom?

In his journal, Justin wrote that he had chosen these "sides" of the cube to use in exploring assimilation: analyze for cause-effect relationships, exemplify, compare or contrast, apply, associate, and argue. He decided that description was not very applicable to his topic of assimilation and that analyzing for elements would not be as useful as analyzing for cause-effect relationships. Below is his cubing.

Justin's Cubing

Analyze for cause-effect relationships--Assimilation would cause a merging of cultures so that we would not have ethnic neighborhoods, maybe not even such things as festivals and restaurants if it went to its highest degree--it might also cause a lack of tension among groups because the groups would disappear--in the long run it might cause a rebirth of ethnic pride if people wanted to get back to their roots. We see that today in

African Americans who seem to want to find the roots they lost--or it might have economic effects on communities that count on businesses and festivals that focus on a particular background--mostly it would be a loss for the richness of our country.

Exemplify--Examples of assimilation--Lots of African American people have merged into the culture, my mother works with business people who seem to me to be just like everyone else--and Colin Powell seems very assimilated to me; I don't think of him as Black or anything else, I guess I think of him as part of the military if I associate him with any group. The problem with finding examples is that the main ones, like musicians or other famous people, belong to another very separate group--sports players, for instance, so that they aren't typical in any way. They're a culture all their own. Maybe the most important group I can think of is Native Americans, and I don't think they've been allowed to assimilate at all.

Compare or Contrast--Assimilation is not like someone just joining a group, because someone from the main culture can join a group and they all already have all kinds of things in common. But very basic things, like the things they did as kids, the language they first learned to speak, the foods they were fed as babies, religion may all be really different. Most little kids my age watched Sesame Street but someone from another culture can't go back and watch S.S. as a little kid, so he missed that indoctrination of cultural values. And, the things that the people in the main culture take for granted may look strange to other people. I don't know what else to say here.

Apply--We could use assimilation to change the way we do some things, like affirmative action maybe, or the balances they try to get in schools. I'm not sure those examples really apply, I think I'd have to ask somebody if that's going too far--we could use it to get rid of prejudice or to make the ideals of all men being created equal really be true.

Associate--I associate my friends with assimilation because I think of Darnell as assimilated, though I know that now, in his new school, he's much more active with other African American students, and I associate Rajesh because he and his family are trying to be assimilated. He would especially like not to stick out, not to have his parents have different rules for him than most of us have and he'd like his mother not to wear a sari. And I think it's great that she does. I think sometimes I value his culture more than he does.

Argue for or against--I think I'm against assimilation. I like diversity and the interesting elements that come with people of different backgrounds. We'd have nothing but McDonalds! I like cities that have a Chinatown. But maybe that's the view of someone in the main culture. Maybe like Rajesh, they don't want to stick out, don't want to live in a "chinatown" but would rather live in the suburbs and don't want to provide entertainment for me when I go to their part of town.

Finding Direction in Cubing

Justin followed his cubing with a journal response that identified the most promising aspects of the cubing exercise in preparation for revising the draft about Reed's essay.

Justin's Journal Response to His Cubing

When I was doing the cube, I could see that I was really against the idea of assimilation as a good thing. Towards the end, though I started thinking about whether people would like to be assimilated. And then I read my draft and came to that last line where I quoted Reed about wanting a world with no heart, no poetry, just robots etc., and suddenly that looked like a pretty far out view. What makes him think that would happen? Why wouldn't we have hearts, maybe we wouldn't have hate. Or why wouldn't we have poets and artists? Most cultures do. Are there only two choices? So now I think that my main idea for the piece is that assimilation is something we really don't know very much about, because it seems awful hard to accomplish, partly because a main culture may not be willing for it to happen, like with Native Americans. It might lead to a utopian world, where everyone could pool their talents and backgrounds, who knows? For right now, I'm glad to know people of all kinds, but I can see how assimilation might be a good thing for people outside the main culture.

PRACTICE WITH CUBING

1. Look through Justin's cubing and his journal response to it. What new ideas does he identify in his response? What ideas does he generate in the cubing that he does not identify in the response?
2. Write a note to Justin about the new material he has generated and its uses in a new draft. What changes can you foresee in his revised draft?

PRACTICE WITH YOUR CUBING

1. Read through journal entries and other writing you have generated so far in this class. Note possible topics of interest. Cube, using a topic you already have some interest in and knowledge about. As you cube, use at least six of the eight perspectives described in this chapter.
2. Discuss your cubing experience with a classmate. How did it work for you? What was easy or hard about it? Which aspects of the topic seemed easy to discuss; which seemed difficult?
3. Look through your cube, identifying at least three of the six perspectives that might provide purposes for a piece of writing. In your journal, write one of the purposes at the top of the page. Use a "to" statement such as "To Explore the Effects of Assimilation Upon Immigrants' Family Life." Freewrite, filling at least a page with information exploring that perspective. State a purpose and freewrite for two more perspectives.

DRAFTING YOUR PAPER

1. Practice planning a draft by returning to Justin's cube. Work with a classmate to write a "to" statement to identify a purpose drawn from the material he generated in his cube. Choose material from his cube, his draft(s), or Reed's essay as the basis of a proposal for a paper that might result from Justin's cube.
2. To plan your own paper, exchange journals with one or more classmates and respond to each other's freewritings from your cube exercises. Which of the approaches seem best? Why? What would the purpose of each be? What would a reader expect to find in such a piece of writing? What information about this topic can you share with your classmates?
3. Working from your cube, your freewriting, and the responses of others, choose a statement of purpose and material you have already generated to propose a paper you might create from your work with cubing. Write the statement of purpose and list of material in your dialogue journal.

RETHINKING A DRAFT

Justin has used cubing to generate a number of ideas related to his earlier discussion of assimilation. Cubing seems to have broadened his perspective, as Monica requested, for his journal entry points out that he now believes assimilation to be a very complicated topic. He has determined that although he may enjoy the richness of a diverse world, people new to a culture may find advantage in being assimilated, and that point comes through in his revision of Paper 2, the response to Reed's essay. Justin seems to have acted on Monica's advice not only in thinking about the perspective of those new to his culture but in reconsidering Reed's remarks about a heartless world of robots. Justin sees that the issue may not be limited to two choices.

This broadening of vision is a good example of the way in which portfolio learning provides opportunities to rethink your ideas. As you read Justin's second draft of the response to Reed's article, look for other examples of changes in his ideas as he combines new material with that from the original draft.

Justin's Paper 2, Draft 2, Response to Reading

The Disadvantages of Assimilation

In the article "America: The Multicultural Society," Ishmael Reed tells his readers that the America of today, in fact, the America of history is a society made up of many cultures. The article focuses on the combining of cultures in such cities as Detroit and the impossibility of identifying a set of beliefs, a culture, or a human activity such as the arts that is not a mix of cultural influences. He identifies the Puritans as the foremost influence on this country's tendency to selectively persecute members of various groups in various times in our history. He ultimately asks what kind of world we want, "a humdrum homogeneous world of all brains and no heart, no fiction, no poetry; a world of robots with human attendants bereft of imagination, of culture?"

I agree with Reed that today our world and our country are a mixture of all kinds of cultural elements, maybe more than ever before in history. And in this country, the issue of assimilation is one that seems to me to be very controversial. Assimilation is minority people actually becoming part of the main culture. We are in the midst of arguments about such things as affirmative action, and new arguments about busing in some parts of the country. Those are attempts to assimilate minority people into the main culture by making sure they are part of the workplace and of classrooms. In both places they would be exposed to majority values and ways of doing things. That would aid assimilation.

I can see why assimilation could be a good thing for minority people. My friend Rajesh, who was born in India, would like to be more assimilated, and would especially like his parents to be more assimilated. They are much more strict than most American parents, and when he is with his mother, he gets embarrassed when she is wearing a sari. He doesn't want to stick out as foreign. Assimilation can be a good thing for people who come here wanting to be Americans, for it allows them to fit into a society and to have the advantages of the members of the society.

But I think I agree with the main idea that Reed is putting across, even though it may be selfish. He thinks that we need to maintain the diversity that comes in a city such as Detroit which has both mosques and an Hispanic population. There is a richness that comes with all those different cultures. When I was in high school, my two best friends were Rajesh and an African American guy named Darnell. I learned about sweet potato pie, about Hindu religious customs, about saris, and heard stories about Darnell's slave ancestors. It's hard to know what they got from me in that way. I would hate to see them and their families become just like everyone else.

It seems like more minority groups are wanting to stay apart from the main culture, not to assimilate. All the African names that people use now, and the lawsuits that Native Americans have started over land and artifacts that belong to them and are important to their religion show that people value their different backgrounds just like many of us enjoy them too.

So, while I want my friends and other minority people to be allowed the rights and privileges of the main culture here, I also want to be able to know about their backgrounds and to have that all be a part of our culture. I don't think total assimilation is a good thing for either the people joining our society or for the rest of us either.

ANALYZING JUSTIN'S DRAFT

In your journal, write a response to Justin's draft.

1. What is Justin's purpose for this paper? What material in the paper supports your identification of this purpose?
2. What elements of the paper make it more appropriate or inappropriate for his audience than was his first draft?

3. How well has he overcome the problems his readers identified in his first draft? What parts of the new draft show the advantages of Justin's cubing as he prepared to revise?

REVISION STRATEGY

1. In your journal, discuss the papers you have already drafted. How could observation enhance that work and help you serve your purposes? What question is raised in a drafted work that could be appropriately and interestingly answered by observation?
2. If observation does have application in any of the papers you have already drafted, amend your proposal by identifying a new section related to the new draft you will create. In this new section of your proposal, plan your observation and discuss how it will help you accomplish your purpose.
3. Conduct the observation and synthesize it into your earlier draft. You may want to see how student writers synthesize various sources into their writing in later chapters.

WORKING PORTFOLIO UPDATE

Justin has worked his way through two papers in this chapter, incorporating sources of information outside himself into his work. He has also continued to receive and consider the responses of others to the work he produces. He has moved back to earlier work and has looked ahead to a new assignment, incorporating material gathered from his reading and his observations.

By now you have added to your Working Portfolio documents reflecting practice with a strategy for reading, the stages of an observation, and cubing. You may also have newly revised work in your growing collection of materials.

In the next chapter Justin will continue to create variety in his work by including material from sources outside himself. This time he will use interviews as a way to enlarge his understanding of his topic and of his own thinking.

CHAPTER 6
Creating Variety

When my grandfather died last January, I accompanied my parents and sister to the flower shop in his southern Missouri town. Florists for thirty years, now retired, my parents seemed unsure about what to order. When the local florist made a conventional suggestion of "nice browns and golds," my mother seemed ready to agree until my sister interrupted.

"Let's do something more interesting, pull in a lot of colors and different kinds of flowers," she said. "He liked pretty colors," and indeed he did. His windowsills were lined with rainbows of sparkling trinkets. As I write today, a red glass goblet from his kitchen window throws a ruby stain across my desk. My mother acquiesced, and, walking through the refrigerated storage area, we chose a few of practically every flower in stock. It made a lovely display, vivid and varied in the winter landscape.

While you may strive to make your writing colorful in a somewhat different way, you can look to variety as a technique, just as my sister did. In the next two chapters you will see an emphasis upon using various kinds of sources to provide information in your work. You have already seen Justin call upon his own experience, use a text, and move outward from the text into a related topic enhanced by his observation. Such variety of sources can add color to your writing and broaden the scope of your ideas.

In this chapter you will see how students create variety and enrich their work by adding information from interviews about their topics. Amy will incorporate the results of informal interviews into a paper that also contains her own ideas and information gleaned from a magazine article. Later, you will see Justin interview his grandmother for use in revising his literacy autobiography. He will also conduct a formal interview in preparation for a new paper. This new paper will include his own ideas about the Reed essay, information based upon his student union observation, and interview results. Lots of variety.

You'll also see Justin at his most frustrated in this chapter, struggling with several problems. Afraid that he's falling behind, he is trying to revise Paper 3, the one that grew out of his observation, to collect information to revise his literacy autobiography, and to grapple with an important professor whom he finds difficult. You will probably identify with the conflicts in his busy life as he finds himself intrigued by his work and the new activity of interviewing but unable to focus on just one paper at a time. Justin is having trouble setting priorities, and his work shows it.

USING INTERVIEWS AS INFORMATION SOURCES

You are familiar with interviewing as a part of news and entertainment programming. However, interviewing doesn't necessarily require that you go to newsmakers for information. Although you may go to expert sources of information, if you choose to write about an experience common to many people, you can play up that commonality, recognizing the enjoyment readers derive from reading material they can identify with. In such cases, the personal experiences and resulting knowledge of others can provide enlightening information that enriches your papers with the authoritative voices of everyday people. They can also add support to your material, give you a frame of reference or point of comparison for your own experiences, and consequently help you evaluate your own approach to the topic.

Amy is a freshman science major. One of the assignments in her writing course was similar to Justin's for Paper 2 in which he responded to the Reed article about our culture.

> *Amy's Assignment*
>
> Choose a magazine article which takes a position of interest to you; develop and support your own position in relation to the author's.

Though she first considered responding to a science article, Amy chose to work with an article that she believed would have more personal appeal to her and to readers in her writing group. She selected an article written for *Cosmopolitan* by Pete Hamill, "The Simple Truth about Love (There Is None!)." As she considered her response to the article, she drew upon her background in journalism when she enjoyed interviewing students for the school newspaper.

PROPOSING A PAPER THAT SYNTHESIZES TEXT AND INTERVIEWS

As Amy prepared for this paper, she wrote a journal entry that analyzed her article, answering many of the same questions that Justin addressed in his journal analysis of Reed's article on page 107. For instance, her journal entry included a summary that she then used verbatim in her paper.

Amy's Journal Entry

Hamill's article is a witty writing that explains that all women are not alike in the world, although most men think they are. A lot of men think that they can treat all women in the same way yet always get the same response. Is this true? Of course not! There are many types of women who like to be treated in many different ways. Hamill writes, "Men still begin sentences in this way, 'What women want is . . .' and you must sit back and wonder: 'which women?'"

Amy's journal entry and a freewriting about the article made up her prewriting for this paper and led her to the following proposal.

Amy's Proposal

In this paper, I want to respond to Pete Hamill's article about the relationships between men and women. Everyone is interested in that topic. And since my relationships haven't been exactly smooth, maybe I'll learn something. When I worked on the school newspaper, I used to like to interview people, so I think that I'll try to talk to some people who have different viewpoints from mine and see if I can incorporate them into the paper. After all, I don't really know very much about this so I don't see how I can do this whole paper on my own.

I think I can just sit down with my friends and get them to talk about their experiences, but I also know that they may get off the subject and I don't have much time to do this paper. I have to work all weekend. So, in my group Susan suggested that I make a list of the major points in the article that I will be talking about in my essay and then ask my friends to talk about those things. I think that's a great idea. Of course, I'm not sure yet just what I'll be talking about, so I'll use the list of the article's main points that I put in my journal response to the article. The main points are: 1. Not all women are alike but lots of men treat them like they are. 2. People expect too much from relationships. Sometimes they go into one already knowing what they want. 3. Some books try to tell people that they can change people. 4. Other books and TV give people an idea of how love is supposed to be. I'm going to make a list of these to use as questions when I talk to my friends. Since I'm a woman and not married, I think I should talk to guys and to someone who is married.

As you read Amy's draft below, be alert for several features of her work. Consider the effectiveness of her summary of Hamill's article. She transferred it from her journal analysis, but she also includes in her proposal a list of Hamill's points that might be the basis for a more complete summary. Consider the advantages of each. Also, watch for her use of sources; some passages are quoted whereas others are paraphrased.

Guidelines for Incorporating Sources

QUOTING: When you quote from a source, you reproduce material exactly as it was presented by the original source whether a written passage or a statement in an interview. Also, you must make clear the source of the material, and you must enclose the quotation in quotation marks.

PARAPHRASING: When you paraphrase, you use your own words to restate the ideas of someone else. You may decide to paraphrase because the original passage used language unfamiliar to your reader or because you want some variety beyond direct quotations. You must, however, be accurate in interpreting the original material, making sure that in choosing words more familiar to your reader, you do not change the meaning.

In her paper, Amy quotes Andrea:

> Andrea H., a college student, believes that, "Everyone wants to be him or herself. I would never act in any other way just because someone wants me to live up to his expectations. If people can't accept you for who you are, then the relationship will never work."

An appropriate paraphrase of this quote might be:

> Andrea H., a college student, believes that we all just want to be ourselves. She could never be untrue to herself while trying to meet someone else's expectations, she says. If relationships are not based upon a mutual acceptance, they will never be successful.

Amy's Draft

Women and Men: The Preconceptions Should Be Given Up

"The Simple Truth about Love (There Is None!)," by Pete Hamill, is a witty writing that explains that all women are not alike in the world, although most men think they are. A lot of men think that they can treat all women in the same way yet always get the same response. Is this true? Of course not! There are many types of women who like to be treated in many different ways. Hamill writes, "Men still begin sentences in this way, 'What women want is . . .' and you must sit back and wonder: 'which women?'" Women are different. Some women may love receiving flowers from a man; others may think a man is stupid for spending money on something that will just die in a few days. Brett M., a college student, has experienced that women want different things. He claims, "The first girl I dated would get so mad at me if I didn't call her at least twice a day. The next girl I went out with broke up because she said I called her too much; I didn't give her enough space. Girls are definitely different."

Some people expect too much out of others in relationships. Instead of starting out a relationship with an attitude that all women or men are the same and like to be treated as such, "Women and men must give up all preconceptions about each other, everything that presumes to be knowledge, and deal with each other one at a time," according to Hamill. Some believe that many relationships are ruined because of high expectations brought into a relationship that cannot be lived up to. Andrea H., a college student, believes that, "Everyone wants to be him or herself. I would never act in any other way just because someone wants me to live up to his expectations. If people can't accept you for who you are, then the relationship will never work."

Others, however, believe that not all preconceptions about the other should be given up because a person may come out of an abusive relationship. If someone does come out of an abusive relationship or have some unfortunate history, it is only reasonable that that person is a little overly cautious when starting a relationship with someone. Rob D., another student, agrees, "I would understand if a girl I dated was cautious or hesitated in sharing her feelings. Hopefully, over time, we could work it out. It is probably wise to be a little cautious with everyone considering all the weird people out there."

Hamill thinks that self-help relationship books seem to make light of relationships, making them sound as if you can take any man or woman and turn him/her into the perfect mate. Romance novels always consist of a perfect man or prince charming. This, of course, is not reality. Not everyone is perfect and not every couple is completely compatible. Relationships, which have a lot of give and take, require compromise. Patty J., a married mother of three, believes that it's mostly a matter of compromise because she says it takes more work and sacrifice than romance to make a marriage when you're raising children and paying bills.

Hamill also suggests that television has had an effect on the expectations and outcomes of relationships. He claims that love stories on television "are never about the difficult system of collision and compromise that is at the heart of mature love." Surely that is true about fictional stories. However these stories are not greatly responsible for people expecting only love, passion, and romance out of a relationship, therefore ruining relationships because they are rarely composed of these elements. Matt S, a college student, believes that women form high expectations about men because of romance novels. He says, "Television isn't responsible for the preconceptions about people. However, these love stories that some women read give them these ideas of high expectations that they think men should live up to." Many, if not most, of the adult society realizes the reality of relationships. The reality is that struggling, fighting, compromise, and much more is required to keep it going.

As the title says, there is no simple truth about love. People are so different that it is almost impossible to fall in love, or even be compatible, with every kind of person. It is not always easy to keep a relationship; it usually takes a lot of work. The one piece of advice that Hamill would give to men or women about each other (advice I agree with) is, "Be patient, ask questions, listen hard, and always try to see the other person as he or she really is, rarely perfect, condemned to being human." Since all people are so different and like different things, it is time and experience that best teach what different people are like.

ANALYZING AMY'S DRAFT

1. How does Amy's identification of her sources give credibility to them?
2. Consider Amy's summary of Hamill's article. According to the information on page 145, has Amy adequately summarized the article? How would you make use of the list in her proposal to revise her summary?
3. In your journal, identify Amy's purposes in including her sources in her discussion of male-female relationships. Where within the essay do you find her ideas that are in agreement with Hamill's? In disagreement? How does she indicate the relationship between her ideas and Hamill's? What is the relationship between her ideas and those supplied by her interviews? How does she indicate that relationship?
4. Pete Hamill's article is the focus of Amy's essay. How could she change that focus to the issue of male-female relationships, using Hamill simply as one of her sources? How, for instance, would the opening paragraph change? How would the main points of the essay change? Choose some sentences that would change; rewrite them to fit the new focus.
5. Examine the ways that Amy has presented information from her sources. She has quoted sources, reproducing their ideas word for word and

enclosing them in quotation marks. She has also paraphrased material from her sources, explaining it in her own words. And she has sometimes introduced her source material with a sort of preview of what the source said. Identify each of these techniques in the essay.

Amy has used Hamill's article to stimulate and to limit her thinking for this paper. She already has many ideas about the topic, but the text presents her with a thesis and a series of points that provide structure and direction for her own discussion. It gives her a jumping off place: she can begin by responding to Hamill's ideas and then move outward, exploring the ideas of others and synthesizing all of these as she comes to her own conclusions. Thus, she identifies her position and develops support for it.

PRACTICE WITH INFORMAL INTERVIEWS

Use the following set of activities to help you plan and draft an essay for which you find a position and develop support based on your own ideas and those of others:

1. Read an essay chosen by a group of your classmates or your teacher and analyze it for main idea and main points.
2. With a group of your classmates, develop a question or set of questions, regarding the issue addressed in your reading. In your journal, brainstorm a list of people you know with whom you could discuss this issue informally. Why are these people qualified to discuss this issue? Do you need to create more variety among your listing? Why or why not?
3. Share your list with a group of your classmates. Each member of your group should leave with an assignment to discuss the question with at least three persons from his list by the next class meeting and to bring written notes resulting from those conversations.
4. In your journal at the next class meeting, write a statement of your position on the question. Then share notes. If your class meets in a computer classroom, put notes on the network; if not, you may bring a copy for each member or may pass them around so that others can copy responses they find interesting or useful. Try to collect material that represents varied positions on the question.
5. In your journal, write a passage that states your position on the question and synthesizes the ideas of at least two other people, including one who disagrees with you. Considering the author of the article as one of your sources, include him in the discussion. Do you and your sources agree or disagree with the author?

6. Exchange dialogue journals with a classmate and respond to the passage, identifying the techniques used to synthesize various points of view.

DRAFTING YOUR PAPER

1. Return to the writing you have done so far in your dialogue journal entries. What experience have you written about that others in your class or of your acquaintance may have shared? Who are those people? Write a proposal for a piece that explores that topic. Include questions designed to elicit the positions or experiences of qualified responders.
2. Move around in your class, asking others about their experiences; take notes on their responses. Be sure to record—and spell correctly—the names of your sources. Or you may want to explain your experience on a computer network and ask your classmates to respond. Contact others listed in your proposal. Collect and record in your journal a total of at least six responses. Categorize them; do they confirm or contrast with your experience?
3. Move toward a draft of your paper by freewriting, getting down everything you know and that you have collected from others without worrying about organization or order.
4. Try beginning your draft with a statement of your own position or a provocative or intriguing statement from one of your sources who agrees or disagrees with you. As you draft your paper, including information from your sources, be sure to identify those sources by name and with any other relevant information.
5. In your Writer's Statement, include questions that ask whether your position is made clear or that ask your reader to identify techniques you used to synthesize confirming and conflicting ideas. One response should come from a person you quoted or paraphrased in the piece. Did you represent her ideas accurately?

INTERVIEWING FOR INFORMATION TO USE IN REVISION

When Justin went home for spring break, he realized that his grandmother could provide him with information useful in getting his literacy autobiography back on track. So he made arrangements with her to tape a conversation about his literacy background. He planned the initial questions, but the conversation went its own direction, as recorded below, prefaced by Justin's comments about the experience.

Justin's Transcript of an Interview

I was interested in getting some more information about my dad to understand why he dropped out of school and what he was really like. Also I wanted to learn about how someone else viewed me as I grew up, especially how I liked to read and what I wrote. I interviewed my dad's mother, my Grandma Cooper. She is 64 years old, and she is getting ready to retire from her job as administrative secretary to the librarian at a small college. She likes to read, too, and also likes to cook and to hike in state parks. My grandma is easy to talk to but sometimes it was hard to keep her on the subject.

When I typed up the transcript, I first tried to get it down exactly the way it was on the tape, but that was too hard. So, I would listen and then paraphrase the conversation except where I thought I needed to get it word for word. I know that means I can only quote those places, but I'll just have to be careful.

Me: *M*   Grandma: *G*

M: Grandma, I'm writing a literacy autobiography for my composition course about things I like to do. It's supposed to represent myself and the world. We've been studying that we have lots of sign systems to use to express ourselves. I've written about some of mine.

As I wrote my essay, I started thinking about my dad, so I'm going to ask you some questions about him. I also want to know what we used to do when I was little that influenced the way I read and write now.

So here goes. How come you've always worked in a library and your only son didn't even learn to read very well?

G: Your father didn't like it when I went to work when he was five. Your Grandpa couldn't make enough money for us to pay our bills, so I went to work. I'd had a year of business school and the college had just expanded its library and needed a clerical person. I like to read and liked libraries and I could learn the new job without having to measure up to someone from the past.

Your dad hated the babysitter's. He threw tantrums and cried every day when I left him. I think he blamed it on the library, like it was the library that took his mommy away. Later when the first grade class went to get library cards, he refused to get one. His negative attitude toward the library got in the way of him wanting to read, right from the start.

M: I remember that you had books at your house. I remember the Dr. Seuss books. You used to read me *Cat in the Hat.*

G: Those books were from when your dad and aunt grew up. Your dad was always so active that he wouldn't sit still to be read to. He liked to be outside running or throwing the football. I'd sometimes corral him, but he'd talk me into going out back and pitching him a baseball instead of reading to him.

You weren't like that. I remember your mother reading to you from right when you were born. I remember going over to your house and finding her reading the newspaper to you when you were less than a month. She said you needed to hear words and it didn't matter what she read, but you needed to hear it.

M: I remember that you had magnets on your refrigerator to keep my pictures and poems. Wow, what lousy rhymes I wrote, but you always read them out loud like they were from great poets. Were you laughing inside?

G: You said you're learning about how people express themselves. Well, you expressed yourself with words in your poems. You'd write when you were happy and when you were sad. Lots of times you would add pictures, or you said that you sometimes drew a picture first and then wrote words.

M: I still write poetry, but I don't show anyone.

G: I still have my magnets!

M: When Aunt Beth's husband died, I wrote her a letter. I couldn't talk with her, but I could write. Did she ever mention that letter to you?

G: Beth only kept a few sympathy cards, with special notes in them, and your letter. She told me that having a twelve-year-old nephew write the way you did was unbelievable to her.

M: I had been thinking that I take pictures when I'm sad, but I guess that time I wrote. How did my dad show it when he was sad?

G: Mostly, he went away from the house. When Grandpa and I would argue, your dad would go out to the woods behind our house. He had a treehouse there. He never wanted to talk about it.

M: Ok, let's switch subjects. I remember that you took me when I was fourteen to a political debate. I didn't even know who the candidates were. You said that I needed to hear them. Why did you take me?

G: Your Aunt Beth got so self-confident when she was on the debate team in high school. I think that's why she became a lawyer. I believe that we should be good citizens, of course, so we have to know about candidates. But I mostly wanted you to hear how people debate. I thought you needed a way to have confidence at that point in your life.

M: My ninth grade year was a disaster. My grade school teachers liked what I wrote. My ninth grade English teacher bled all over my papers. I couldn't understand the red marks, and I got scared of writing. I even had trouble writing lab reports in biology. I was good at the experiments, but I blocked at writing up results.

G: How did you get past that? I remember that you even won an essay contest later. Was it in your junior or senior year?

M: My mom said I should take pictures. I should take a picture every time I wanted to write something to get myself started. You know, it really worked. When I had a picture to describe, I felt more confident about writing. Oh, I even took pictures when we read *Julius Caesar.* I thought the crowds were so hypocritical when they praised and then booed the same person when their mood changed. I went to a basketball game and took pictures of the supposed fans. They did the same thing. They yelled for the team when they were making hoops. Just let them miss a basket or two in a row, though. The boos were loud. You should have seen the evil looks on some of the faces.

G: How did taking the pictures help?

M: This time I got the pictures developed at one of those one-hour jobs. Then I made a list of words under each picture, whatever came to my mind. I used those words to begin writing about the fickle crowds in the play. I actually tried to write a comparison of the kinds of crowds, but that seemed so farfetched that I dropped it.

Anyway, I learned that for me pictures and words are both important.

G: What was your favorite book that you read in high school?

M: That's easy. I liked *To Kill a Mockingbird.* I probably liked it for different reasons than most people. I tried to imagine what it would be like to be living with my dad instead of my mom. I thought that I'd like a dad just like the attorney in that book. He was smart, cared about his kids, cared about human beings.

G: You are like that, you know. You gave me that book about Rosa Parks and told me that you admired someone who wouldn't let anyone push her around because she was black. Didn't your winning essay argue against hate groups like the Ku Klux Klan and the John Birch Society?

M: You know, from reading about those groups I found out how much I despised them. Then when I started writing, I got real mad. In my essay I argued that groups like that should be outlawed by the Constitution.

> *G:* Well, I'm getting ready to fix dinner. Do you want to ask any more questions?
>
> *M:* Just one more. If you were me writing this literacy autobiography, what would you think was the best thing to put in?
>
> *G:* That's a hard one. I guess I'd mention that you show other people how you feel really well in writing. And that you plan to write your Grandmother often while you're away at college!
>
> *M:* Thanks for the interview, Grandma. I'll be sure to quote you so you'll go down in history as the relative of a famous writer.

REVISION STRATEGY

1. If you have already drafted a paper that would, like Justin's, be enhanced by the addition of information drawn from informal interviews, amend your proposal to include the question(s) you would ask of your sources, a list of appropriately varied sources, and your rationale for including such information.
2. Ask a reader to help you find places in your paper that would be improved by adding the material you will collect in an informal interview. Conduct the interview. As you add the new material, consider whether you should quote or paraphrase your source. Use Amy's essay as an example when you feel unsure of the technique. You will also find information about incorporating source material into an essay in chapter 8 on pages 199–200.
3. Amend your Writer's Statement to explain the additions that you made to your paper. New questions should address the effectiveness for the reader of the material you added. If possible, include as a reader of your paper one person whom you interviewed.

CONDUCTING FORMAL INTERVIEWS

Although the information collected from others who have personal experience with your topic is relevant and often enlivens a paper, you may find that you need information available only from a recognized authority. You may be accustomed to finding that authoritative information in books and articles, rather than going directly to an expert. But conducting an interview can be extremely helpful. It allows you to bring primary research, brand-new material, to your writing. This interview has, after all, never before been published. That makes it timely as well, giving you a chance to ask up-to-date questions that already-published material cannot possibly address.

Interviewing an Experienced Source

Kathleen Schuckel is the social issues and family reporter for the *Indianapolis News*. Because she is an experienced interviewer, I asked her to step out of her usual role of asking questions into the less familiar role of providing answers. I, therefore, conducted a formal interview with her, in my office, working from a list of questions I had prepared and organized before the interview. I wanted authoritative information about conducting effective interviews.

As you read the interview with Kathy, list in your journal the guidelines she offers for conducting a formal interview and for working with the resulting material. You will use this list later in this chapter and for your own interviewing.

> Preparation for an interview is vital, Kathy says. "First I have to consider my purpose; is it a personal profile of the mayor or a story about the failure of one of his programs? I target my questions so they will accomplish my purpose in the time I have. I don't go in and say, 'Tell me your life story in twenty minutes; instead I ask, 'Who do you ask for advice?'" Talking informally with other sources or reading to gain background information is necessary homework, she adds.
>
> Kathy combines another information strategy with interviewing. "Observation is part of it too. If I were interviewing you, I'd note that you have dangling earrings on, how you use your hands, that you have lots of pictures in your office. All those details would be important in a personality profile, for instance."
>
> Getting the interview started can be tricky. "I often start off with general questions, some background information that just lets the person talk a bit: 'Explain to me about your project,' or if I'm interviewing about a personal experience, 'Tell me about your situation, what happened to you.'" Some people, she says, like to have a list of questions before the interview, and though she worries about a contrived interview resulting, she notes that it can also make an efficient interview. Rarely, however, does she employ a tape recorder as a way to be efficient. "I don't have time to transcribe," she says, so she just depends on good notes. On the rare occasions when she does tape—"when I expect lots of material I need to quote directly"—she makes sure the interviewee agrees and is aware of the recording.

Successful questions, she says, address the purpose of the interview and depend upon doing the homework to create them. The questions must keep the conversation headed toward the needed information. "When the interviewee gets off the subject, you have to have a focused question that pulls him back." At the same time, Kathy cautions, "You want to avoid 'yes, no' questions; make them open-ended. You want to invite the person to talk, so a simple yes or no isn't very useful." Success also depends upon the ability of the interviewer to seem sincerely interested, "not skeptical or in the position of prejudging or already knowing the answer."

Kathy's concern about journalists' preconceived notions about an interview raises an important classroom issue. Some students have a tendency to do that as well, deciding what they want to find before they conduct their research. Perhaps they deliberately look only for those materials that support their views or perhaps that's a subconscious decision, but they end up with materials that offer only one perspective. And although interviewing people who will tell you what you want to hear may be efficient or confirming, it simply isn't honest.

Choosing people to interview is hard. "Lots of times," Kathy says, "the first interview doesn't work. Sometimes, I have to interview ten people to get good information. I think students might be afraid to do that, especially to call someone they didn't know. But what happens when you finally start getting some good interviews is, 'Wow, this is fun,' or 'This material is really going to help my reader understand.' Often it's the interviewer who gains understanding. That's one of the best things about interviewing: talking to other people about something you're interested in makes you even more interested in it. If you just go read about it, you don't get the emotion, the personality, the enthusiasm, the rage that will come through in an interview."

As an interviewer gains all this information and insight, she should constantly network. "Today, for instance, I'm doing something on whether sports are too structured, the little league syndrome. And so I called a professor who has served on a physical fitness task force, and he said, 'You should really talk to this guy at Michigan State.' It was a great tip. He had done all kinds of good research; he was better than anyone I could get here. You just always have to be asking and reading. That's how you'll find people's names, and then you can call them and say, 'Do you know somebody else who might talk about this?'"

Kathy further reminds interviewers to use networking to find authoritative sources who are not public officials, researchers, or people in the limelight. "There might be a gem of an old lady in a neighborhood who's worked for months in one of the mayor's programs developing the best strategy for keeping litter out of her neighborhood or working against crime, but she doesn't have a press secretary."

Such interviews let you inform readers with totally new material which is "probably the best aspect of conducting interviews." It allows you to focus on the exact information you need, to be thorough, and to clarify what you are told. When you're asking the questions, you can search for the exact information you need and you can take your reader into account. If the person makes a very general statement, you can ask for an illustration or example that will help you explain her point to the reader; if she uses a term you don't understand, you can ask for a clarification, so that you can use the term just as she would.

Kathy agrees, "Ask questions; that's the whole point of interviewing. Whether you're a student or a journalist with fifty years' experience, when you don't understand something, you have to be willing to say, 'Can you please slow down,' or 'I didn't quite get that.' We're hesitant to show our ignorance, but people want to tell you more, they want you to get it right. They're almost always happy to repeat or give you more detail. Lots of times, they give me additional written material. I love that."

Portfolio learning encourages students to analyze their own writing processes. Kathy certainly has a firm grasp on hers. Once she has conducted the interview, she works with her material right away. "I may try to get it down in the elevator as I leave the office. I highlight important things, put in little words or even do some organizing, put it in categories or subject areas." Notes in the margins or highlighting material about the same aspect of the topic with one color of ink and material about another aspect with another color could be helpful.

Kathy then moves to the computer where her hardest decisions often concern what material to leave out. "One writing coach calls it 'Killing babies.' It's so hard to give up good material that you just can't use. I make that mistake all the time. I get all this information and I get really interested in a topic, and I realize that I didn't stay on task. So I have to go back."

To solve such problems, "One suggestion someone made is to put a line up over the computer screen, stating the purpose of the piece you're writing. If it doesn't fit, leave it out. It's self-discipline. You just stick with your purpose. The smaller amount of time and space you have, the narrower the topic has to be."

"If you have two evenings to do this entire piece, you can't talk to ten people. You have to choose carefully who to include. That affects purpose and narrows your topic even more."

And as she writes, Kathy's process sometimes also includes a follow-up interview or contact. "I was doing something with asthma last week, with a pediatrician. I assured her after the interview, 'If there's anything that I'm not quite sure about, I'll check back with you.' People like that. They open up to you more if they know you're going to check back with them in case you make a mistake. And sometimes you just get more information if you go back. You talk to them at a time of day when they're clearer headed."

ANALYZING INTERVIEWS

1. As I wrote up the information from Kathy's interview, I synthesized points that she made with points I wanted to make as well. Answer the following questions in your dialogue journal. How can you identify material as mine or as Kathy's? What passages, if any, confuse you as to the source of the information?
2. A useful technique for incorporating source material into your own is to summarize or preview the main point offered in an upcoming quote or paraphrase. Identify that technique in the account of Kathy's interview.

Preparing for an Interview

Using your list of interview guidelines from Kathy, evaluate the questions that Justin proposed below for his interview of a well-known sociology professor on his campus. How would you revise the questions that do not fit the guidelines? How would you order the questions? Record your suggestions in your dialogue journal.

Justin's Interview Plan

When I wrote that third paper using my observation, I knew that it needed help. I thought I should use my observations more in the paper, but I was also worried about the conclusions I drew. Was I right about people mixing more in small groups than in large ones? I took the advice to go and talk to someone in sociology. My friend Todd told me that Dr. Callahan is an expert on group dynamics, so I went to see her. She told me I had to make an appointment. She seems like a serious woman, so I think I had better really get ready for this interview. My questions are below and I would really like some feedback on them before I go to talk with Dr. Callahan. When I get her ideas I hope that will help me know what to do with my observations and whether they amount to anything.

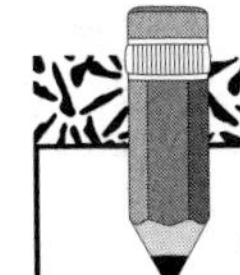

Justin's Interview Questions

1. How did you get your experience and knowledge about group dynamics?
2. Do you think that most interracial groups are small groups?
3. How are most intercultural or interracial groups formed?
4. Are friendships between an American and a person from somewhere else more likely to form before or after that person is assimilated?
5. What are the main difficulties mixed friendships have to overcome?
6. Are mixed friendships more common among college students than other people our age?
7. What is your definition of assimilation?
8. Do you think assimilation is a good thing for America? For the people being assimilated?
9. Do you see very many mixed friendships on this campus?
10. Do you think the union was a good place for my observation?

PRACTICE WITH INTERVIEWING

1. In chapter 2 you may have done a brainstorming activity to help you find a topic. This time, make a list of topics that you already know a lot about. Think of all the topics you are an expert in, anything from what your grandfather eats for breakfast to how to use a new computer system in the library to how to find a place to park when you're late for class.
2. Choose one topic from your list, write it on a slip of paper, pair up with a classmate you do not know well, and trade slips. In your journal develop a list of at least five questions that you will ask in a formal interview of your partner, recognizing that doing background homework will be difficult unless you can identify someone else in the class who does know your partner.
3. Conduct the interview, taking notes as you do.

4. In your journal discuss the effectiveness of the interview process and of your questions. Did you find out what you wanted to know? What questions were productive or nonproductive? Exchange journals with your partner and respond to the analysis of the interview conducted with you. Did you evaluate the questions similarly? What would you have liked to be asked? What questions were hard to answer? Why?
5. In your journal write up the results of your interview.
6. Exchange journals with your partner. Evaluate the accuracy with which the information you gave was reported.

DRAFTING YOUR PAPER

1. Working within an assignment or with an idea gleaned from material you generated earlier, such as journal entries and lists of ideas for topics or proposals you wrote in chapters 1 and 2, write a proposal. Include a passage explaining why you think formal interviews with experts or authorities would enrich the paper.
2. Use some of the journalistic questions to help you determine who would be good sources for an interview: Who are the authorities or experts concerning this topic? What qualifies them as experts? Where on your campus or in your community would you find experts on your topic? How can you find out?
3. In your proposal, identify at least one expert source whose knowledge could enhance your paper. Include a passage explaining your plans for contacting and setting up a formal interview with that person.
4. Include in your proposal a list of questions you intend to ask of your source in the interview. Exchange your proposal with a classmate to obtain a response to your questions. Revise, if necessary, and submit the proposal to your instructor before you conduct the interview.

REVISION STRATEGY

1. If you have already produced a draft that you think would be enriched by the addition of an interview with an expert, explain in your journal your rationale for including such material.
2. Then follow steps 2 through 4 in the previous exercise, amending your Writer's Statement rather than your proposal as you prepare to conduct the interview and to synthesize the material you collected into your draft.

Interviewing an Expert

Justin reported in his write up of the interview with Dr. Callahan that it had taken a turn he did not expect: she took over the interview, asking to see his list of questions.

Justin's Notes on His Interview

My interview with Dr. Callahan seemed more like a classroom lecture than someone being interviewed. But she really had a lot to say, and she made me look at the paper in a whole different way. She does a lot of research, and so she was thinking about my paper and my observation in that way. She really liked what I did in conducting my observation, and she said I had developed an interesting hypothesis, but she didn't think I could draw any conclusions. She said she'd be glad to work with me on this hypothesis, to see what is true on our campus. She told me that the first thing I would have to do is a literature search, to find and read whatever has been done on this topic before. She says that there is some work on this topic out there. She said that in many papers like mine, you have to include the main ideas presented in the research. Then she said that I needed to understand that nothing is as easy as I wanted it to be. That it's hard to call assimilation a good or bad thing. She said that assimilation is something that happens, and we have to consider "both the benefits and the drawbacks for the dominant and the minority groups as well as the individuals." She said that's true of most questions about social changes and group dynamics. "Evaluating human activity and events is tricky business," she said. She said that it's better to "stand at a distance" and observe and draw conclusions, often without evaluation. She said my own experience is "anecdotal" and "valuable as one person's experience or as an example" but she says I can't pretend that "it is representative of the general social experience in this country or even this state." She said that the idea that college students are more inclined to accept people from other backgrounds is "another hypothesis, far from proven." When I asked her what she thought I ought to do about my paper, she didn't really know. She said I should review my notes and think about what I should do. I didn't find that very helpful.

I think I'll try to revise, mostly to sort out my own ideas and to make sure I understand about this issue, but I'm not going to do the research right now because I don't have time and maybe I won't even put this paper in my portfolio. If I decide to use this paper in my portfolio, then I can take the time to go to the library and see what I can find. I'm not feeling very excited about this paper anymore.

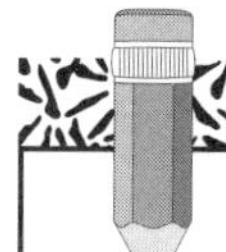

Justin's Paper 3, Draft 2, Observation

In our society today, relationships between members of different racial or cultural groups is a big issue. It's on the front page or on the news every day. The big question seems to be the one that Rodney King asked after the LA riots. "Can't we just get along?" One way to try to find that out on a college campus is to watch the people in the student union. That's where people gather to eat snacks or meals and to talk and to watch big screen TV.

This topic is important to everyone first because it's a part of everyone's life, living with people who are from other backgrounds. And also, when a person has experience with friendships with people from other backgrounds and they will find it to be a good thing. Darnell, an African American guy and Rajesh, whose family came here from India are both my friends. We have spent lots of time together and I have learned a lot about their backgrounds from our friendships. I like having that as a part of my life, and I think it's helped me see the value of other cultures and how they add to our society.

But I don't know if other people see the same value. An observation in our student union showed that most people, especially those who gather there in large groups tend to choose the company of people from their own background. Over three observation periods the large groups of people in the union, groups of up to ten people, were more likely to be made up of only one group. As the groups in the observation got smaller they became more likely to be a mixture of two races or cultures, but a mixture of three was not observed.

On the basis of that information it seems as though it might be worthwhile to conduct more research to find out if the integration of America is taking place on an individual basis, among small groups of people or pairs of people. Maybe, if that is true, we are going in the wrong direction to try to create diversity in all parts of our society. Maybe people have to learn to live and work together in small groups instead.

That would mean a gradual assimilation. And assimilation, the merging of the minority group into the dominant group can be both good and bad. It depends on the goal and upon each person's life. According to Dr. Grace Callahan, assimilation has "both benefits and drawbacks for the dominant and the minority group." Maybe the most important benefit of the merging and friendships of people of different cultures is that it will mean a more authentic blending of groups in our society.

Justin's Writer's Statement Amendment, Paper 3, Observation

This is the worst paper I have ever written. I don't even see what it's about. It goes all over the place, talking about my friends and assimilation and Rodney King and observation. The worst thing is I really am interested in this topic but I don't know what to do with it. I have nothing else to say except help! I revised and I made it worse.

ANALYZING JUSTIN'S DRAFT

1. Write a response to Justin's amended Writer's Statement. What can you say to someone who is so discouraged?

2. How do you evaluate Justin's paper? What will you say about the quality of the paper? Is Justin right?

WORKING PORTFOLIO UPDATE

Make sure, as you add drafts and other documents to your Working Portfolio, that you keep a record of your own frustrations. How have you solved them? What strategies have your classmates developed? Your Working Portfolio is the place for all your writing experiences this term, the problems as well as the successes.

If you are worried about Justin or just want to see how he solved his problem, perhaps because you are experiencing a similar difficulty, you can look ahead to chapter 10 where he returns to work on the troublesome Paper 3. In the meantime, however, in the next chapter you will see another student, Darren, working with still more sources of information. Justin will begin a new assignment, finding more success than he has in this chapter. All writers have their ups and downs.

CHAPTER 7 Drawing from Different Media

In previous chapters you have read about and tried various ways of gaining knowledge, including drawing on personal experience, reading, observing, and interviewing. Each of these is a medium through which you have made meaning.

Different people communicate meaning through the medium of a letter, the radio, a painting, a lecture, an advertisement, a poem, a poster, a song, or a symphony. All these methods of communication provide an astounding amount of stimulation that both directs and creates ideas in us. A sermon or a piece of scripture in a church service may direct your thinking about your own life in a particular direction. A scene in a movie may suddenly open a door to understanding about a topic that is part of your classroom studies, or an old song on the radio may call up a strong memory.

As a writer, you are stimulated by media, and you join the media. You may write a personal essay as a result of that church sermon, you may incorporate elements of that movie into your answer to an essay question, or you may write a letter to the radio station in response to that song. In such cases, you are putting forth information from your own perspective and creating a piece of work that has never been created before. You can use such sources as a sort of genesis point for writing and thinking or as a way to add development to work and thinking already in progress. Sources often interconnect and can be synthesized in a piece of writing.

SYNTHESIZING SOURCES

Your college or university may have as one of its objectives for you as a student to become a critical thinker. Although the term *critical thinking* is defined in many ways, the ability to synthesize is usually a part of the definition. The word *synthesize* has a Greek root meaning "to put" and a prefix *syn* meaning "together." When you synthesize two or more ideas, you are bringing them together to make a different idea.

Synthesizing is not as easy as it might seem on the surface. Remember the first time that you did a research paper in which you had to have a variety of sources. Did you do what most inexperienced writers do? Novice writers often line up the sources, conscientiously reporting what each said. Basically, they list the information from each source and feel that they have covered the topic. Perhaps you were a more sophisticated researcher who knew that parroting back the ideas of others, however well presented, did not constitute a new idea. You were aware that synthesizing the sources, calling on them for what they could contribute to a new idea, was the point of your learning from multiple sources.

Synthesis can happen naturally as we call on all that we might bring to bear on a topic. We can help ourselves, however, by consciously drawing on many media to make our new meanings. Darren, a junior majoring in English and philosophy, decided in a cultural studies class to use directed freewriting and cubing to explore an assigned topic. His assignment, to represent his culture, seemed so broad that he knew he would have to focus. First, he did a freewriting on the subject of tackiness in modern culture, especially his own fascination with the tacky, a topic that both interested and disturbed him.

Darren's Freewriting

I have an attraction to the tacky. I have an attraction to the tacky that, at its roots, is condescending. I love the tacky to show the world that I have "taste" or an "aesthetic sense," but am often so cool that I can ignore it. I laugh at those who confuse "the tacky" with "the beautiful," an entirely different thing that your average American Jane or John couldn't possibly access. Most people are so stupid.

Or perhaps not. Although I've always thought of it as an innocuously elitist fascination, on my last road trip I began to wonder. Jeremy, my traveling buddy, repeatedly asked himself the question "What is the difference between me saying 'this is so cool. I've got to have it,'" showing me a Fabulous Las Vegas serving tray or a Genuine Petrified Wood trivet, "and Mabel from Omaha saying 'This will be so beautiful next to the toaster oven'? Is there really any difference?" I blew him off, naturally: "Of course there's a difference, dumbass. Don't make me kick your ass again. Huh, huh, huh." (Doing my best Butthead impression.) But it bothered me at the time, and more so now, that I couldn't pin down just what the difference was.

Using Modified Cubing to Generate Ideas

Having settled on a general topic, Darren then did a cubing exercise. However, he modified the strategy to make it work for this assignment. Instead of using various approaches to his topic such as comparison and contrast or argument, he used various media influences such as music or television programs that he connected to his topic. He wrote for ten minutes on each medium he chose.

Darren's Cubing

Music

I bought a "Romantic Pan Flute" CD at Target last year. I enjoyed it because it was terrible. "Listen to this," I would say to my friends, "It's 'Don't Cry For Me Argentina.' Honest to God. Isn't it terrible?" The reason why I enjoy it, although it's terrible is the realization that someone, somewhere, some fellow Target shopper, thought it was beautiful, actually found it "romantic." Here, I see a real difference between my enjoyment and another's but what is it? It's the same physiological response. I would have been disappointed if the album actually was "romantic" for me. My Target comrade would have been disappointed if it didn't come up to her standard of "beautiful." But is it right for me to look down on her sense of beauty? Isn't my "pleasurably terrible" a standard of beauty, if beauty is that which gives pleasure? Is my pleasure more noble than hers?

TV

Beavis and Butthead seem to me the epitome of all that is tasteless and stupid. It is amazing. The writers must be brilliant to be able to maintain complete meaninglessness and moronity through the numerous episodes. Beavis and Butthead sometimes brushes with issues and leaves an unmistakable mark, with such banality and thoughtlessness that the world looks absolutely absurd and therefore wonderfully simple. This is a show written purely to be stupid. The folks in Omaha don't think it's adorable: they want it banned. No one can reasonably come to the show expecting to see something "beautiful." Except maybe Jeremy, myself, and a few others. We see a difficult to capture, real beauty in Beavis and Butthead. It's almost transcendent. I'm sure reasonable people think of us what we think about Mabel in Omaha with her trivet in the kitchen.

Literature

In one essay in his book *Staying Put,* Scott Russell Sanders considers the lawn ornaments that grace the property of many of his fellow Bloomingtonians. In an uncharacteristically didactic manner, Sanders resists the temptation to laugh at the pink flamingos that are currently popular and scolds those who would belittle the landscaping taste of others. Sanders recognizes that, for the most part, people put flamingos on their lawns because they feel that it makes their homes more beautiful. We should respect that. If I put a flamingo on my lawn, I wouldn't be doing it to beautify my property: I would be doing it to put down those without my supposedly more refined sense of taste. This hit me hard when I read it.

Spoken Performance

I recently went to the Monroe County Civic Theater production of *Faust.* The performance dragged a bit--they probably should have cut some more scenes--but the performance was saved by the spirited and deftly funny performance of the actor playing Mephistopheles. Of course, she was intentionally funny. I got the sense that the crowd was laughing at what was supposed to be humorous and not at the moments intending to be serious. However, for some reason that is beyond me, the director decided to include a dance sequence. The ballet dancer was a muscular black man with long gericurled hair dressed in some sort of pseudo roman loincloth getup. Although I am fairly certain it wasn't intended, he looked ridiculously funny. We probably could have overlooked that, but, at the apogee of one of his tolerably graceful jumps, the rear flap of his loincloth was blown up so that the whole audience got full southern exposure. We couldn't stop laughing for the remaining hour of the play. I wonder, what is the difference between the two kinds of humor we enjoyed? Is it the cliched difference between being laughed with and laughed at?

Film

There seem to be two types of cult films: films that were made to be stupid and films that are stupid by accident or necessity. An example of the first type would be *Attack of the Killer Tomatoes,* an incredibly funny film that is completely mindless fun. A mad scientist character makes the tomatoes large, mutant, alive, and bloodthirsty. It's supposed to be funny because it's so stupid (like Beavis and Butthead). In contrast, there's *Plan Nine from Outer Space,* a sci-fi film from the sixties(?) that is hailed by many as the worst film ever made. But it doesn't appear that it was made to be funny. It's obviously low budget: the props are cheap and the technology was out of date before even then. The acting is hapless, but tragically sincere. One gets the impression that the movie was made to be an actual honest-to-goodness horror movie; they meant for it to scare you. But they couldn't have written a more funny (in this case, meaning worse) film if that was their explicit goal. Both films are hapless, stupid, and sloppy,although different in intent. Do I like *Plan Nine* because I laugh at the thought of someone actually finding it scary? If so, why do I like *Attack*?

Other Print Media

One of Jeremy's and my primary sources of the location of the tacky on our roadtrips has been the *New Guide to Roadside America.* The book features hundreds of tasteless and peculiar attractions such as Wendell Hansen's Bible Bird Show, The World's Largest Concrete Egg, and The World's Smallest Church(es) (there are seven that claim the title if my memory serves). It is written in the condescending tone that I have always used to justify my fascination with the tacky. The last entry in the book is entitled "A Curator Alone." It describes Max Nordeen's Wheel Museum in Woodhull, IL. They make Max out as a dirty, tedious, old man that no one seems to want anything to do with. Max, however, is most incredible. He has an eclectic collection of thousands of items, from world's fair souvenirs to hood ornaments and knows everything about all of it. He is a man of passion and purpose and finds it strange that others don't understand. We understood.

Darren's modification of cubing enabled him to explore the media he judged most influential. He is an avid music fan, attends the theater often, and reads and travels extensively. Focusing his cubing on the media's relationship to the tacky enabled him to think widely about his topic and his experiences with it.

Some material from Darren's cubing appears, virtually verbatim, in his essay. Other material, like the analysis of *Faust,* is not included in his paper. Obvious and admirable in his essay is the interrelatedness of his various experiences and influences through the mass media. As you read, note the intersections between media influences and the transitions that Darren builds.

Darren's Paper

Cornering the Tacky

I have an attraction to the tacky. I own a red foam cap with white wrap around stripes, featuring the slogan **"TIME FOR FOOTBALL"** and a working clock on the front. I drove through a tree and liked it. I've made a 500-mile pilgrimage to the "Official Future Birthplace of Captain James T. Kirk," Riverside, Iowa. I lust after an autographed picture of Elvis and Nixon shaking hands and plan to visit the Agricultural Drainage Hall of Fame some day.

I have an attraction to the tacky that, at its roots, is condescending. I love the tacky to show the world that I have "taste" or an "aesthetic sense," but am often so cool that I can ignore it. I laugh at those who confuse "the tacky" with "the beautiful," an entirely different thing that your average American Jane or John couldn't possibly access. Most people are so backward.

Or perhaps not. Although I've always thought of it as an innocuous, if somewhat elitist, fascination, on my last road trip I began to wonder. Jeremy, my traveling buddy, repeatedly asked the question, "What is the difference between me saying 'This is so cool. I've got to have it,'" showing me a Fabulous Las Vegas serving tray or a Genuine Petrified Wood trivet, "and Mabel from Omaha saying 'This will be so beautiful next to the toaster oven'? Is there really any difference?" I blew him off, naturally: "Of course there's a difference, dumbass. Don't make me kick your ass again. Huh. Huh. Huh." (Doing my best Butthead impression.) But it bothered me at the time, and more so now, that I couldn't pin down just what the difference was.

Last year, I bought a "Romantic Pan Flute" CD at Target. The album features arrangements of such lovers' classics as "We've Got Tonight" and "Up Where We Belong," each performed on the pan flute, an instrument from the Andes, with occasional piano accompaniment. Immediately, when the CD caught my eye, I could see it, the perfect romantic evening: candlelight, pasta, true love, and . . . the pan flute. I enjoyed it because it was terrible. "Listen to this," I would say to my friends. "It's 'Don't Cry for Me Argentina.' On the Pan Flute. Honest to God. Isn't it terrible?" I think that the reason why I enjoy it, although it's terrible, is the realization that someone, somewhere, some fellow Target shopper thought it was beautiful, actually found it "romantic." Here, I see a real difference between my enjoyment and hers, but what is it? Isn't my "pleasurably terrible" a standard of beauty alongside her "romantic," if beauty is that which gives pleasure? Do I have any reason to believe that my pleasure is more noble than hers?

My friend Scott Sanders addresses his attraction to the tacky in his essay "Yard Birds." He proposes to his family adorning their yard with a few of the yard ornaments that grace the lawns of many fellow Bloomingtonians. "No flamingos . . . And no peasants or lantern boys. Just geese." To which his son Jesse replies, "If you put plain old geese out there, people will think you *mean* it." At this remark, Sanders realizes that he could not display ornaments in his yard "without also putting [his] tongue in cheek." He concludes that decorations, while funny in some contexts, are often meaningful for those who display them: "Surely they are not all meant as jokes. Surely some are meant as art. And a few, at least, must be icons to household gods." Writing of the sign promoting tacky merchandise showcased in The White Rabbit, one of my favorite stores, Sanders concludes that "'camp' and 'kitsch' and 'cool' all rhyme with 'condescension.'" To Sanders the tacky is only funny at the expense of those who find it beautiful. The very term "tacky" is probably problematic because it implies an exclusionary standard of taste.

However, Sanders is not entirely an aesthetic pluralist. At church some months ago, Scott and I were discussing the wildly popular *Bridges of Madison County,* which had owned the *New York Times* Bestseller List for months. Agreeing that *Bridges* was basically fluff, Scott commented that it was a shame that the novel was so popular, since people only have a limited amount of time to read, and there is so much superior literature available that would make more worthwhile use of that time than the *Bridges* brand of popular fiction. It seems that Sanders chooses to retain his standards of taste but finds it important to be sensitive to the standards of others. As he says in his essay, people "buy the art they can understand and afford." Perhaps Scott longs for "the masses" to be able to understand and pay for classier art but respects the pleasure that the tacky gives them.

I was very disturbed when I first read Scott's essay. My attraction to the tacky had previously seemed to me an innocent quirk. In light of the essay, it was beginning to look like a character flaw. Reviewing my encounters with the tacky, it was easy to see them as snobbish insult, as elitist egoism. This reevaluation did not end my quest for the tacky, however. It simply added a tinge of guilt. My attraction to the tacky was now a minor vice, something to be superficially embarrassed about.

It took Max Nordeen to change my mind. One of Jeremy's and my primary sources of the location of the tacky on our road trips has been *The New Roadside America.* This book features hundreds of tasteless and peculiar attractions such as Wendell Hansen's Bible Bird Show, The World's Largest Concrete Egg, and The World's Smallest Church(es) (there are seven that claim the title if my memory serves). It is written in the condescending tone that I had sometimes used to justify my fascination with the tacky, the attitude that Scott Sanders's essay made me question. The last entry in the book is entitled "A Curator Alone." It describes Max Nordeen's Wheel Museum in Woodhull, IL. They make Max out as a dirty, tedious old man whom no one seems to want anything to do with. Jeremy and I thought it would be fun to go see his museum.

Max, however, is most incredible. He has an eclectic collection of thousands of items—antique toys, clocks, lamps, radios, railroad items, milk glass, watch fobs, purse mirrors, an extensive world fair souvenir collection, auto radiator caps and emblems, Indian relics, Civil War items, a Studebaker race car, John Deere's death notice, and a naked picture of Marlene Dietrich when she was seventeen. He knows everything about all of it; he asks you to quiz him. He is a man of passion and purpose and finds it strange that others don't understand. We understood. Jeremy and I took Max's guided tour in reverent awe. We weren't laughing at him. We were enjoying ourselves in a way we couldn't explain.

I am beginning to think that my need to explain is key. I can't explain away my enjoyment of Max's museum as condescension as I could with the huge orange carrot wall hanging that I put up in my room. Yet I feel a need to differentiate the pleasure that tacky things give me from the pleasure that "real" art brings. One possible distinction is insult versus actual appreciation. As Sanders's essay made me realize, I had been using condescension all along as a way of justifying my attraction to the tacky. I needed an excuse for liking something I wasn't supposed to. I was willing to accept the guilt of being an elitist in place of the uncertainty of not having a well-defined sense of proper (or fashionably proper) taste.

I'm listening to the pan flute again and I am not sure that it isn't, as Jeremy says, "Just cool." In truth, I like the pan flute arrangement of "Up Where We Belong" infinitely better than the original Top 40 version. Everything I know about established standards of music appreciation, both traditional and contemporary models, ethnomusicology to grunge, tells me I ought not to enjoy this. Yet, I do. To say "I like this" constitutes a personal risk; I expose myself to the ridicule of friends and critics. Therefore, I need to explain away my pleasure as something less substantial than an authentic appreciation of beauty. I can do this at the expense of my less educated fellow Target shoppers, or I could formulate a political rationale: In enjoying this work of popular culture, I am transgressing the boundaries of the Western phallocentric aesthetic hegemony and deconstructing the dominant conception of the "canon" in bourgeois society. However, to so distance myself from my emotional responses seems untruthful. The most courageous approach simply may be to say, "It's just cool," and leave it at that.

PRACTICE WITH ANALYSIS

1. In your journal, identify the sources Darren has knit together as he explores his fascination with the tacky.
2. Then analyze Darren's use of direct quotation and of paraphrasing in some passage that combines both. Direct quotation involves using the exact wording of a source. Paraphrasing involves deriving meaning from a source but using one's own words to express the idea. How does Darren build the connections between direct quotes and paraphrases in the passage you are analyzing?
3. In your journal, offer examples of concrete language that create strong sensory appeal in Darren's essay. Remember the earlier analysis of strong language in the apple-coring essay in chapter 4.
4. In Darren's essay, he makes meaning of his own experiences. What conclusions does he draw? How broad or narrow are they? How are they appropriate for the evidence that he supplies?
5. Describe the tone of Darren's essay? Imagining the essay read aloud or reading portions of it aloud, listen to the tone of the sentences. Is the tone consistent? Explain by referring to certain passages.

PRACTICE WITH VARIED MEDIA AS SOURCES

1. In your group, choose a social problem that is of interest to you all. Do a group brainstorming on a blackboard, computer network, or a big piece of paper, following Darren's general plan of using multiple media. Everyone should contribute to a list of sources related to the problem you chose and drawn from each medium you decide to use.
2. Explain sources unfamiliar to others in your group.

DRAFTING YOUR PAPER

1. In the materials in your Working Portfolio, look for topics, issues, and concerns that appear more than once, preferably several times. Put a topic at the top of a journal page. Then do the sort of cubing exercise that Darren did,

choosing the sources you will use from the media mentioned throughout this chapter. Add others if you like.

2. In your journal, discuss the sources and their influences. How credible are they? Which ones offered new perspectives? Which ones made you feel good, disturbed, sad, or angry? How did they contribute to your understanding of the topic?
3. Write a proposal for a piece that will use varied media sources to help you fulfill your purposes. In your proposal include a discussion of the sources you will use and how they have influenced you in regard to your topic.

REVISION STRATEGY

1. Survey your draft(s) and responses. Has a reader expressed a need for further development? Has your teacher asked you to lengthen a draft? Does a draft seem flat or uninteresting? Are you too dependent upon your own ideas? Are you too pressed for time to conduct an interview or an observation? Try the cubing exercise described in this section. You may be able to pull in a discussion of a television special news report that you watched last week when you should have been revising this paper. Or you may be able to quote your favorite lyric from the Beatles or a bumper sticker you saw in the campus parking lot or graffiti in the restroom. Instant, painless sources!
2. Redraft. Amend your Writer's Statement with a rationale for adding the sources you have identified. What problems will their addition solve? How do they help fulfill your original purpose? Are they credible and appropriate to your audience?

Guidelines for Using Media Sources

1. Use only source material that applies to your point.

When you progressed in school from writing book reports to book reviews, you went from describing a story to analyzing and evaluating it, an advance in critical thinking. Instead of retelling a plot, you included only those plot elements that provided examples for the point you were making about the book.

As you consciously seek media sources, you may be tempted to tell too much about the source, to describe the entire context for the source in your life, or to comment unnecessarily on all aspects of the source. In alluding to Barbara Walters's interview techniques as you describe your own, you need not list all the important interviews she has done: you are using the source to further the readers' understanding of your own technique. In using Pearl from *The Scarlet Letter* as an example of an isolated child, you need not recount the intrigue between Chillingsworth and his rival. Mariah Carey's voice range is not pertinent if you are using her to exemplify the combination of singer and entrepreneur necessary for success in the business world of modern music. Be sure that the elements that you pick from your sources are carefully selected for synthesis with elements from other sources to make your own point.

2. Use the source to make your own point.

You may use a source differently than the originator so long as you do not falsify the source. Darren, for example, used the roadside attractions book in a way that its author probably would not even have imagined. Although the book was written to locate unusual attractions for curious travelers, Darren used it to ponder a philosophical point. He synthesized what he learned from visiting one of the attractions in the book into an analysis of aesthetic pleasure. The author of that book also hardly expected to be treated alongside the work of Scott Russell Sanders, a professional essayist. Out of his experience with both books, Darren was able to bring them together as he made his own point about satisfaction.

3. Record your reactions to various media.

In your journal you might practice reflecting on different media to expand your sensibility to the diverse influences that color your thinking and decision making. For example, an e-mail posting may stick in your mind because of its candor: you may recall that directness later as your speech communication class studies rhetorical strategies. If you have recorded your observation about the posting in your journal, you can use it to make a point about the appropriateness of directness in various speech acts.

After seeing a film, you might experiment with routinely comparing it to another film that you've seen recently. You could compare on the basis of technical features, character development, or suitability to audience. Comparing two films chosen arbitrarily by chronology of viewing challenges you to see similarities and differences that you might not otherwise notice. For example, I recently saw *Sense and Sensibility* on screen and *Howard's End* on home video: the happenstance made me think about the constancy of the nineteenth-century British attitude toward married versus unmarried women. That insight was useful as I wrote a letter of complaint to an editor about the newspaper's identifying women by their husbands' names rather than their own names. In almost the twenty-first century the paper was reinscribing the nineteenth-century practice of classifying and valuing women by their marital status.

4. Seek out new media for expanding your knowledge base.

Recently, Julie started attending the symphony. Unfamiliar with classical music, she wasn't sure how she would experience it, but she learned that it is satisfying to her soul. If she writes in the future about spirituality, she might refer to her interaction with classical music as one source of her knowledge of the sublime.

If you watch the same news program every night on television, switch to another channel for a change, or listen to *All Things Considered* on public radio. If you always read fiction for pleasure, try a book of essays. If you've never seen ballet, go to a performance. When a football coach of a well-known team did so, he signed up his players for ballet classes so they could work on their agility. The way in which different media will expand your thinking and feeling may be unexpected. The expanded base of knowledge and experience will be invaluable as you write.

DEVELOPING AN ESSAY USING VARIOUS MEDIA AS SOURCES

Justin was assigned an essay in which he was to use multiple sources. Anticipating his summer plans, he decided to write on the advantages of traveling. He first brainstormed a list of all previous trips and experiences that had influenced his ideas about travel.

Justin placed an asterisk beside the items that interested him the most when he reread the list. He then decided to freewrite these starred items for a maximum of three minutes each in order to see if any commonalities emerged from his writing. He was concerned that the list was so random that it would not be useful unless he could identify some larger points that were embedded in his many entries on the brainstorming list.

When Justin finished his freewriting, he was intrigued that some of the items on his brainstorming list could be grouped based on what he had learned from this freewriting. He identified four interesting ideas. First, the items involving other people's travel exemplified traveling vicariously. Second, from his early experiences with travel, first to his friend's house and later to his cousin's, Justin

Justin's Brainstorming

National Geographic
Grand Canyon
Chicago
grandparents' farm in Illinois
travelogue on Greece
exchange student from Germany
Washington, D.C.
Mother's trip to London
Florida
Sesame Street in Europe
French jazz
Kabuki theater
sister's band trip to San Francisco
staying with cousin in Maine
Mammoth Cave
overnights at Matthew's
world history in high school

learned to identify the feelings associated with traveling to new places. Third, the places he visited with his family or with friends or classmates all widened his sense of the diversity of the world. Fourth, he realized that arts themselves were a form of travel.

Justin decided to write on travel as an activity that takes one away from home, whether in the body or in the mind. He hoped to expand his readers' definition of travel as he expanded his own. His first draft shows how he used a variety of media, some identified in his brainstorming list, to illuminate his thinking.

Read Justin's Writer's Statement for Paper 4 in order to respond to his draft in your dialogue journal. You may choose to write answers to his questions as you read or after you finish reading. Be prepared to discuss your answers with classmates.

Justin's Writer's Statement for Paper 4, Using Media

1. The purpose of this piece is to show that travel is possible in many ways and has many positive outcomes.

2. The audience for this piece is anyone who has a curiosity about travel. Since most people have traveled somewhere, I think that the audience should be most people.
3. I learned in my freewriting that I had a broader definition of travel than I had thought to begin with. I noticed that I considered travel not just in physical terms. Does my writing make clear that I like traveling in different ways although I prefer going places myself? Why or why not?
4. I feel good about the specific examples. Please read to see if each example makes a point, though. I want each memory to contribute to some point that I'm making about travel. What do you think?
5. Do I draw enough conclusions about travel? What I mean seems obvious in some places to me, but I may need to explain more. If you see a conclusion I only imply, would you mark the spot or even write what conclusion you think I could draw?
6. Do you have any other suggestions for revision?

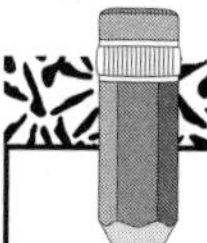

Justin's Paper 4, Draft 1, Using Media

Boundless Travel

About January, I start to think of summer vacation. Sometimes I get out albums from past vacations to recreate the pleasurable feelings associated with family trips. Other times I gripe about not having enough money to travel to California or New York or wherever I'd like to go at the time. Sometimes I even get practical and think about saving my money so I really can go somewhere. This year I'm thinking about how to convince my mom that I need to go to Europe after all I'm a college student who is supposed to be broadening my horizons.

Although most people may think of traveling as going far away from home I remember that my first travels were not far in physical space but were far in psychological space. My first overnight to my friend Matthew's house was when I was seven years old. Although I had stayed at my grandparents' house my mom had always been there too. This time I was on my own. I remember the scary feeling of being alone but also the exciting feeling of not quite knowing what went on in this new house: just things like locating the bathroom at night, eating different foods at a table where they said grace and talked about politics at dinner, and having a dad who played pool with us were novel. I felt pretty independent. My next travel experience was to my cousins in Maine. This time my mom and sister were along, but my cousin and I got to explore anywhere we wanted in the woods around his house, hike to the town near their place by ourselves, and stay up as late as we wanted in the treehouse in his back yard. That great feeling of doing something different and of being on my own is one that I associate with travel even today.

My mom tried to see that my sister and I got to travel to places that are well known in the United States. Because we lived in the Midwest we went several times to Mammoth Cave and to Chicago, two very different experiences. In Mammoth Cave, where we would take the day-long trip, I was awed by the large rooms within the cave and by the stalagmites and stalactites. I learned to appreciate nature, including what lies beneath the surface of the earth. In Chicago, I loved the museums. Although I got sick of my sister wanting to see every stuffed bird in the Museum of Natural History, I never got tired of going into the coal mine in the Museum of Science and Industry. I learned so much in both museums about the natural and human worlds. I still have a souvenir, a miniature model of the submarine at the Museum of Science and Industry, on my desk right now. Travel increased what I knew in a fun way.

Sometimes you can travel vicariously. My sister went on a band trip to San Francisco. Part of her required preparation was reading about the city, so I heard about it whether I wanted to or not. Pretty soon I wanted to as she talked about the bay, the steepest street, and Chinatown. When my mom graduated from college and got an accounting job she took a trip she had always wanted to, to London. You'd have thought she was studying for a test the way she read Fodor's Guide to England was dogeared before she ever went. But, I was really excited by her explanations as she showed us pictures when she returned. She pointed out differences in daily life and British attitudes toward certain things but also the similarities in life styles and forms of amusement between the United States and England.

Travel helps you understand how you're alike or different from other people since I believe that differences among people are interesting and good I am especially interested in learning about different customs. That's why I enjoyed having a summer exchange student from Germany stay with us when I was fifteen. Although sharing my room was a bit (notice my British term) cramping Berthold and I had a great time, especially because we liked the same rock bands. He had CDs of many European bands I didn't, though. Also he was strict Roman Catholic, had had a grandfather who was an unwilling Nazi in World War II, and spoke three languages because his family traveled regularly in Italy and France. We had deep discussions about religion, politics, and cultures.

As I've thought about traveling I realize that I can travel in different ways. One way that some people probably don't think about is traveling through the arts. After all, art makes you think and feel in ways that expand your awarenesses. For example, I can remember way back to watching Sesame Street when Big Bird traveled to Mexico. My mom tells me I called her in to watch Big Bird do a hat dance and go to a bull fight. I told her I wanted to go to Mexico because the people had fun there. One time our neighbor took my family to a travelogue on Greece the slides of the Acropolis touched something in me that connected me with the distant past in a way I can't explain. Also we always subscribed to National Geographic. The great photographs brought the places described to life, in fact, when I got a camera in elementary school I declared that I was going to become a photographer for National Geographic. I could think of nothing more exciting than traveling to faraway places and taking great photographs to show others what I'd seen and done. The media of television, film, and photography have sent me on many wonderful travels.

The most important art form for travel for me, however, is music. Since I play the saxophone I like

```
jazz especially. If you play enough jazz you begin to
learn what influences have been on what players. I
learned that the musicians in New Orleans, the American
center for jazz, were influenced by the French culture
that was so important in that town. When I play certain
pieces I get transported to New Orleans or to Paris
through my feelings. I believe that I participate in
their cultures almost as much as if I were there.
Someday, however, I hope to travel to France to play and
listen to jazz there.
    Which brings me back to next summer. Don't you think
my mom should support my travel to Europe? Think about
all the education I would get. I've gone far through the
experiences of others and through the arts, but now I
want to go far physically. Wish me luck!
```

PRACTICE WITH USING MEDIA FOR EXPANDING THINKING

1. For one week explore a different medium each day. For example, if you do not regularly read the newspaper, read it and record in your dialogue journal reactions to different articles, columns, cartoons, advertisements, or other sections of the paper. If you never watch soap operas, watch two or three to see if you can understand some people's fascination with the soaps. Choose an art gallery you've never visited to see a current exhibition. Take a set of photographs of your neighborhood: what did you learn through that experience? At the end of the week, exchange your dialogue journal with a classmate to react to the media he chose and wrote about and to get responses to your experiences.
2. For a topic you are considering or have been assigned, brainstorm a list of sources of information with which you are familiar. Then, brainstorm a list of sources that might be helpful. Freewrite about each item on each list if the lists are not too long, or freewrite on the items on each list that seem most promising as important sources for your paper.
3. Although multiple sources are often helpful, you may discover that one source is rich enough to supply you with material for your topic. If you decide that a single source might be sufficient, cluster that source. If you generate many offshoots from your source at the center of the page, you may want to concentrate on that source as the chief information base for your paper.

4. Just as Justin tried grouping sources in order to achieve focus in his paper, you might want to classify entries on your brainstorming lists. Or you may want to do looping from a general entry on your list in order to focus more narrowly for your paper.
5. Would cubing like Darren did be potentially useful for your topic? You could choose media that might lead to good sources or ideas for your paper. After you have cubed, ask a classmate to respond to your cubing, looking for revelations in the cubing that you might not have seen.
6. By this time in the portfolio process, your classmates have read drafts or finished products that reveal your writing style, interests, and perspectives. Ask a classmate to recall from any of your previous writing ideas, examples, or perspectives that you can use in your current writing. Having the written drafts or pieces on hand in your Working Portfolio for referral will jog memories. Your own past writing becomes a medium for your current writing project.
7. Write a draft that plumbs one source or synthesizes multiple sources to express your main idea for the piece. In your Writer's Statement include a question for readers that asks them to identify other media that you might use in revising.

WORKING PORTFOLIO UPDATE

Keep all your explorations about media sources in your Working Portfolio. The exploration that you did for this paper may, in fact, yield information for another paper or revision. You may have noticed, for example, that Justin used in his paper on travel something he had learned in writing a previous paper about interactions among people of different races and cultures. You may be able to synthesize knowledge gained from a new source with previous knowledge as you continue writing about a wide variety of topics. Critical thinkers are able to apply both old and new knowledge to new situations to solve problems in fresh ways. Portfolio learning enables you to continue to incorporate your learning as you proceed to your next writing project. In the next chapter when you choose your own topic about which to write, you will be free to select topic, perspective, and sources. Your broadened array of media sources will be an asset as you begin your next paper.

CHAPTER 8
Conducting an Investigation

A common task in school, work, community, or personal life is conducting a research project that leads to an informed position on an important topic. Such a research project may involve any or all of the strategies for gaining information that you've practiced in this book so far.

BEGINNING AN INVESTIGATION

In Justin's class, each student was given the opportunity, for the fifth paper, to choose a topic for an investigative project. Justin joined his classmates in returning to journal entries, papers, and other documents generated earlier in the course, including the brainstorming for his literacy autobiography, as he began the initial stage of the project, choosing a topic.

> Assignment: Choose a topic that you would like to know more about. Use strategies of your choice, drawn from your experiences in this course or others you have found successful, to plan an investigative project. You may find it helpful to pose a research question that your investigation will help you to answer. Use written resources as your main source of information for this paper; document according to MLA style.

Justin wrote his initial ideas about the assignment in his journal.

Justin's Dialogue Journal Entry

I might write about photography. I would have to narrow it down alot. Or I see some topics in my brainstorming from the first of the class, like how important is a college degree anyway, and how much influence teachers have on their students. I also see one that says "convince myself I am literate." That seems dumb. I know I'm literate. That's about my dad. I wonder if I would be so literate if I had grown up with him and he was not. In fact, I wonder alot about how I'd be different if he had been there for me. I read something about a group of men that meet in football stadiums, something about promises. It said that they are trying to keep men involved with their families, and I wonder sometimes just how important it is to have a father's influence. The media tells us that crime and school problems and all kinds of things are connected to families without fathers. But I did okay, our family is okay, and so are lots of my friends. And, I know people from families with both parents who are in trouble. So I might try to find out just how important it is.

In his journal entry, Justin has begun to identify some potential topics for the next paper, including a general question related to his father. When he showed Suellen a list of possible topics, he discovered that she was not surprised by his many concerns about the importance of fathers.

Suellen's Response

You seem to know a lot about photography, but if this project is an investigation, why investigate something you already know about? And please don't write about "people who influenced me." I've written too many of those to want to read another one. I think you've been wanting to write about your dad all along. He keeps showing up in your writing. Unless you think it will upset you, you should go ahead and do it. It doesn't have to be a talk show paper, like "here's my sad `story." There must be things you want to know for this assignment.`

While Justin was deciding about his topic, his classmate Natali was further along: "I'm in a class on current issues and we're looking at the criminal justice system, including juvenile justice. That is interesting to me because sometimes kids are a problem in my neighborhood and my neighbors have been talking about better enforcement of the curfew laws. I said I would try to find some information about what they do in other cities and how well curfew laws work."

You may think that Natali seems much more focused and ready to begin an investigation, but Justin is also in a good position. Because he has not narrowed his topic, he can survey the available resources, read some of the materials, and thus develop a sense of the conversation that experts are carrying on in the literature about fatherlessness. He will discover what issues they think are important and what questions they are trying to answer. He may find studies focused on the economic effects of growing up fatherless or psychologists' discussions of the long-term effects of fatherlessness upon other relationships. Other articles may attempt to determine the effects of fatherlessness upon educational progress or self-image.

His broad question may require him to find a specific direction through reading and discovering the perspectives of different people. Justin's question and Natali's more focused question imply different but viable starting points for their investigations.

PRACTICE WITH PLANNING AN INVESTIGATION

1. Use a strategy such as brainstorming or freewriting to find a topic of interest to you. Think about issues in your classes, on your campus, in your work, or in your personal life. Survey the writing you have already done in this course for possible topics.
2. Choose another strategy such as cubing or journalistic questions to help you narrow your topic. Give a classmate a statement of your intended topic or perhaps several you are considering. Together, brainstorm a list of research questions for your investigation: what do you want to know about this topic? Then try to limit your questions to three or fewer.

WORKING WITH SOURCES

No two investigations are the same. Natali and Justin have begun in different ways; but as they begin to look for sources of information, they can both apply some general guidelines to their searches. Such guidelines are necessary because in the present information age, so many people make so much information available that the answers writers seek may be hidden in the myriad research studies and articles that fill libraries and expand databases. That very abundance of information can create confusion about which sources to consult. It also places a heavy responsibility upon writers to evaluate the sources they use to support their points.

Guidelines for Evaluating Sources

What advantages-disadvantages do your sources offer? Apply each of the following questions to each of your potential sources.

1. How timely is the material?
2. Who is the audience?
3. How reliable is the information?
4. How accessible is the material?

Books

1. Because preparing a book for publication takes a long time, information in books may not be as timely as that in other kinds of sources.
2. The audience will vary widely; look for cues in the level of language and the amount of background information for readers like you who are unfamiliar with the topic.
3. Information about the author should be available in a preface, on the book jacket, or elsewhere in the book. A bibliography will show you what sources of information the author used; you may be able to find a review of the book that discusses the credibility of the author and his book.
4. Library catalogs will tell you whether the book is available in your library or library system. The book's index may lead you quickly to the specific information you need.

An article in a magazine or newspaper

1. Because these periodicals are published frequently, they can offer timely information.
2. The huge number of periodicals makes it possible to serve very specific audiences, for instance, pheasant hunters or gold prospectors. Articles in periodicals often include helpful background information for those not familiar with the topic.

3. An article may be written by a free-lance writer whose credentials are often identified in a brief paragraph or by a staff writer knowledgeable about the topic. In both magazines and newspapers, writers usually identify their sources of information in the text of an article.
4. Paper or electronic indexes in your library can help you locate articles. Many indexes are available on-line in a database or electronic service.

An article in a scholarly or professional journal

1. A journal article usually offers the first information about the results of a research study. Newspapers and magazines often report such a study as soon as it appears in a journal.
2. Because their audience is professionals in a specific field, these articles may include technical language and statistical information that is difficult to understand. They may take for granted a certain knowledge base in the reader.
3. A journal article offers the firsthand account of the researchers themselves and includes a list of the sources they used; additionally, many of the articles appearing in such publications have been "juried," read and approved by a panel of others in the field.
4. Paper and electronic indexes help you locate such articles; many are available on-line. Sometimes a professor in the appropriate field subscribes to a journal and will let you copy an article you need. Most journal articles include an abstract or summary of the article.

Material from the World Wide Web

1. Information on web sites can be updated instantly; that also means that information available on the web yesterday may be gone today.
2. The audience varies widely; take cues from the level of language and information.
3. Material comes from all kinds of sources; you must be careful to identify the source. You may want to verify such information with a second source if you have any reason to doubt its accuracy.
4. The web offers a huge variety of topics; home pages and search engines can connect you with information from states, cities, organizations, and businesses among others. Some web sites allow you to participate in a dialogue with your source.

When Natali decided to look into curfew laws, motivated by events in her neighborhood, she drew three sources from a computer index: a popular source, *USA Today,* and two others that address current issues in more depth, *Governing* and *Commentary.*

She wasn't worried about understanding information about curfew laws because it was not likely to be technical. She chose those sources from the index list primarily, she says, because they were all from the same time period. Although she scanned several other articles, she did not copy or print them out because, although they did address her research questions, they were older. She did not want to mix articles from different time periods, for they all used some statistics and she wanted the numbers to be "comparable." She also wanted articles that did not have overt biases. "I didn't want something from a police journal or from something aimed more at kids, like the kind of commentary you might get in *Teen* magazine or something like that. You can even find letters to the editor from teenagers about curfew. I hoped these articles would be more objective."

Because she could print out two of the articles from the library computer and copy the others, she employed a system for marking on the texts rather than taking notes.

Natali's Investigation

As I read, I found myself wanting to highlight important things in the articles. But I've done that before, and I still have to go back and read and reread everything I highlighted and find what I'm looking for. This time I just made marks in the margin as I found important things while I read. Then, later, I went in and highlighted all the statistics in blue. I highlighted all the examples of what they are doing in different cities in yellow, and all the other important ideas and quotes that I liked in green. I made myself a key--you know, a chart that showed that green was good quotes, blue stats, etc. It wasn't a perfect system, but it helped. I do something like that every time I use several sources in a paper. Working with copies of the articles is really better because you've got page numbers and everything right there.

PRACTICE WITH CHOOSING SOURCE MATERIAL

1. Conduct a search for materials related to the topic you have chosen. Record in your journal some of the decision making that you employed. What kinds

of sources were available to you? Which did you choose and why? Ask your peers to respond to your entries. Do they have suggestions about your process or about your sources?

2. What difficulties did you experience in your research? What successes? Share them with others in your class. Try to solve each other's research problems. You might try pairing up for a research trip; talking it through with someone can make the process easier.
3. What important ideas and information did you find as you read your source material? What points of agreement or disagreement did you find among those writing about your topic? What new questions or unexpected answers did you discover? How will these discoveries affect your own thinking?

WRITING A PROPOSAL FOR A PAPER USING RESEARCH

Natali's proposal for her paper included her research questions, indicating that she wanted to explore curfew laws and their effectiveness and to apply her investigation to her own neighborhood. Her research fulfilled her expectations, providing a great deal of information about curfew laws, the problems associated with them, and solutions being undertaken in several cities. She knew that she could successfully answer her research questions and use the information to work with her neighbors, developing some ideas applicable to their concerns.

Natali did not write her proposal until she had conducted her research and read the sources; too many writers make the mistake of deciding on the topics of their papers and the positions or ideas they will defend before they gather information and educate themselves about their topics.

Determining a position too soon can be a waste of time because new information about the topic often emerges during an investigation and changes the writer's thinking. When this happened to K. C., she was unhappy. Like Natali she also had very specific research questions, but she followed a different process: "I had already written a lot of my paper about mandatory AIDS testing. Then I went out to get the research to plug into it. As I read, I found out that I was all wrong, and I had to completely rewrite my paper," she told the class on the day drafts were due. But as Ana pointed out, "Wouldn't you rather have to rewrite and be right? I thought you wanted to know about this, not just express your opinion."

Justin's search was different from both Natali's and K. C.'s, for he found himself adrift in a sea of information, none of which was exactly what he was looking for. Resources that directly addressed the effects of fatherlessness were hard to find. He began by reading an article in *Newsweek* that he thought might refer to research studies that he could trace. But the article also indicated that no long-range research on the topic was available. As he scrolled through lists of articles, Justin found that warning to be true, but he also discovered a number of related topics that intrigued him. He wrote the following proposal.

Justin's Proposal for Paper 5, Research Investigation

Purpose: I will discuss the importance of the absentee father.

Audience: People who still have marrying and having families ahead of them so that they will understand how big a responsibility it is to be the father and have influence over other people's lives.

Sources: I have articles from *Newsweek,* from a counseling journal and from *Demography.* I will also use an interview, maybe my interview with my grandmother or maybe I'll find an expert on family issues. I haven't decided yet.

Concerns: I didn't find the kind of information I was looking for, statistics or factual statements about the effects of absentee fathers on kids. I probably need to do some more looking.

PRACTICE WITH PROPOSALS

1. Write a proposal for your paper. Include information about your purpose and audience for the paper. Offer specific information about the sources you intend to use and how they will serve your paper. How did the availability of sources affect your plans for this paper? State any concerns that you have about writing the paper.
2. Share your proposal with a classmate or your instructor. Ask for response to the writing situation you have chosen: do the purpose and audience seem appropriate to each other? What kinds of sources are you planning to use? Have you adequately discussed their usefulness to the paper? Considering responses of your reader, revise your proposal if you need to.

DRAFTING A PAPER INCORPORATING RESEARCH

Before Natali drafted her paper, she brainstormed a list of ideas that she wanted to be sure to include in her paper. Then she numbered the listed items to indicate their order in her paper. For instance, "Kids in my neighborhood" is labeled "(1)" meaning that it will appear first in her paper. Sometimes she added notes to those items. For instance, she identified "Things that can happen to kids late at night" as one reason supporting curfew laws. She also identified material that adds to her support, as she did in noting that "The Indiana torture case" would function as an example to illustrate what can happen to kids late at night. This system of numbering and note taking was Natali's attempt to keep control of the process of writing a long paper. She created a record of what she had done and still had to do as she wrote. Here is her list.

Natali's Brainstorming List

Things that can happen to kids late at night (2), this is a reason in support of curfew laws

The Indiana torture case (2a), an example of what can happen late at night

Kids in my neighborhood (1), my reason for writing this paper

Phoenix etc.--other cities (4) examples of ways to deal with curfew

Reasons for curfew laws--vandalism, crime, bothering people in Broad Ripple (2b)

Opposition to curfew laws (5)

How effective are curfew laws? (3)

How can we make Indianapolis laws more effective? (6)

As you read Natali's draft, check it against her list. Did she adhere to her projected order?

Natali's Draft

Indianapolis Should Enact New Curfew Laws

It is a Thursday evening, close to midnight, and I hear the familiar voices of the local teenagers, yelling obscenities and kicking what sounds like an aluminum can as they make their way down my street. Indianapolis has an eleven o'clock curfew for all teens under eighteen, but these kids obviously have no fear of breaking curfew. As I watch a city police officer whiz by in his patrol car without giving these juveniles a second glance, I understand the lack of concern kids have about city curfew laws.

Even though police seem to lack commitment in enforcing curfew laws, such laws should be enforced in order to decrease violence perpetrated by and against juveniles.

That crime perpetuated by juvenile offenders is a growing problem is a view shared by many and proven by statistics. Alfred Blumstein of Carnegie Mellon University has estimated that the rate at which young males between the ages of 14-17 commit murder has gone up dramatically for white youths and even more so for black youths. Between 1985 and 1992, the homicide rate for young white males increased by almost 50 percent and tripled for young black men (Wilson 26). Although most people are not personally touched by juvenile homicide, the annoyance created by young people congregating in public places at night has received a lot of attention lately, particularly in Broad Ripple, a favorite haunt for this city's teenagers. Patrons in Broad Ripple have reported being harassed and intimidated by gangs of kids crowding around popular restaurants with no adult supervision. A ten o'clock curfew would certainly help to alleviate this problem if a commitment to enforce the curfew could be agreed upon by the local police.

Putting a roadblock in front of juvenile offenders is an important reason for enforcing strict curfew laws, but protecting kids from crime might provide an even stronger argument for the enforcement of curfew laws. Data gathered by Purdue University sociologist Kenneth Ferraro shows that young people have the greatest fear of being victimized by crime and that this fear is not unfounded (Fox 12). Young black males comprise 14 percent of the victims of homicide despite constituting only 1 percent of the U.S. population ("Who" 25). While instances of teen violence are increasing, the reasons for violence and aggression perpetrated by young people seem to become more trivial with each new police report. In California, two teenaged girls confessed to murdering their best friend because they envied her beautiful hair. Indiana residents may refer to the horrific slaying of New Albany teen Shanda Shearer. Her killers were four teenage girls, the youngest among them being fifteen-year-old Toni Lawrence. The terrible ordeal, instigated by one girl's jealousy of the popular Shearer, began at eleven p.m., after the victim was coaxed into the car by the young perpetrators, and didn't end until six the next morning when Shearer was doused with gasoline and burned alive on a country road near Madison, Indiana. The four teens responsible for Shanda's death were out on the streets for an entire evening, at one point stopping at a gas station for gasoline with the wounded girl unconscious in the trunk of their car. Perhaps the parents of these killers could have thwarted this savage act by keeping tabs on their daughters and enforcing a curfew. And maybe if Shanda had felt worried enough by the penalties of breaking a curfew, she might have refused to go with her killers and avoided her untimely and tragic death.

It is the above reasons that have galvanized many cities into enacting stricter curfews. Phoenix, Baltimore, and Little Rock are among a tidal wave of cities overhauling and tightening curfew laws (Watzman 20). Parents, fearing for the safety of their children, generally support curfew legislation. "I would rather have gotten a call to come pick up my child than to come identify him," laments Sophia Lopez, founder of Mothers Against Gangs, Phoenix chapter. Lopez's sixteen-year-old son was gunned down during a gang incident (Watzman 20).

Resistance to curfews definitely exists, though, from the police and the American Civil Liberties Union. Police concerns regarding curfews are legitimate and need to be overcome to successfully combat curfew violations. The lack of manpower available to round up violators and the financial burden that processing apprehended juveniles will place on the department are chief concerns. As it stands in Indianapolis, there are no fees required of parents when their children break curfew laws. To cover the costs of the extra manpower needed to handle teen violators, the city could charge a fifty-dollar fine for the first violation. Each violation after that could incur greater fines for the parents of curfew-breaking juveniles. Not only would fines defray the costs of this service, it would let apathetic parents know that they will have to pay for refusing to impose a curfew on their children.

Indianapolis might follow the example set by the North Little Rock police department when dealing with curfew violators. In North Little Rock, where a 10 p.m. curfew is in effect on weekdays and a midnight curfew applies to the weekends, officers have detained over 1,300 youths for curfew violations since 1991 when the law was enacted. Their department employs a "juvenile intake" officer who processes teens so that officers can return to the streets quickly after bringing a teen violator to the police station. A police spokesman in North Little Rock claims that the new system "hasn't inconvenienced us at all" (Watzman 21).

ACLU opposition to curfew laws creates problems in enforcing curfew laws. Claiming that curfew laws violate constitutional rights of teenagers, the ACLU has taken some cities to court with inconsistent results. A strict curfew law for the District of Columbia was ruled unconstitutional in federal court four years ago, but other curfew laws have survived challenges brought by the ACLU. Last year in November a federal district court decision that struck a Dallas curfew law from the books was reversed (Watzman 20). Some individuals side with the ACLU, claiming that the government has no right to strip parents of their legal right to impose curfew on their children that they, the child's legal guardians, feel is appropriate. This may be true but the fact remains that kids are on the streets late into the evening and that the parents of some of these juveniles simply do not impose reasonable curfews on their children.

The biggest question regarding curfews is whether they really work. Complete data on this is not available because many of the cities enacting new curfew laws have done so only recently, but some findings support the enactment of curfew laws. In Charleston, South Carolina, Chief Reuben Greenburg ordered his officers to take all truant children back to the classroom and to return all kids violating evening curfews back to their parents. Because of this policy, gangs of school-age children no longer haunt the local malls in the afternoon or roam the streets late at night. Although findings were not acquired scientifically, in 1991, rough figures show a drop in the crime rate after strict curfew enforcement in San Antonio. Police there reported a drop in the number of juveniles victimized by crime from about 3,600 offenses against underage kids before the curfew was enacted to 826 during the second year of the curfew (Watzman 21). These facts certainly prove that teen curfews can have a very beneficial effect on the communities that enforce them.

Although many problems facing the enactment and enforcement of curfew laws in Indianapolis do exist, the need to consider overhauling our current system is apparent. Picking up a child and holding him at the juvenile center, then releasing him without further consequences may be more of an inconvenience to the police than to the violator and his family. The legislation should be changed to include a small fee for the first offense as well as higher fees for successive violations. Also, the eleven o'clock cut off time should be changed to 10 p.m. One reason crimes are committed later in the evening is that fewer people are out in public, allowing perpetrators the secrecy they need to commit criminal acts without detection. Another reason for changing the curfew to 10 p.m. is that 11 p.m. seems terribly late for a school day. If children are expected to attend school in the morning, they need to get some sleep at night.

Creating new curfew laws may or may not stem the tide of juvenile crime in Indianapolis, but we will not know the outcome of these laws until we try them. Cities like Charleston and San Antonio obtained positive results from their new curfew campaigns. Indianapolis must get with the program and address the problem of violence perpetrated by and against juveniles. Curfew laws may only be a small part of the solution in protecting our kids from crime, but in this era of dangerous streets and schools, we must use every small weapon we have to combat juvenile crime.

Works Cited

Fox, James, and Glenn Pierce. "The Young Desperados." *USA Today* 21 Aug. 1992: 12.

Watzman, Nancy. "The Curfew Revival Gains Momentum." *Governing* Feb. 1994: 20–21.

"Who Is Most Afraid of Crime?" *USA Today* 22 Jan.1994: 24–26.

Wilson, James. *Commentary* Sept. 1994: 25–35.

INCORPORATING SOURCES INTO YOUR WRITING

You probably noticed Natalie's use of in-text documentation supplying information about her sources. Note the parentheses in this example.

```
    A police spokesman in North Little Rock claims that
the new system "hasn't inconvenienced us at all"
(Watzman 21).
```

In this sentence, Natali gives her reader information drawn from the article by Watzman, including a quotation found on page 21. Her use of parenthetical citations instead of footnotes or endnotes conforms to the MLA stylebook, the official publication of the Modern Language Association. Because different audiences and writing situations call for different systems of documentation, you will need a guide, such as a handbook, to systems commonly requested by your professors.

Whatever system you use, however, you should consider your audience as you incorporate source material into your work. Many students simply drop quotations or other information drawn from sources into their texts with no introduction or identification of the source beyond the parenthetical citation. Although that is technically acceptable, you may want to use your sources to better advantage by identifying them in your text, letting their authority add to the credibility of your paper. When she first uses Nancy Watzman's information in her paper, for instance, Natali might identify Watzman as a social worker with twenty years of experience working with juvenile crime. That background gives Natali's source an authority that can strengthen her argument. She might even identify the publication *Governing* as a publication for municipal workers, again enhancing readers' sense of the authority and purpose behind her source. That sort of identification is necessary only when a source is first introduced into your paper. After that, the parenthetical citation is enough.

Documentation systems are designed to add authority, to give credit to other writers, and to help a reader to locate a source in case she wants to read it for herself. In addition to the in-text parenthetical citations, the Works Cited page at the end of a paper lists all the sources used in the paper and the information necessary for a reader to find them. There the sources are listed alphabetically at the left margin by each author's last name or the title of an article when no author is identified. A reader who encounters Watzman in the parenthetical citation can easily find that source on the Works Cited page. The citation ("Who" 25) indicates the first word in the title of an article for which no author is identified. A reader looking for that source on the Works Cited page should be able to find it easily.

As you gain experience with documentation systems, you will find that they allow you some choices. For instance, when you include the author's name in the text before you quote from an article, only the page number appears in the parentheses. A page number is necessary when you quote a source directly, when you use specific information such as a statistic or other factual item, or when you use an idea that clearly belongs to the source, even though you may paraphrase that idea by putting it into your own words. The principle to remember is that the reader must be able to move with ease from source material in the text to the full identification offered on the Works Cited page to the quoted passage in the original article. The combination of the parenthetical citation and the Works Cited page allows that movement. As Justin includes sources in his next draft, pay attention to his need for documentation.

Before drafting his paper, Justin, too, did some preliminary planning. He "drew" his paper (see below) to get an idea of the order in which he would discuss various points and where he would use sources. He also wanted to "see" how the parts of the paper would balance out and to estimate their relative sizes.

This is my paper. Divorce comes speeding through with effects on everyone, the mother, father and kids, but the kids have more effects. Which one of the boxes is the "kids"?

As you read Justin's draft, try to "see" his paper as he did, imagining the "parts" of the paper as they appear in his visual version of the paper.

Justin's Paper 5, Draft I, Research Investigation

One of the most talked about problems today is the problem of absentee fathers. All the discussion about the overhaul of the welfare system, crime and problems in schools seems to come down to pointing a finger at families where the fathers are gone. If you listen to some of the talk on television the male influence is supposed to be so important that it's a miracle families without it survive. But is it really that big of an influence? Who is affected by the absence?

An article in *Newsweek* says that David Blankenhorn, chairman of National Fatherhood Initiative and president of the Institute of American Values, "calls fatherlessness 'the most urgent social problem of our generation.'" The article goes on to say that a 1993 *Atlantic Monthly* article says that kids raised without fathers are "'more likely to drop out of high school, to get pregnant as teenagers, to abuse drugs, and to be in trouble with the law.' They were at higher risk for physical and sexual abuse and an array of emotional problems that would persist into adulthood." A father's absence can even put a child at higher risk for accidents and injuries.

That's a lot of influence to have on a kid. And I'm not sure it's right. The article also says that the research collected about this influence is from the field, people noticing that kids in trouble in school, for instance, are often being raised by their mothers alone. But it also says that more academic research is needed and says that lots of people grow up very successfully without their fathers. I have grown up without my father, and I have never been in any sort of trouble. And I've been thinking about the generation from World

War II because lots of men who had families were killed in the war, and you don't read much about all these social problems in the years following that war.

Maybe we should look as well at the effect this situation has on the fathers. In the *Journal of Counseling and Development,* associate professors Janice and Michael Wilber wrote an article called "The Noncustodial Parent: Dilemmas and Interventions." It says that noncustodial parents experience "feelings of loss, self-doubt, and ambivalence and a generally diminished sense of their importance as parents." If the children are doing well, noncustodial parents feel unneeded. In my life, my father is a noncustodial parent, by choice. He never has tried to be a custodial parent. After he left us, it was a long time before we heard from him. My Grandmother Cooper did, and she would tell us that he asked about us, but I can guess now that he was ashamed. She said he felt like we might be better off without him. But that was for a different reason.

He wasn't very literate. So he thought that he couldn't make a good living, and he couldn't. Then after he left, my mom went on to get a degree, and it would have been hard for him to deal with that. He has remarried now and has two more kids. We haven't met them, though my Grandma has. She says that he has been back to school and has learned to read and write so that he can have his job as a dispatcher for a trucking company. A report in an article in *Demography* says that when parents divorce when the children are young, they frequently give little in monetary or emotional support, and that even when child support is required by law, the child-father tie is no stronger.

Absentee fathers is a big problem today, but the answer to the question about the effect of absentee fathers is that their absence has an effect on every member of the family. It may have an adverse effect upon a family's finances, but it may also encourage the woman to continue her education so she can support the family and find fulfillment outside the home. It may encourage kids to become their own people, not to try to be like their father and to take responsibility at an early age. And it has an effect on the fathers. They may suffer from leaving their families, whatever their reasons, and from not staying in contact with their children. It is possible for children to grow up successfully without their fathers, and we can only hope that they will understand the importance of being a more involved father when their time comes.

Justin's Writer's Statement for Paper 5, Research Investigation

Purpose: To look at the effects of absentee fathers on their families and themselves.

Audience: It's supposed to be young people who can maybe keep from having bad effects on their future families.

Thesis: I have two main points, I think. First I ask just how important a father's influence is. Then towards the end, I say that the absence of a father affects everyone in the family.

Strengths: I think I have a good idea and that it's an important subject. I have experience with the topic and I would like to have some information that would help me to be a better father than mine has been for me. But, as always, I worry about how to put the personal slant into a paper, especially a paper like this that is supposed to be a research paper. This one looks like all my other papers and I think it should be different. I am happy that I think I stayed on a focus this time--how are different family members affected by an absentee father. I did that!

Weaknesses: I think that by talking about all the family members that are affected, I copped out. I don't think I did enough research. I should go get that *Atlantic Monthly* article and I should find out more about the football stadium group. And I really am not happy with using my grandmother. The thing is, I didn't answer the questions I wanted answered. I just wrote a paper and I already knew most of those things, except the effects on the father himself. I read Natali's paper and it looks much more like I think this one should. If I really can't find what I need when I go back to the library, I guess I'll change my topic. And, I know I didn't do all the page numbers for documentation but I will in the next draft.

Questions: My main question is how can I find the right material about this topic? How can I make this more like a research paper? The other important thing to me right now is the age old problem of how much personal stuff I can put in.

ANALYZING NATALI'S AND JUSTIN'S DRAFTS

1. Justin believes that Natali's paper looks more like a research paper. Do you agree? Why? How do the characteristics that make Natali's paper different serve the purpose of a research paper?
2. How well do the two writers meet their statements of purpose for their papers? What would you suggest to either of them to make their papers better meet their purposes?
3. Compare Natali's planning list to her draft. Did she conform to her plan? What rationale for her order can you provide? What alternative orders can you offer? Explain your rationale.
4. In his Writer's Statement, Justin has pointed out two important statements as representing his main point or thesis: "First I ask just how important a father's influence is. Then . . . I say that the absence of a father affects everyone in the family." Which do you think best represents his main idea for the paper? What are the advantages of locating the thesis early in the paper; why might a writer choose to save the thesis for the end?
5. Identify material in Justin's draft that requires documentation. What should be included in the necessary parenthetical citations?

DRAFTING YOUR PAPER

1. Try one of the strategies used by Natali or Justin in this chapter or a planning strategy you have used before, drawn from an earlier chapter in this

book or from your own background in writing. Let the strategy help you create an order for the main ideas that you want to discuss in this paper.

2. How will you address Justin's concerns in planning your own paper? How much personal material will you include? How will this paper be different from earlier papers you have written in this class?
3. Draft the paper.
4. In your Writer's Statement, include information about your sources.

WORKING PORTFOLIO UPDATE

With the drafting of his paper on fatherlessness, Justin has produced drafts of all five papers required in his course. Now he must decide which three of the papers he will revise and polish for inclusion in the Course Portfolio. In the next chapter you will join him in that decision making, sorting through the contents of your Working Portfolio, weighing the merits of your papers, revisiting your goals, and considering how best to showcase your work.

CHAPTER 9 Making Choices

My son Andy collects things. Since he was little, he has been intrigued by railroads. Living not far from a track, he has taken many excursions along the tracks, returning each time with souvenirs: rusted railroad spikes, flattened pennies, or twisted metal in multiple shapes. Andy also likes junk mail. When he was old enough, he opened a post office box in which he received replies to entries in contests, letters to celebrities, and requests for ads and publications. He kept the replies "in case he wanted" them. You could probably predict the accumulation in our basement of toys, stuffed animals, vacation souvenirs, costumes and props from holidays and plays, sports equipment, and memorabilia of all kinds. Admittedly, Andy has put to use many of his collectibles for unexpected purposes. For example, many items have been important in videos he has filmed in the past few years. Yet our basement is full, Andy is going off to college, and it's time to make some choices about what to keep.

During the term you have been collecting all your writing: dialogue journal entries, heuristics, responses from readers to your ideas and drafts, proposals, drafts, Writer's Statements, and other informal and formal writing. In fact, you now have a Working Portfolio of material, a collection of many possibilities. You have ideas for future writing, suggestions about different ways to approach certain writing tasks, and both partial and complete versions of papers. In a Working Portfolio you, like other writers, have stored everything that you have produced, thereby having the materials ready for an emergent occasion or purpose.

For example, several years ago I gave a talk on feminist pedagogy at a national conference within my discipline. The talk is stored in a kind of Working Portfolio, a file on my computer named "conference presentations." When later I was asked to talk on a similar theme at a higher education conference, I brought up my earlier conference paper from that file: I could use ideas and even sections of the paper in my newer presentation. At about the same time I was interviewed for an article in a professional journal: I had both papers in front of me to help me answer questions coherently and substantively. You can use your writing in similar ways as you move from your Working Portfolio of papers to your Course Portfolio. As you near the time for revision or final revision, you must make choices about what to discard, keep for later use, or finish for presentation in your Course Portfolio.

You may be in a class that has finished papers as you have gone along: you revised, received responses, revised some more, and produced a finished product on which you were evaluated. You may have even received a grade on the finished paper.

In portfolio learning, however, you can revise even after you have received an evaluation. In fact, you can use your instructor's responses to guide your revision and editing process. Your instructor may or may not grade this later revision, but the revised piece becomes substantial evidence of your learning since the original grading and can help make a case in your Course Portfolio about your improvement over the term.

On the other hand, you may be in a class that has produced pieces that are open to revision throughout the semester. You may have done single drafts and put them aside as you began another piece of writing. You may have taken a piece to a certain stage at which you needed to move on, knowing that you could return to the piece later. You may have put a paper in the best shape it could be at the time, received some response, and now are ready to revise, if you choose that piece for your Course Portfolio.

SELECTING WORK TO REVISE FOR THE COURSE PORTFOLIO

The reasons that you choose pieces to revise are dependent on your course; your instructor; and your own goals, roles, time, and motivation. Three bases for selection that often guide choices are evidence of best work, established criteria, and particular audience.

Best Work

Sometimes students can choose their best work to submit in their Course Portfolio. They generate for themselves the criteria on which to base their selections. Writers may reason quite differently about these criteria. For example, I learned a lesson from a student the first time that one of my classes used best work for selecting writing to include in a Course Portfolio. Joe reasoned that he could show progress toward his individual goal of using correct punctuation by including in his portfolio his last paper from both his previous semester's developmental writing course and his current beginning composition class. Indeed, his earlier paper had errors in the use of the apostrophe to show possession, the semicolon before a conjunctive adverb in a compound sentence, periods to mark ends of simple sentences, and quotation marks to note direct quotations. Joe reasoned that because many college writers already had punctuation uses such as these under control, his claim for control in his final paper would not be impressive. When he contrasted his earlier papers with his later ones, however, readers could see how far he had come in his ability to use appropriate punctuation. Joe went one step further, however, by revising and editing his last term's paper, demonstrating dramatically how he could apply his new knowledge. Although you will probably revise and edit papers exclusively from this term's work, remember that you may be imaginative in demonstrating your abilities.

You must have some basis on which to judge your pieces. You may use the goals you set at the beginning of the semester: department, class, and individual goals. If, for example, you want to show that you have learned how to use sufficient evidence to support your main points, you may select to revise and edit a draft on which your readers noted the comprehensive scope of evidence. Afterward, you will have an excellent example of your best work.

As you choose your best work, you may include material that traces how you got to your finished pieces. Although you will not revise this earlier material, you can refer to it as you later describe your writing process and products. For example, after doing a cluster, you may have changed your original idea about writing on surrogate parenting to writing on single parenting. The resulting paper is well done because you had a wealth of information from your single mom, your neighbor who is a single parent, and material from your sociology of the family course. In other words, the signal from the cluster that you had more to say about single parenting than surrogate parenting is borne out by the ease of finding information from your own experience. Because the paper was initially well received by readers, you may choose to revise it for your Course Portfolio, responding to their suggestions about a more relevant introduction and a sharper focus on your main point.

You may devise other criteria for best work, but listing those criteria is an effective way to keep yourself focused as you make decisions about which pieces to revise. From among the possibilities in your Working Portfolio, you can choose those pieces that have the greatest possibility of exemplifying your best work for your Course Portfolio.

Established Criteria

Your department or instructor may have stipulated the kinds or genres of writing that should go into your portfolio. For instance, requirements for a beginning composition Course Portfolio might include an introductory essay, a narrative, a critical analysis, a piece using sources, and a position paper. Students in the class may have drafted two narratives, two critical analyses, an interview write-up, a contrast of articles from two periodicals on the topic of the interview, and a position paper. These students, therefore, would have some choices about what to revise for the Course Portfolio. Although everyone would presumably revise the one position paper draft, students might choose either of the narratives or critical analyses. Also, they might revise the interview or the contrast separately or merge the material into a piece using sources. Although starting a new piece from scratch is more difficult at this stage in the term because the papers lose the benefits of early writing and of reader responses, students could revise through merger or through using a draft in a new way. If a student in the class just mentioned had written two effective critical analyses but had a poorly drafted piece using sources, that writer might turn one of the critical analyses, on a recent film, into a piece using sources. The writer could incorporate reviews of the film that supported or refuted points in the analysis, leading to some new analysis and an effective piece using sources.

You must be clear about required or selected criteria before choosing pieces to revise for your Course Portfolio. If your instructor or department has established criteria, be familiar with them so that you make choices that lead you to a successful portfolio.

Particular Audience

You may be creating a portfolio for a particular audience. Although it is more likely that you will have alternative audiences for a portfolio at the end of your undergraduate years, you may have an audience beyond your teacher and peers for at least part of this portfolio. Some colleges and universities see a Course Portfolio as part of a more comprehensive portfolio that records learning across disciplines and across the undergraduate program. If you envision using your portfolio as part of the unfolding of your literacy history, you may include pieces that are indicative of work in this course but, more importantly, demonstrate your learning over time. Joe's pieces showing punctuation mastery are one such example, but yours may be embedded in your major, your vocational goals, or your personal goals.

If you are a poet in a composition course, for instance, you may have written no poems for class assignments. You may, however, have used metaphor effectively in a piece for the course, an important application to prose of your poetic ability. In the long run, for your creative writing major, you may be interested in including that prose piece to connect your learning in this class with your main genre of writing. The piece may need revision to make it acceptable for this Course Portfolio, but the revision will be worthwhile for your larger purpose.

In her portfolio letter for her Course Portfolio, Julie talks about the importance of "the aural aspects of writing."

Julie's Portfolio Letter

Like Richard Selzer, whom we read, I appreciate the aural aspects of writing: the sound of words and syllables. My drafts are full of crossed-out words and entire sentences that have failed to achieve the desired euphonic effect. Since studying poetry last year, I have enjoyed trying to use alliteration in my writing as I did in a poem that I wrote for that class. (I am enclosing the poem, "Middle Age," in the portfolio.) Although alliteration is a device used more frequently in poetry, I find it challenging to employ it in essays as I did in "Lifelong Learning." When Karen, Cynthia, and Maureen praised the readability of my papers, they gave examples of interesting word usage and imagery in my first essay. In my opinion, this ability to use applicable and poetic language is my greatest strength in writing.

Julie identifies one reason for her revision and inclusion of this piece in her portfolio: she unites her ability to use figurative language in both poetry and prose, laying the basis for a claim about the range of her writing ability in the portfolio she will complete as an English major. She is thinking about her current audience and about her future audience.

Another audience consideration as you choose which pieces to revise may be political. In rhetoric, we learn to consider the interests, biases, backgrounds, and abilities of our audience. If you learned through early response to a draft on the benefits of genetic engineering that your instructor has strong, religiously based objections to genetic manipulation, you know that you have to build an especially persuasive argument. Although your instructor will be a good reader of your piece because she is a professional, as a reader she must deal with her own convictions as she tries to understand and to appreciate your points. Do not put aside a piece that is important to you because of your worry about an instructor or peers who may not be able to understand initially your choice of subject or perspective, but do be alert to the responsibility you take when you write about topics or from viewpoints that are difficult for your readers. You can always come back to a piece in another context if you decide that the context of this audience is not amenable to this piece of writing. Or you can accept the challenge of addressing the audience through making yourself familiar with the kinds of evidence and arguments that are most likely to be persuasive.

FINDING CUES ABOUT WHAT TO REVISE

Recently, a student faced with the decision of what to revise for his Course Portfolio told me that he didn't have anything that looked promising enough to revise: he despaired about proceeding. I advised him to look back into his Working Portfolio dialogue journal entries both before and after submitting drafts to readers, his Writer's Statements, his reader response sheets, and his e-mail exchanges about his drafts. In one or more of those sources, he might find encouragement about what to revise and why.

Dialogue Journal Entries

As Amy recounted in her dialogue journal, she used a tried and true heuristic to help her get started in deciding which drafts to revise.

Amy's Dialogue Journal Entry

When I sit down to compose something, whether it is academic or creative work, I first check in with my e-mail account. Before I even put my disk into the computer, I log on to the Internet to send mail to friends at other universities. Call it a warm-up exercise. It is a great way to get the blood pumping in my fingers before I have to pound out some work. I have heard that some writers have special rituals that are involved with their work, and so I seem to have developed my own.

After reading this entry from earlier in the term, Amy recalled how an e-mail session served to help her thinking and writing. She wrote e-mail messages to friends before she began the task of deciding on her pieces for revision. The cue from her journal about a way to start the decision-making process was useful.

Other dialogue journal entries may provide more direct cues. Jeremy had written after the last version of his piece on the pleasures of fishing that he wanted sometime to expand his piece by contrasting the emotional effects of various kinds of fishing: he wanted to complicate the simple picture of fishing that he had painted. Although Jeremy had needed to move on at that time to the next required writing, he had the dialogue journal in his Working Portfolio to remind him of an idea for further revision. When he reread his journal, he decided to choose the fishing piece to revise for his portfolio and, possibly, for submission to a local sport fishermen's magazine.

Your dialogue journal may also contain other people's suggestions about future possibilities for your pieces. After Rafael read Mary's draft of a paper on diversity and her thoughts about revision in her dialogue journal, he advised her not to pursue the subject. He believed that her life in a small, rural northeastern town had not prepared her to make the claims that she did about tolerating diversity. Although she had read widely about other cultures, at college she was for the first time living with people different from those in her hometown. Speaking from the personal experience of having lived and gone to school in Los Angeles, Miami, and Indianapolis, Rafael told Mary that she would be taken more seriously when she had had more opportunities to confront cultural differences that cause conflict. Her present draft was unrealistic about what is possible. Although Mary disagreed with Rafael that she would have credibility only on subjects with which she had had life experience, she did understand that her classmates might agree with Rafael. Because she had other pieces that had as much or more promise, she used Rafael's dialogue journal response to help her make her choice about postponing revision of her diversity piece.

Writer's Statements

Writer's Statements are useful at the time of first revision because you receive specific answers to your questions addressing immediate needs. You learn if a piece of evidence is pertinent, a paragraph is too long, or a certain argument is persuasive. Writer's Statements can also be useful over time, however, including when you are deciding which papers to choose from your Working Portfolio to revise for your Course Portfolio.

Discovering the Real Subject

In my classes students sometimes decide on the content of their Writer's Statements; other times they respond to a set of questions chosen by me to emphasize what we are currently studying. Because most of us wish for more time for our writing, I often ask the question "What would you change in this piece if you had more time?" The answers are excellent cues for future revising.

When Charlotte took on the topic of the "sandwich generation," she did so because she and her husband were rearing children and caring for parents simultaneously. With a firm knowledge base, she stated that she could provide important information for anyone beginning this double duty. Then Charlotte added this section to her Writer's Statement.

Charlotte's Writer's Statement

When I began to do research on the sandwich generation, I planned to write an informative paper with suggestions I might add based on my experience with my parents. As I began to add the *I* to my paper, it seemed to take off in a direction not planned by me. I began to express some of my resentment and anger toward my siblings and that was not something I had wanted to do. I would now have to say that my purpose for the paper has changed to an airing of grievances or resentment about being caught in a situation not of my planning. I also have to admit that my perspective has changed, and this paper will not be an unbiased, informative paper.

Because Charlotte discovered the real purpose and perspective of her paper as she wrote, her draft was uneven, sometimes providing information and other times describing her frustrations. In the addendum to her Writer's Statement, Charlotte had already identified the shift, although she had not located in her text the spots that suffered from an incomplete movement from decontextualized data to personal account.

Choosing to revise the piece for her Course Portfolio in order to move completely to her new focus, Charlotte used her Writer's Statement to prompt her revising. The title of her final piece signals her completed shift: "Caught Like a Rat in a Trap."

Building a Knowledge Base over Time

Listen to Julie again as she explains in her Writer's Statement why she wants to continue with a topic and papers about that topic.

Julie's Writer's Statement

Choosing a topic about which I had very little knowledge but a strong interest was an important decision for me. My initial awareness of tenure stemmed only from an observation that it is rarely looked at in a positive light outside academia. After reading John

```
Silber's book in which he discussed the pros and cons of
tenure in a straightforward manner, my interest was
piqued. It also seemed a natural transition to
investigate this topic further after seeing many
references to it in my research on academic freedom for
my last paper. My most difficult problem in writing this
paper was a failure to develop an opinion on the
subject; both sides of the issue were convincing. I have
reached the conclusion, however, that three weeks does
not an expert make!
    It was important for me to continue with the theme
of academia in this paper. I have a need to be informed
about that area of my life in which I am involved. Now
that I am part of the university and hope to remain for
awhile, I will be more comfortable if I have an
understanding of the system. Perhaps because of my
previous highly structured experience with education, I
am thoroughly enjoying the freedom and encouragement to
examine and debate matters of importance in the academic
arena.
```

Julie's strong desire to continue to investigate issues central to the structure and role of academia and her strongly felt awareness that she needs and wants more time to study the system are strong cues that her pieces are appropriate for revising for her Course Portfolio. In addition, she states that she is "thoroughly enjoying" the freedom of studying and writing about that which interests her: surely the joy of writing is a pertinent reason for continuing with a writing project!

TURNING TO READER RESPONSES

You have already collaborated with other writers to give and to receive help during the writing process. As you choose pieces to revise for your Course Portfolio, reader responses can again be central in your decision making.

Using Reader Responses to Make Alternative Decisions

In a piece called "Football: A Justification," Gordon associates football with what he calls the "magical" season of fall. Gordon reviews various reasons that people love fall, coming to football as the central reason for him. He then explains the virtues of football, including the constant competition, the beauty of the movement, the "inextricable bonding of order and chaos," and the emotional high of the spectators. He concludes that "football ranks with Halloween and the return to classrooms as the watermark indicating the presence of that fall feeling."

In my response letter to Gordon's piece, I wrote this entry among others.

> As a person whose older son plays college football, whose television blasts forth ESPN statistics and highlights when my other son is not watching Sunday or Monday night games, and who has attending football on her own list of reasons to love fall, I appreciate your effort in this essay. I'm wondering, though, if someone who knows little about the game or who doesn't associate it positively with fall will be persuaded by your piece. When I read Heidi's response, for instance, I was intrigued by her suggestion to connect your feeling with something that might evoke emotional response on the part of more of your readers. Did you consider such a move?

Gordon had Heidi's suggestion and my affirmation of one possibility for change to consider as he chose drafts to revise for his Course Portfolio. Did he want to try for a wider audience, or was he satisfied to connect with readers like me who could understand through description rather than persuasion the point of his piece? Although Gordon did choose to revise this piece for his Course Portfolio, he did not make the connection suggested by Heidi. Later in his Course Portfolio letter, Gordon wrote as part of a longer paragraph: "When I received feedback from my instructor and my peers, I looked long and hard at their comments, looking for their value. I welcome criticism, now more than ever, because I see that I miss a lot of things which can hamper my writing. I am not so proud as to dismiss these comments, although I will decide on occasion to overrule my rough draft readers." Reader response to Gordon's piece motivated him to revise it for his Course Portfolio, but his revisions were alternative changes to those suggested by his readers.

Using Reader Responses to Shape Decisions About Revisions

When Melanie received my letter of response to her first paper in her composition class, she was apprehensive. Although she had received grades on papers in past classes, she had no experience with letters of response to drafts. Based on the letter, however, she decided that the paper was worth revising. Melanie had this record of her reaction to my response to her paper because students write reactions to my comments immediately after receiving them and keep them in their Working Portfolios. These reactions are useful to me in understanding how a writer has made meaning of my comments and to the students in deciding what to do next.

Melanie's Reaction to a Reader Response

My initial reaction to my instructor's reader response is a really good one. For the most part, her response to my paper was very encouraging, and gave me a good feeling. The criticism was constructive, and instead of feeling insulted, it gave me something to keep in mind for my future papers. I have been really worried about this paper, not only because it has been a long time since I have written for anyone other than myself, but also because this was such a personal topic, and I focused on the personal perspective. I am pleased that the response was a good one, and feel encouraged and more confident about my writing in this class, and in general.

The next step I need to take as I revise is to read each sentence separately, and ask myself, "Does this contribute to the theme and purpose of this paper?" My instructor made the suggestion of not telling all my experiences in chronological order, but instead, grouping general or like experiences together to get the point across better. Possibly telling this in chronological order is better suited for a story instead of an essay.

Although Melanie moved on to the next writing assignment immediately after she received my reader response and wrote these reactions, she has a written record to help her decide if she later wants to turn this story into an essay. Melanie, in fact, did revise this piece for her Course Portfolio, partly because she had the confidence to do so and partly because she had a suggestion about how to reorganize her material.

Reader responses can raise questions that you may decide to answer in your own way: the cues in reader responses, however, can add to your own thoughts as you decide whether a piece is worthy of revision and what should be revised.

Using E-Mail Exchanges

E-mail exchanges can be the source of cues about revising. A general conversation about an issue of evidence, focus, or organization can prompt you to read a draft with a new eye for application of what you learned in the on-line discussion. If you learn from an exchange among Darrell, Laura, and Latoya about techniques for interviewing, you may choose to conduct a new interview as you revise your paper on safety standards in fast-food restaurants in your town. For your former draft you may have interviewed employees within earshot of their supervisor or a regional manager who had little direct experience with local restaurants. Discussing effective interviewing practices with your classmates, you may decide that your piece, which was critiqued by readers as unpersuasive, can be made substantive by the substitution of more reliable, quoted testimony.

The following e-mail exchange helped Ruth decide to revise her draft on the parking problem at her university.

Ed: Ruth, I agree that parking here is really bad. But, you write as if you are the only person who has the problem. After your third story about being late to class because of not finding a parking spot, I was getting pretty bored.

Lynx: Man, I ain't found a place yet less than three blocks from this building.

Leslie: I've read about this problem in the school newspaper already twice this year. That doesn't mean it isn't a problem, but you'll have to provide some new twist if you want to have anything new that anyone will want to read. Just whining isn't enough. Did you find any suggested solutions to the problem when you interviewed people?

Ruth: I did talk with the head of the physical plant who says that more parking garages are planned for the future. That doesn't help now, though, so I didn't use the information in my paper.

Ed: I'd have liked your piece better if you'd included the garage info because, at least, I'd know that the university cares. I know also that the rates at the current garages are lowered between 7:00 and 8:00 a.m. so people who are willing to come early can get a spot. That doesn't help everyone, but it's one thing.

Elizabeth: My friends at other schools have the same parking complaints. Did you check to see if other schools have done anything different about their facilities? I agree with Ed that you need to branch out. It's so frustrating, though, I know.

This exchange, which Ruth printed out, contains several suggestions that Ruth can use if she decides to revise later in the term: she could investigate the university's attempts to alleviate the problem, or she could even move beyond her university to gain information about other schools, perhaps turning her piece from a complaint into a set of recommendations.

Although this exchange occurred in class, you can get cues about revision from e-mail on your personal computer as well. You can post a draft, ask for responses, and use the feedback to decide whether a revision for use in your Course Portfolio is worthwhile. If a draft has an external audience, this method is particularly appropriate. For example, if you are arguing for more girls' varsity sports at your former high school, you might send a draft of your paper to the athletic director or to a school board member who has some authority in determining athletic policy. If the director or board member encourages your writing by offering additional information or by challenging your points in ways that you can address, you might choose to revise for your Course Portfolio. A printout of the e-mailed response would be sound evidence for your revision strategies.

CHOOSING TO REVISE AS A DEMONSTRATION OF LEARNING

Students in a class taught by a professor friend of mine sometimes write and revise one piece throughout an entire term. "What an easy class!" you may think, but listen to what the revision entails. Each student uses the material from the first paper for different purposes and for different audiences. For example, if the writer first chooses to write a narrative about working at McDonald's for classmates considering working there, that writer might subsequently write a complimentary letter to the regional headquarters about her manager, a report for the school paper's health column about moves McDonald's has taken to lower fat content in its offerings, and a collage of descriptions of unusual customers for the college literary magazine.

As the writers change their purposes and audiences, they discuss the new demands on their writing. Do they need more material? Must they change the tone of the piece? How much evidence is sufficient for the new purpose? Will the audience be initially interested in the piece or need to be persuaded to read it? One advantage of switching purpose and audience is the possibility of using the same knowledge base; another advantage is that the original piece is reexamined as the revision goes forward.

You may decide that the piece that goes into your portfolio would better represent your writing if it were revised for a different purpose and audience.

You might choose, however, to include the original piece and a revised one in order to demonstrate how you altered the material to fit the occasion. The original piece need not be revised: you could explain in your new Writer's Statement the reasons and the ways that you shifted your purpose and audience. Although the warning about starting new pieces at this stage of the term holds, you are more likely to complete a successful new piece if you are transmuting a former one.

When Todd wrote his portfolio letter at the end of the term, he commented on an opportunity that he had let pass. "One fear that I have about this portfolio is that readers may assume I am a humorless individual. I am really not as serious of an individual as most of this writing would suggest. Perhaps I could have expanded the framework of the assigned papers to include a more humorous perspective." Because Todd had had an open invitation in several assignments to choose his tone and perspective, he could have originally written in the humorous vein that he identifies. He, however, had an alternative. As he reviewed the pieces for revision before inclusion in his Course Portfolio, he might have rewritten one piece with a lighthearted tone or used the ironic tone that he had sometimes revealed in class discussions. Although he may have had to shift his purpose or audience, he could have generated a piece that revealed a part of his identity as a writer that is important to him.

Jacqueline also passed up a revision opportunity when she did not alter the audience of a piece that she wrote regarding the deficiencies of the large metropolitan school district in which she was enrolled during high school. In her Writer's Statement Jacqueline identified her paper's readers as "either anyone attending public schools or anyone that has anything to do with the selection process of public school teachers and the distribution of money and books to various public schools." My reader response to Jacqueline warned her that the previous knowledge and the need for different kinds of knowledge would be very different for the two, or even three, targeted audiences. I advised her that the selection of evidence in the paper would be quite different for these diverse audiences, so she needed to choose one primary audience.

Although Jacqueline decided to revise for her portfolio, she changed her paper in only superficial ways. Had she wanted to show her ability to address specific audiences, she might have written a piece for an audience of students and another piece for either personnel officers or service personnel. The resulting papers would have signaled her skill in adapting material to diverse audiences.

Although you will most often revise one piece, rather than creating multiple new ones, remember that the piece can be significantly changed to demonstrate your learning. In unusual circumstances in which you have a start toward accomplishing mutually exclusive goals, you may consider heading in both directions in different papers that signify your versatility and abilities.

PRACTICE IN MAKING CHOICES: ANALYZING ANOTHER WRITER'S WORK

As you make decisions about what to revise for your Course Portfolio, practice by doing some of the following exercises. The first set of exercises asks you to read and consider another student's essay. The second set focuses on your own writing.

Read the following essay by Gordon. His assignment was wide open: he could choose any topic and audience. Gordon rather likes this piece, but he knows it would need some revision before inclusion in a Course Portfolio. The Course Portfolio is to contain best work, so without reading the rest of his work, you cannot help him decide for sure on this piece. You can, however, give advice about revising: does the piece have enough possibilities that you can imagine it among the best pieces of work of a writing student? After you read this essay, you'll be asked to answer several specific questions about its strengths and needs for revision and to respond to his instructor's comments about the piece.

Gordon's Draft

The Project Write! Experience

It was only a few short months ago that I received in the mail a letter from my friend Chainey. I had moved away from Philadelphia to start a new life for myself in Indiana, but ours is not a friendship easily severed. Many a time, friends say "I'll write" or "Stay in touch," knowing full well that neither party intends to do so. There's no malice present in these situations, just the parting of ways without wanting to call it that. It's easier to assure one another that things won't change, and then allow time to clear the slate gradually, almost imperceptibly. I know this to be true because I have been guilty of this "negligence," having moved often in my younger years. I only bring this up because, despite my lack of initiative in letter writing in the past, I want very much to continue my correspondence with Chainey for as long as I am capable. She is that kind of a person and a friend. Perhaps that is what prompted me to think of her, write to her yesterday, and, finally, write this essay on the valuable relationships that can be formed in a literacy program. One can meet special people and become better teachers. You see, Chainey was my 77-year-young learner. I tutored her in literacy skills through Temple University's

Center for Intergenerational Learning and Project Write!.

I originally volunteered to become a Project Write! tutor because my Multicultural Education professor offered Write! as an alternative to working on what I deemed to be worthless class projects emphasizing what students universally term "busywork." I felt that I needed to expand my horizons, and I get satisfaction from helping people, but I am not uncomfortable in admitting that there were some selfish motives involved: namely, a good opportunity to gain teaching experience for myself and further develop my resume. I felt tutoring in a volunteer capacity would look impressive next to my coaching stints in YMCA youth soccer. Little did I know that I would reap far greater rewards than this. A literacy program partnership is most successful when a social relationship is established between the parties. Today, I am an advocate for literacy training and volunteering in general.

After a very brief training session replete with role-playing, strategies, and punch and cookies, I was paired with an older adult who sought help in improving reading skills. I had never done anything like this. This beginning was awkward as many are. My learner's name was Chainey Jones--she is seventy-seven. Chainey is a large woman with skin of dark chocolate. You would swear she isn't a day over sixty, for she is in excellent health, and her silver hair is ever complemented by large spectacles she uses for reading. Chainey warmed up to me slowly; upon my initial telephone call, she claimed she'd have to sit down and look at me to tell if the tutoring would work out.

We met initially, and every week after that, at the Senior Center on Broad Street, six blocks from Temple's campus. I would walk from African American Lit with Hill on Wednesdays along red brick walks, past the belltower, the food trucks' generators jackhammering the pavement. The nondescript brick and cement buildings quickly gave way to subway stairwells, Hardees, and convenience stores and jewelry shops with barred windows. The Senior Center sat nearby, a stone building guarded by wrought iron fencing.

I approached Chainey with the right attitude, it seemed, because we got along well in our first session. We both were relieved to find out that we had many things in common. For instance, we agreed on voting Democrat, exhibiting caution with alcohol, and the need for a love of learning. For an entire semester we would spend time talking, enjoying a relationship that cut across decades of difference in age. We also read. Chainey read at a fifth grade level, having never advanced beyond the fourth grade.

I remember reading mini biographies together from a text focusing on famous African Americans. We would sit at a desk in the nurse's office at the Center, decorations from past Christmas pageants in boxes at our feet. We both learned things about the men and women in the book: Chainey was impressed that Harriet Tubman carried a revolver that she used to motivate runaways in the event they changed their minds about fleeing to the North. Prior to our studies, neither of us had known why Louis Armstrong had such large cheeks: it seems that, as a boy playing for coins on New Orleans' streetcorners, he placed coins in his mouth while playing as he had no pockets. Her reading improved and we both learned a lot. I'm sure I learned far more than she--specifically, effective teaching measures via crash course 101.

The fill-in-the-blanks worksheets featuring the Beatitudes were very popular with Chainey. We also worked on writing small letters to one another, and together composed a letter to an Alabama branch of the Social Security federal offices concerning Chainey's entitlements. But aside from that which is relative to academia, there was simple enjoyment in conversation. I learned that Chainey's father was threatened by whites in a part of North Carolina where lynchings were not uncommon. However, it seems no one really wanted to tangle with this very large man. Chainey told me about her life in the South working for Jewish families. She is a devout woman, always thinking of others, but stubborn, too. Chainey treated me like I was her only grandson. There were as many times the conversation turned towards my life, too, and I tried to keep the flow of words from honing in on the subject of my love life.

The semester after my Project Write! Experience was concluded, I made sure I was updated on her life and progress in reading. We talked once a week on the phone. I know Chainey and I both learned (the ultimate goal for any teacher). We learned to trust, to become better students and teachers, to read (in Chainey's case), and lastly we learned how valuable a friendship can be, how valuable a literacy program can be. It can be magic in a bottle. I know.

During the holiday, I sent a collection of bath oils (Chainey loves baths) to my friend and ex-learner. Big deal. You can get a nice box of Epsom salts at the corner store for almost nothing. Chainey mailed me something much better: a letter, received in July and scrawled in her hand. She addressed me as "Brother Gordon" from "Sister Chainey."

Answer the following questions about the essay you have just read.

1. What are the strengths of this essay that might make Gordon consider revising it for an example of best work in his Course Portfolio?
2. What revisions would you recommend if Gordon wants to include this essay in his Course Portfolio?
3. Gordon received a letter from his teacher that may help you decide about your recommendation to Gordon concerning this paper as a candidate for his Course Portfolio. Notice the strengths and areas for revision that his teacher notes in this letter.

Dear Gordon,

Two aspects of this piece are striking to me: your language and your images are graphic and evocative; also you evoke positive emotions around your friendship with Chainey. The specific scenes and specific benefits for you of this relationship are clear.

Yet, I wonder what you want readers to gain most from your piece. Just as you admitted that volunteering for the project first attracted you as an entry for your resume, I suspect you want the reader to feel good about you after having read this piece. But, I think that the purpose must be larger. Is the purpose to advocate for literacy programs? To explain the unexpected benefits for teacher and student if their relationship thrives?

The paragraph on page three about your mutual learning from the mini biographies and the paragraph on page four about the conversations succeed in showing readers what you mean about what I think might be your main point: there are many kinds of literacy, one being reading written texts and another being reading human beings. Are you implying that volunteering for literacy work is successful when it results in both kinds of literacy, including the kind of a wonderful and unexpected relationship you describe so well in this piece? Are you simply advocating volunteering? Is volunteering successful even if such friendship, the second kind of literacy, doesn't evolve? Or, are you talking more about enduring friendship, as you ponder in your introduction?

You title your piece "The Project Write! Experience," but I'm unclear if you are just telling your particular story or are trying to help us readers draw some conclusion from that experience, such as volunteers "reap far greater rewards" than they might expect. In other words, I'm asking for something difficult: can you still do your wonderful describing and yet make your point clearer while adhering as you now do to the well-worn advice of showing instead of telling?

I'll be interested to read a revision of this piece if you choose it for your Course Portfolio. I hope that you will submit it to the literacy newsletter that is published here in Indianapolis. I think that your story affirms the experiences of those who receive and give the most in literacy programs. Please let me know if you're interested in the address of the newsletter editor.

4. Write a note to Gordon in which you advise him about this paper's inclusion in his Course Portfolio.

PRACTICE IN MAKING CHOICES ANALYZING YOUR OWN WORK

1. If you are using the standard of best work as the basis for choosing papers for your Course Portfolio, assemble all the possible pieces that you might include.
   a. Lay out your papers, putting on the left the most successful paper and on the right the least successful one. Then arrange the remaining papers on a continuum between the most and least successful. Make this arrangement of papers on a holistic response to the papers, that is, based on your feelings, the prior responses of peers, or grades or responses from your instructor.
   b. To each paper attach a three-by-five-inch card on which you write all the reasons that you consider that paper successful. Be as thorough as possible, writing both major and minor reasons for your rating. On the basis of this listing, rearrange the papers, if necessary. Number your papers, with 1 being the most successful paper.

c. Stack the papers with the most successful on top and the least successful on the bottom. Bring the papers to your writing group. Exchange stacks. Read the writer's rationales for the rating of the papers. Scan the papers again: presumably you will be somewhat familiar with the writer's work from your writing group experience. On the cards offer more reasons for the writer's rating, question the writer's reasons, and suggest any reordering that you think appropriate.

d. In your writing group discuss instances in which the writer and reader had different opinions about the best pieces to revise for the writer's Course Portfolio.

e. Affirm or change your choices based on the writing group analysis.

2. If you are using established criteria to determine which papers to revise for your Course Portfolio, assemble all the possible papers that you might include.

   a. Take out your list of criteria, which may have a variety of sources: they may have been furnished by your teacher, generated by your class, or determined by yourself. Be sure that you understand thoroughly what each criterion means. For example, if one criterion is focus, be certain that you know how focus differs from organization or clarity. Check with whoever determined the criteria about precise meanings.

   b. For each paper, write out evidence of ways that you have fulfilled the criteria in that paper. Write references to the evidence on a three-by-five card for each criterion. For example, if correct sentence structure is a criterion, note that you had no fragments or run-on sentences in the piece. If organization is a criterion, allude to your use of markers like "most important" and "least important," your peer's reference to ease of reading because the points seemed logically related, and your instructor's response that this piece is your best organized so far in the course. Attach the cards to the paper.

   c. In class ask a writing group member to verify your evidence. Does the feature you have referred to support your claim about adherence to the criterion or about excellence in reference to the criterion? Why or why not? Is there other evidence that the reader sees that would bolster your contention? Analyze each paper that might be included in a Course Portfolio.

   d. When you have received your reader's response, rate your papers. Choose those papers that demonstrate excellence or potential for excellence in relation to the established criteria.

   e. As a writing group, discuss the process of choosing papers according to established criteria and the next steps that you will need to take to revise papers to meet the criteria.

3. If you are choosing a paper for a Course Portfolio to revise for another particular audience, sort your papers according to audience or potential audience.
   a. For each paper, identify on a three-by-five card the characteristics of the audience of that paper.
   b. On the card, indicate the ways in which the paper has been written to serve that particular audience. List the choices that you made as a writer such as tone, amount of evidence, and level of vocabulary. Cite evidence from the paper.
   c. In your writing group, determine which papers might be revised for another audience. Consider the success of the first paper, the reason for revising, and the way(s) in which the revision would show the ability of the writer.

WORKING PORTFOLIO UPDATE

At this point you have all your drafts in your Working Portfolio. You will want to retain all drafts and other written documents in your Working Portfolio so that they are available as sources for evidence when you write your reflective piece for your Course Portfolio.

Through work done in this chapter, you have determined which papers you want to include in your Course Portfolio. Now you can place those drafts at the front of your Working Portfolio. You will then decide whether each paper is ready or needs revising. You may have previously worked with the paper enough that it needs no more revision, or you may have identified ways in which you want to make the paper better. The next chapters suggest strategies for revision that may benefit you during the next stage of your process. You will see what choices Justin has made about pieces to revise and learn about his process of revision.

CHAPTER 10
Revision: Taking Another Look at Purpose and Focus

When my dad taught me to drive, one of his rules was to always take a second look, a warning to look twice before pulling out into an intersection, turning a corner, or making any other final decision in driving. Taking a second look is a good rule for writing, too, one you should incorporate as a part of your writing process before coming to a final draft or, in this case, a portfolio draft. Revision is the second look a portfolio class allows.

You have taken a second look at your own and others' work many times already: as you developed your Writer's Statements, as you offered feedback to others, as you discussed your work with your teacher and classmates, and as you recorded your ideas in your journal. Reviewing the documents in your Working Portfolio is a reentry into the chaos of creation. By returning to your work, rereading it, analyzing it, evaluating the comments of others, and making decisions about what to do next, you experience writing as a dynamic activity.

In this chapter and the next you will find examples of students working with four major issues within their work. You will first see them revising their essays to better fulfill their purposes and to narrow focus. In chapter 11, you will see them revising to create organizations that serve their purposes and to develop their papers. Once you have identified the revision tasks you must undertake, you may want to use only the relevant parts of these two chapters, or you may want to test these elements of your work by trying out some of the strategies included in both chapters.

You have already seen Justin revise, trying to overcome a tendency to stray from his intended purpose. He believes that revision helped him as he wrote successive papers. In his Writer's Statement for Paper 5, he remarked that he felt confident he had stayed on the topic and remained true to his purpose in that draft. He attributes that success to the learning gained through his revision of Paper 2. You may have had similar experience. But whether you have revised along the way or are just now preparing to do so, revision allows you to put your learning into practice and to showcase your best writing in your Course Portfolio.

In this phase of the course, you will first identify the elements of your work that require revision. Justin and the members of his class did this by pulling together all available information: responses from other students and from their teacher, dialogue journal entries, Writer's Statements, revision plans, notes in the margins—anything at all that contained discussion of their papers. Interpreting that information and making your own decisions about a response to it are your first steps toward revision.

IDENTIFYING ISSUES FOR REVISION

How do you know what your paper needs? Although most writers depend upon their own analyses and the responses they receive from others, sometimes it's hard to know what those responses call for. What does it mean when a teacher writes "Dev" in the margin or when a classmate says "I'm having trouble following this" or when you yourself ask "Why is this here?" Some responses are indecipherable, such as the favorite of a professor I once had in a Shakespeare course: "Mayonnaise"; others, fortunately, can be translated. Next you will find some frequent reader responses and an interpretation of their probable meaning. You may want to add others you've received and work with your teacher and classmates to break the code.

Guidelines for Cracking the Code

Unclear Purpose

What is this paper really about?

What is the point of this paper?

So what?

What was the assignment? (a gentle nudge sending you back to the syllabus or assignment sheet)

For revision strategies related to purpose, see pages 232–239.

Too Broad or Undefined Focus

You're talking about a lot of things.

You're trying to accomplish too much.

You're just skimming the surface.

This topic is so general; you're not saying anything new.

The choices are to write a book or just write a lot of very short paragraphs.

For revision strategies related to focus, see pages 239–247.

Lack of Development

Tell me more.

I don't understand.

Dev.

For example?

Illustrate.

Detail.

When? Where?

Who says?

Evidence.

Prove it.

For revision strategies related to development, see pages 254–262.

Lack of Organization

I'm confused.

How does this fit in?

This paper doesn't seem to flow.

Why is this here?

Org.

The paper seems choppy.

For revision strategies related to organization, see pages 248–253.

As you analyze your readers' responses, double-check your interpretation by writing back to a responder, restating the message in the response. Tell your reader, for instance, that he seems to want more information in paragraph 5. If you have understood his response, he will confirm; if you have not understood, he should explain more clearly.

SUMMARIZING RESPONSE FOR REVISION ANALYSIS

To begin his revision efforts, Justin summarized in his journal the responses he had received to the three papers he chose to include in his Course Portfolio.

Justin's Summaries for Revision Analysis

Paper 1--Diving Into the Wreck--I've done a lot of work on this paper. I got a better focus by leaving out a lot of stuff about my dad and really thinking about my own literacy. I did that by putting the title up over the computer and looking at it again and again. I took out the material that wasn't really related. *Autobiography* means it's about me. This paper is in good shape I think. I hope I can make the others as good.

Revision Plan: I don't know. I think it's very good. All the feedback I have says so too.

Paper 3--Getting Along--My worst paper. But I liked doing the observation and would like to know how to use it better. I like the topic, too. I think it would be good if I had a paper in my portfolio that uses observation and maybe ties in Reed, and maybe even uses an interview. When Laura wrote to me about it she said that I didn't have any details. She told me that she really liked reading about my friends from other backgrounds in earlier papers and she thought I should put that in. She also said that she didn't find out enough about my observation in the union. She said she really wanted more details about that too. I'm going to think of Laura as my audience. My teacher told me that I should look at the assignment again, that I was trying to go too far. She said that I didn't do a very good job of evaluating just how useful my interview was. She also said that she could understand why I would be sort of overwhelmed by what Dr. Callahan said. She said to remember our different purposes in our writing and research. I think that means that Dr. Callahan is a bigtime researcher and my assignment was just to address activities in a public part of our campus. "On our campus" must be the operative word. Actually, when I read my first draft of Paper 3, it's much better than the second. In fact, I like it.

Revision Plan: Go back to purpose. I think I've had this problem before! Add details. My audience should be students and maybe teachers on this campus. That should help me keep things in perspective. I also don't like my introduction and ending. It's really good on the autobiography, especially the introduction. I want to make this one better.

Paper 5--Absentee Fathers--I was happy with the way I stayed on focus, but my teacher thought that I didn't get it as tight as I should. It was all about absentee fathers, but my main point overall was not as clear as it could be. I said in my Writer's Statement that my paper didn't look as much like a research paper as Natali's did but I don't know why. When I told Natali that, she said some of my quotes didn't fit in very well. She said that the stuff about fathers and money and emotional support could be tied better to what I am talking about. And Robin told me that my intros in 3 and 5 were alike. I see sort of what she means. I had trouble finding material for this paper. In my proposal I said that I wanted statistics or more specific material about the effects of absentee fathers on kids. I think I should look for more of that again. I really want this paper to be a practice for the kind of research papers I will have to do in other classes. I need to work on the intro and conclusion too. I have a lot to do on this.

Revision Plan: Be more sure about what my purpose is. Work on finding sources that are very connected to my points. Work on my introduction. I also want to find out how much I can say about my own life in a research paper. I wrote this because of my own experience. But it's a research paper. And document better.

PRACTICE WITH ANALYZING YOUR WORK FOR REVISION

1. As Justin did, read through all the materials related to the papers you have chosen for your portfolio. In your dialogue journal summarize your own comments and those of other readers for each paper. Be sure to include comments pointing out your successes in a paper as well as those identifying problems.
2. What elements of your papers as a body of work are successful? What elements of your work must you be sure to maintain? What major revision tasks lie ahead? Can you identify tasks related to improving purpose fulfillment, narrowing focus, developing your ideas, or organizing the paper? Name the writing problems that you must take on. Then add notes about your revision plans.

TAKING A SECOND LOOK: FULFILLING PURPOSE

In his notes about his Literacy Autobiography, Justin remarked that putting the title up over his desk helped him to stay on task when he revised that paper. You might try the same strategy, this time posting your purpose over your desk or screen and using it as a guide to help you identify material that does not fit your purpose.

To determine where a paper strays from its purpose, do an activity similar to what Patti did on Anne's apple paper in chapter 4. Identify the main idea in each paragraph. Which paragraphs relate to your purpose? Which do not?

As he worked on Paper 3, Justin used a combination of these techniques. He wrote a statement of purpose to tape over his desk.

> TO SHOW HOW PEOPLE OF DIFFERENT RACIAL OR ETHNIC BACKGROUNDS SOCIALIZE IN OUR CAMPUS STUDENT UNION

Then he read each paragraph and identified what each paragraph of his paper said, making notes about what he found.

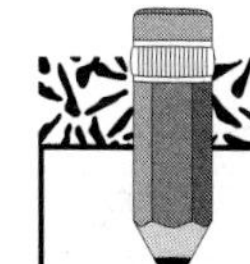

Justin's Analysis, Paper 3, Observation

In our society today, relationships between members of different racial or cultural groups is a big issue. It's on the front page or on the news every day. The big question seems to be the one that Rodney King asked after the LA riots. "Can't we just get along?" One way to try to find that out on a college campus is to watch the people in the student union. That's where people gather to eat snacks or meals and to talk and to watch big screen TV.

Para. 1: Identifies race relations as a problem. Sets forth college union as a place to find out if people can get along. Notes: Why am I using the union? I need to explain that to tell that it is our union. All the ideas I have here are important.

This topic is important to everyone first because it's a part of everyone's life, living with people who are from other backgrounds. And also, when a person has experience with friendships with people from other backgrounds and they will find it to be a good thing. Darnell, an African American guy and Rajesh, whose family came here from India are both my friends. We have spent lots of time together

Para. 2: Explains why race relations is important and gives my own experiences with friends from other backgrounds. Notes: Paragraph 1 already shows that this topic is important and I should be talking about the observation, not my friends, because the para. before brings up the union. I do think the stuff about my friends is important, and Laura said she liked that part. I need to

and I have learned a lot about their backgrounds from our friendships. I like having that as a part of my life, and I think it's helped me see the value of other cultures and how they add to our society.	make it fit and maybe give more details. But I don't know if other people see the same value.
But I don't know if other people see the same value. An observation in our student union showed that most people, especially those who gather there in large groups tend to choose the company of people from their own background. Over three observation periods the large groups of people in the union, groups of up to ten people, were more likely to be made up of only one group. As the groups in the observation got smaller they became more likely to be a mixture of two races or cultures, but a mixture of three was not observed.	Para. 3: Back to the observation, the conclusions not the details that Laura asked for. I need to keep all this and add details that show how I came to these conclusions.
On the basis of that information it seems as though it might be worthwhile to conduct more research to find out if the integration of America is taking place on an individual basis,	Para. 4: Two ideas here--conduct more research and the idea of diversity working better in small groups than in the whole society. Notes: I don't think my

among small groups of people or pairs of people. Maybe, if that is true, we are going in the wrong direction to try to create diversity in all parts of our society. Maybe people have to learn to live and work together in small groups instead.	audience, Laura and others like her, care about conducting more research. The other point is a conclusion or an idea about what would work. I think this whole para. should go.
That would mean a gradual assimilation. And assimilation, the merging of the minority group into the dominant group can be both good and bad. It depends on the goal and upon each person's life. According to Dr. Grace Callahan, assimilation has "both benefits and drawbacks for the dominant and the minority group." Maybe the most important benefit of the merging and friendships of people of different cultures is that it will mean a more authentic blending of groups in our society.	Para. 5: What would happen if people related in small groups, the idea I had in the para. before. Defines assimilation, says it's good and bad, talks about one benefit. Notes: Where did assimilation come from? This paper is about interracial friendships! I think all the assimilation should go. Terrible thought!

Finally, after the analysis and note taking, Justin underlined the material unrelated to his purpose, marking it for deletion. He then wrote the following entry in his journal.

Justin's Journal Entry

I was worried about taking so much of my paper out, but Laura said that I should look at my first draft, that she liked some of the stuff there and I should think about putting it back in. I did find things about my friends and about the observation that I'll put back in the next draft. I'm glad I saved the original one.

Justin marked the following passages for deletion because they did not serve his purpose. Can you support his decision to delete this material? Why or why not?

Purpose: To Show How People of Different Racial or Ethnic Backgrounds Socialize in Our Campus Student Union

Para. 2: This topic is important to everyone first because it's a part of everyone's life, living with people who are from other backgrounds. And also, when a person has experience with friendships with people from other backgrounds and they will find it to be a good thing.

Para. 4: On the basis of that information it seems as though it might be worthwhile to conduct more research to find out if the integration of America is taking place on an individual basis, among small groups of people or pairs of people. Maybe, if that is true, we are going in the wrong direction to try to create diversity in all parts of our society. Maybe people have to learn to live and work together in small groups instead.

Para. 5: That would mean a gradual assimilation. And assimilation, the merging of the minority group into the dominant group can be both good and bad. It depends on the goal and upon each person's life. According to Dr. Grace Callahan, assimilation has "both benefits and drawbacks for the dominant and the minority group."

PRACTICE WITH REVISING FOR PURPOSE

1. Employ one or all of the same strategies that Justin did.
   a. Post a statement of purpose on a sheet over your desk or computer screen. Read your draft carefully, marking anything inappropriate to your stated purpose.
   b. Perform a descriptive analysis on your draft. What does each paragraph say? Make notes about how the elements of each paragraph function to meet your purpose.
   c. Underline material you intend to delete from your next draft.
   d. Discuss your plans with someone already familiar with your draft. In your journal, record your ideas about necessary revision for this paper.
2. Write a revision plan for your paper; use it as a guide while you work on the paper.

Justin's Paper 3, Draft 3, Observation

Observations on Getting Along

On the front pages of every newspaper in the United States are stories about the difficulties of good relationships between people of different racial or cultural backgrounds. College campuses and college newspapers are no different. The big question everywhere seems to be the one that Rodney King asked after the LA riots. "Can't we just get along?" One way to try to find out whether people are getting along on a college campus is to watch the people in the student union, where people, no matter what their living unit, gather to eat snacks or meals and to talk and to watch big screen TV.

During a recent set of observations in our student union, most people, especially those who gather there in large groups, tended to choose the company of people who appear to be from their own racial or ethnic background. Over three observation periods, set at times of the day or evening when the union is busy, the large groups of up to ten people were more likely to be made up of members of only one racial or ethnic group. However, among the groups recorded in this observation, the smaller the group, the more likely it was to be a mixture of two races or cultures. Friends or couples of two backgrounds was not unusual, but during this set of observations, a group that included three people of obviously different backgrounds was never recorded.

While this small sample from our campus can't really tell us anything definitive, it does have a sort of two-fold effect on me. First, I think it's sad that more people don't have the advantage of friends from other cultures. When I was growing up, I had two friends from other backgrounds. Darnell, an African American guy, was my friend from grade school. We've been in and out of each others houses nearly all our lives. By doing that I've learned about sweet potato pie and I've heard the family stories about their slave ancestors. I understand history better because I have been friends with Darnell. I also understand math better because he has always helped me with my math.

That's how we both got to be friends with Rajesh, our Indian friend. We met in math class. Darnell and I have learned a lot from Rajesh. Some of the things are food and traditions, but also about what it's like to be an immigrant and to want to be a part of this country. Rajesh and his family work hard at their store, and he wants more than anything to be "American." I think that knowing Darnell and me has helped him to get closer to that goal.

Which brings me to the second part of my reaction to the findings from the observation, and that is a hope that people are learning, slowly, to know each other. It's been that way for me and my friends. We are just a small group and we don't really spread our friendship into our other groups of friends. Some people probably think that's wrong, but it is what works for us. For right now, we are friends with each other and we understand each other.

That's what's hopeful about the observation. If people are getting to know each other on a one-to-one basis, that is probably how we spread intergroup relationships into the larger society. Whether people meet and form friendships in college, in their jobs, or later in life in community or church activities, they begin to get to know each other as people. That would make the observation carry a positive note that maybe one of these days, we will all get along.

Here's what Justin says in his Writer's Statement.

Justin's Writer's Statement

I'm glad I took out all the material that I did. When Suellen read it, she said that it could still use some more information about the observation, that I should think about the journalistic questions, like when did I do it and how did I do it and why did I do it, and who . . . anyway, she's probably right. It probably means another pass through this draft before this paper is in the final form for the portfolio. But I've still got a little time, and I want it to be right.

PRACTICE WITH REVISING FOR PURPOSE: ANOTHER WRITER'S WORK

Do you agree with Justin that he has more fully met his stated purpose for this paper in his revision? Do you agree with Suellen about the need for more information about the observation? Why or why not?

PRACTICE WITH REVISING FOR PURPOSE: YOUR OWN WORK

If you have worked to make your paper adhere more closely to your stated purpose, compose new questions for reader response and share your revisions with a classmate. Consider the response and revise your Writer's Statement. Include any further revision tasks that you or your reader find necessary to complete.

TAKING A SECOND LOOK: NARROWING FOCUS

As he worked to fulfill his purpose, Justin also addressed his problem of focus in Paper 3. By reminding himself that he was discussing intergroup friendships on his campus, he was likely to regain his focus, the original narrow one appropriate for readers at his school. In the first draft of Paper 5, however, focus is still a problem. In his notes for revision, Justin said that he was happy with the focus on absentee fathers but that his teacher did not think it was as "tight as it should be."

Consequently, Justin took another look at focus in that paper. His purpose in Paper 5 is to "discuss the importance of the absentee father." His conclusion in the paper says that everyone in the family is affected by the absence of the father. That's not a particularly surprising conclusion; most readers could make that assumption, as could Justin, on their own. Remember that "you're not saying anything new" was pointed out earlier in this chapter as a common reaction to a paper with a too-broad focus. To find out if he had stayed with his focus on the importance of absentee fathers, Justin performed part of a descriptive analysis, noting what each paragraph said.

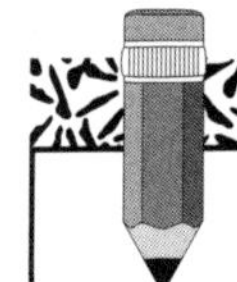

Justin's Descriptive Analysis for Paper 5, Research Investigation

Para. 1: Families without fathers are said to be the cause of many of kids' problems. Is it really that important?

Para. 2: Kids without fathers are more likely to have every kind of problem there is according to Blankenhorn and an *Atlantic Monthly* article.

Para. 3: Those ideas may not be based on good research and what about kids like me and kids during other times, like during WW II when fathers were away?

Para. 4: Being away from their kids is hard on fathers too. My father left us by choice and he thinks we might be better off that way.

Para. 5: My father had trouble keeping a job because he couldn't read and that led to lots of other problems. Some of those are solved now--he can read, but there's not connection between us.

Para. 6: The absence of a father affects everyone in the family, sometimes to the bad and sometimes to the good by making everyone learn to be responsible.

When Justin started this paper, he had hoped to find very specific material about the effects of absentee fathers on their families, particularly their children. He wanted to find out if more daughters of absentee fathers get pregnant, or if more kids get into trouble with the law or drop out of school. When he failed to find that, he wrote instead, as his analysis shows, about all members of the family: mother, father, and children. And, since he saw himself as an example of a child who had succeeded without his father, he moved toward that point, offering many details from his own family as he continued throughout the paper to question the importance of paternal influence.

Justin realized that he could choose between two focus points in Paper 5. He could try to make the case that some families do just fine without the presence of a father or return to an analysis of the effects of fathers' absence. Returning to his original question would require further research to help answer it more fully.

After addressing these aspects of his paper in his dialogue journal and talking with members of his class, Justin headed back to the library. This time he felt better about his search for material, as he noted in his journal.

Justin's Journal Entry

A librarian said I had not used a good search term when I put my topic into the computer. I used the term *fatherlessness* when I looked for material the first time, but there were only a few articles. I tried lots of other things, but finally the librarian told me to try "divorced parents." That's when I finally found that *Atlantic Monthly* article that one of my sources talked about. It's called "Dan Quayle Was Right." It still doesn't do exactly what I wanted, but it must be important because after I got into this new listing under "divorced parents," lots of other articles mentioned it. The author kind of summarizes lots of studies, and because it's a magazine it doesn't have a Works Cited page, but she seems to be respected by a lot of other people who wrote about her article. So, I decided to use it to help me get back on my focus for that paper. That will let me get better practice with a research paper approach.

Justin's problem of focus may be solved by locating more information that allows him to create and sustain his focus. The material he found as he intensified his search addresses more directly how fatherlessness affects children, the information he needs to return to his original idea for the paper. Later in the section on solving organizational problems in chapter 11, you will see Justin's second draft for Paper 5 as it incorporates his newly discovered material.

REVISING TO NARROW FOCUS

Another student with a different problem of focus is Greg, a freshman who has always liked to write and thinks of himself as a good writer. In high school, he says, he got good grades and was always able to organize his work in a way that made his teachers happy. Although he did not expect to work too hard in his introductory writing class, to his surprise, he learned to revise his work with particular attention on focus. Early in the semester, Greg was asked to write an essay that drew on personal experience as the main source of knowledge. In a brainstorming exercise, he settled upon a summer camp experience when he was fifteen. "The camp was an Outward Bound kind of thing," he wrote in his dialogue journal. "I learned a lot there, and I had lots of different experiences. So I decided to write about them."

Greg's Essay, Draft 1

Summer Camp

When I was fifteen years old, I went to camp in Kentucky. The camp was in the hill country and most of the kids there were from Kentucky and Indiana. While I was there, I participated in many different experiences.

We participated in many physical tasks like climbing a huge tree or crossing a river on a rope bridge. Later we did other things like spend the night alone in the woods. I didn't have any trouble with the bridge but I was surprised how hard it was to be alone in the woods all night. I am an only child, so I'm used to being alone and even when I was a little kid I've never been afraid of the dark. Plus, by then, we had been in camp for two weeks, and I thought I was used to the woods, but the night went slow. I heard noises I had never heard sleeping in the cabin with the other guys. I had built a good shelter, but I never did sleep that night, and I was glad when it was morning.

Another thing we did was work on a trail. I was in charge of a project to clear a part of a trail. I had to read about erosion and go to a meeting about tools to use and how to do the clearing. Then I was in charge of five guys. First we marked the trail with string. We tried not to include any trees, though we did have to take down two small ones. It took several days, and my

```
job was to keep people working. That was hard because it
was hot and everyone got tired. It was hard to be in
charge of people my own age and to tell them what to do.
But after awhile I got people to work in pairs and it
all got done.
    I had to work in the kitchen too. I hated that
because Tom, a guy from Chicago, was in charge and he
took it very seriously. In fact, he was obnoxious. He
stayed away from the grease and heat and just told the
rest of us what to do. Our cook team had some meetings
about him and we even talked to a counselor about him,
but in the end, we just had to put up with him. The rest
of us got to be good friends that way, it was fun to
complain about Tom.
    I think anyone would like to go to camp and do all
these different things so I would recommend it to anyone
who likes the outdoors.
```

Greg needs a focus. He has a wide-ranging topic that invites him to tell his reader about many different experiences, but he makes no significant point about his time at camp or how his experience was different from that of anyone else who has gone to camp. The essay simply relates a number of events.

Greg might have found a focus if he had looked for a thread that runs through the whole piece of writing, something that comes up in more than one paragraph. In response to that suggestion from a reader, he sat down with his dialogue journal to look at each paragraph in his paper and to identify the most important idea in each.

Greg's Paragraph Analysis

Para. 1: Introduction

Para. 2: I didn't really like being alone in the woods all night.

Para. 3: It's not easy to be in charge of people your own age.

Para. 4: The rest of us learned to work together on the cook team even though Tom wasn't a good leader.

Para. 5: Most people would probably enjoy these experiences.

Later he wrote in his journal about his revision decisions.

Greg's Journal Entry

I could see that two of the main paragraphs were about working with other people. And, when I looked back up at my opening paragraph, I could see that two of the camp goals were about that too. So I wrote my new revision plan, saying that I was going to write about learning to work with people. When Lisa read that in my group, she said that the part about being alone in the woods was connected to the idea of working with other people because it showed that I didn't like to be alone. So I added that part back into my plan. I decided to write about my experiences at camp and how they showed me how I relate to other people. I can see that as my focus gets narrower, my purpose statement will have to change some too.

Greg has found a single point of focus that his experiences at camp will illustrate. Before he settled down to his revising, he explored that new focus in a directed freewriting.

Greg's Directed Freewriting

At camp I worked with other people a lot in all the situations I already talked about in my essay draft and I have worked with other people in sports and a mentor program. My dad encouraged me to play sports but not just because he likes them. In his work, they use the Japanese system a lot, working in teams to solve problems, and he thought I should learn to work with other people like you do on sports teams.

In this directed freewriting, Greg has found a way to take his focus, his orientation toward working with others, beyond the camp experience, to apply it to the experiences of his father and to his own future. As you will see in his portfolio draft, he decided to extend his focus forward toward the future rather than backward toward his mentor and his sports experiences before he went to camp. As you read, watch for the ways the essay has changed to maintain this single focus.

Greg's Essay, Portfolio Draft

A Summer in the Woods

When I was fifteen years old, I went to camp in Kentucky. The camp was in the hill country, and most of the kids there were from Kentucky and Indiana. We participated in a lot of different activities, and I learned a lot about myself. The main thing I found out was that I'm better with a group than I am by myself.

I am an only child. My parents both work, and I was a latchkey kid from the time I was about eight. I always came home in the afternoons, had a snack, and then went out to play. Sometimes I fixed my own dinner and did my homework alone in our house when my parents had to work or had something else to do. So I thought I knew all about being alone. But then at camp, I had to spend a night alone in the woods. I thought that would be easy. But I was wrong because I hardly slept at all. I kept trying to figure out what every noise was. I knew there wasn't anything to be afraid of, but I'm embarrassed to say that I kept remembering those Freddy movies and all the horror shows I used to watch on TV. I kept trying to hear the other guys. I even tried yelling out into the woods to them, to see if anyone could hear me. When it was time to go in the next day, I could hardly wait to see everybody else. As I walked through the woods carrying my gear, I started grinning because I was glad to hear voices. I felt like I'd been away on a long trip.

But I was good at working in groups. In one group I was part of a cook team. We were under Tom, this guy from Chicago. He was in charge! He made us do all the hot greasy work, and he never got close to any work. Some of the guys on the cook team wanted to beat him up they were so sick of him. But we started having meetings at night just to complain about him and make jokes, and I helped people blow off steam so they could go back and do the kitchen work and not get in a fight with Tom. I would look at another guy when Tom was obnoxious, and we'd just laugh.

When it was my turn to be in charge, I tried to think about Tom and how to keep my team working better. We had to clear a trail through the woods. It was hard work, and two of the guys lost interest pretty fast. I decided to make pairs. I would pair with one of them, and I got Steve to pair with the other problem guy. The pairs spread out along the trail, so Steve and I were always right with the problem guys, and nobody else was around. Since we were working hard, I guess they felt like they had to. I also remembered how we got together and made fun of Tom, and I decided that these two lazy guys shouldn't have a chance to do that, at least while we were working on the trail. We got the trail cleared, and I thought I was a good leader for that project, with Steve's help.

I think that working in a group and knowing something about how to lead a group is more important than being able to work alone or liking to be alone. At my Dad's job, they have had training for how to work in groups. Management training sessions always have information about working with other people and lots of companies encourage it. I think the Japanese system has had a big influence on this idea.

By going to camp and getting a chance to be in different situations, I learned that I am better working with other people than being alone. I think that will be a good characteristic to have when I go into business in the future. So, camp was an important experience for me.

PRACTICE WITH REVISING FOR FOCUS

Review the materials you have collected during the semester. If responses to a paper included remarks such as "You're talking about a lot of things" or "This is very general," you may need to narrow the focus in that paper. The following strategies should be helpful.

1. Do part of a descriptive analysis of your paper, recording what each paragraph "says."
2. In your journal, write the answers to these questions.
   a. How many different aspects of the topic did you find?
   b. What words occurred frequently in your text?
3. Examine your answers. Can you identify a main point for the paper?
   a. Write the main point in your journal. Underline all the material in your draft relevant to your point. If you need more material, do directed freewriting.
   b. If you cannot identify a main point, try cubing your topic to find a focus that will help you accomplish your purpose. Do a directed freewriting to help generate additional material for your new focus.

4. Write a revision plan that identifies any changes in focus that you have decided upon. How will these changes serve the purpose of your paper?

WORKING PORTFOLIO UPDATE

In the next chapter, Justin will continue revising the papers he has chosen for his Course Portfolio. You will see examples of his work and that of other students as they take on issues of organization and development. Justin will add the materials generated during this revision process to his Working Portfolio, and you should similarly continue collecting all your materials for possible inclusion in your Course Portfolio.

CHAPTER 11
Revision: Taking a Second Look at Organization and Development

In writing, as in architecture, form is a function of purpose. Marble gothic arches evoke the awe appropriate to a cathedral; they would appear overly ornate in a school gymnasium. Formal letters seal business agreements; they would be needlessly official for a simple thank you. As a writer, you must choose for your paper the form, material, and order that best accomplish your purpose.

TAKING A SECOND LOOK AT ORGANIZATION

The term *organization* refers to the structure with which you order your ideas and material in a paper as you work toward your purpose. We see an example of the connection between purpose and form in Natali's paper about curfew laws. She has a double purpose to fulfill: first, to argue in favor of strict enforcement of curfew laws; second, to provide solutions to the problems that may prevent the strict enforcement she calls for.

In the second paragraph she sets up her argument that curfew laws "should be enforced in order to decrease violence perpetrated by and against juveniles." That statement also establishes the early organization of the paper. Readers may expect first to read about violence perpetrated by juveniles and then about violence against juveniles, two reasons supporting her call for strict enforcement of curfews. She uses a common organization for presenting an argument: a statement of position and the reasons that support it. The paper does indeed follow that general order through the first five paragraphs.

Midway through the paper, however, Natali's second purpose becomes apparent. Because resistance to curfew laws creates a problem of enforcement, solutions to this problem must be found if such laws are to be successfully implemented.

> Resistance to curfews definitely exists, though, from the police and the American Civil Liberties Union. Police concerns regarding curfew are legitimate and need to be overcome to successfully combat curfew violations. The lack of manpower available to round up violators and the financial burden that processing apprehended juveniles will place on the department are chief concerns.

For her advocacy of curfew laws to be realistic, Natali needs to provide solutions to these problems. For the next four paragraphs, Natali then organizes her material to serve her second purpose, offering examples and discussing recommended solutions. Finally, both parts of her organization come together in her concluding paragraph.

> Indianapolis must get with the program and address the problem of violence perpetrated by and against juveniles. Curfew laws may only be a small part of the solution in protecting our kids from crime, but in this era of dangerous streets and schools, we must use every small weapon we have to combat juvenile crime.

Building Organizational Maps

As you can see in Natali's draft, writers often provide their readers with organizational maps. The order that emerges from the writer's purpose is translated into directive sentences that show the reader the path of the paper in fulfilling its purpose.

In the opening paragraph of his literacy autobiography, Justin also uses sentences that create a map of his paper's direction. The map on page 250 shows the expectations those sentences create for a reader. A reader knows what points the author will make and in what order they will appear.

This organizational map shows the relationship between those directive "map" sentences and the plan they provide. It also illustrates the author's responsibility, within the structure he has chosen, to reassure the reader that he is fulfilling the promise of the introduction by providing support sentences that alert the reader to each new point or topic of discussion.

"I've been avoiding a wreck using language like Rich and also pictures and sounds."

Brief discussion of his dad's "wreck"

Justin's use of language

Justin's use of photography

Justin's use of music

Providing Support Sentences

Support sentences often appear as a writer moves to a new point in a new paragraph, but long papers may devote two or more paragraphs to the discussion of a single point. In Justin's literacy autobiography, he uses support sentences to introduce his major points. Note that as he did in the introduction, Justin sometimes uses more than one support sentence.

> Paragraph 2: "Although my dad left our family when I was three partly because he couldn't advance on his jobs with his lack of reading ability my mom supported me in every way. The most important way was in promoting reading."
>
> Paragraph 3: "Two experiences with photography taught me that pictures are another way of understanding the world, the goal of all kinds of literacies."
>
> Paragraph 4: "In this most original research paper I have written to date I wrote about the way that Stieglitz talked about framing."
>
> Paragraph 5: "Another way that I am literate is through music."
>
> Paragraph 6: ". . . I have the advantage of reading and writing and having other ways of expressing myself and understanding the world that my father did not."

ANALYZING JUSTIN'S ORGANIZATION

1. With others in your class, analyze Justin's literacy autobiography for its adherence to the directive "map" sentence in his introduction. Where does it follow the sentence; where does it depart?
2. Evaluate Justin's organization for the literacy autobiography. Is it effective? Would you recommend changing it? How? Why?

PRACTICE WITH MAPPING ORGANIZATION

1. Map the organizations indicated by the following directive sentences. What expectations do these sentences create in you as a reader? When a sentence depends upon general terms, as does 1c, add specifics to help the reader see the direction of the paper.
   a. Many people think that life as a sailor is just one big worldwide vacation; in reality, though sailors may travel to such exotic places as Australia and Portugal, they often remain on board ship, continuing the everyday maintenance, clerical, and service tasks that keep a ship afloat.
   b. Life in my former high school and life in a B-grade prison movie have many things in common, such as restriction of movement, bad food, a rigid schedule, and sadistic wardens.
   c. My Swiss army knife is a tool I use every day for many purposes.
   d. Showing appreciation for their fans by allowing tape recording at concerts was just one of the many ways the Grateful Dead created their enormous success.
   e. Although a third party presidential candidate such as Ross Perot may have many qualifications for the office, Americans should not vote for such a candidate.
2. Choose one of the previous sentences, and write support sentences that could introduce each of the points included in your map.
3. As you mapped the previous directive sentences, you may have noticed that they indicate purpose, in each case a purpose that might have been drawn from cubing. Remembering that cubing directs thinking toward description, analysis into elements, analysis for cause and effect, exemplification, comparison and contrast, application, association, or argument, identify which of these is reflected in each of the previous directive sentences.

REORGANIZING A PAPER

Even though Justin did not choose Paper 4, the multimedia paper about his travels, for inclusion in the Course Portfolio, that paper provides a good example of a piece that could employ a different organization. When Justin wrote "Boundless Travel" to fulfill the assignment for a multimedia paper in chapter 7, simply fulfilling the assignment appears to have been his main purpose. That purpose is most apparent in his Writer's Statement as he identifies the audience for the paper as "anyone who has a curiosity about travel. Since most people have traveled somewhere, I think that the audience should be most people."

Writing for an audience as broad and varied as "most people" is difficult. Such a statement of audience is often an indication of an undefined purpose. A further clue to Justin's lack of direction in this paper is the absence of a directive sentence to indicate his purpose and organization.

About January, I start to think of summer vacation. Sometimes I get out albums from past vacations to recreate the pleasurable feelings associated with family trips. Other times I gripe about not having enough money to travel to California or New York or wherever I'd like to go at the time. Sometimes I even get practical and think about saving my money so I really can go somewhere. This year I'm thinking about how to convince my mom that I need to go to Europe after all I'm a college student who is supposed to be broadening my horizons.

Despite a lack of direction in the introduction, Justin wrote an interesting paper replete with specific examples of his own experiences with travel. But the lack of direction becomes more obvious when you analyze the organization of his points, for you can see that they could probably have been ordered in any number of ways. Following is one example of an alternative organization he could have employed.

Justin's Paper 4 Organization

Original Organization	*Alternative Organization*
Wide-ranging intro.	Intro.
Nearby travels	Traveling via the arts
Vicarious travel	Traveling via music
Traveling via the arts	Nearby travel
Traveling via music	Vicarious travel
Conclusion indicating European travel hopes	Conclusion

Although this alternative organization would require some changes, it would not change Justin's message or his purpose. The fact that nothing in this paper ties organization to purpose may indicate a lack of purpose because organization and purpose should go hand in hand.

What would happen if Justin clarified his purpose, focusing on the hints he offers in the introduction and again in the conclusion? Then he could turn this paper into an argument attempting to convince his mother of the wisdom of a summer European trip.

PRACTICE WITH REVISING ORGANIZATION: ANOTHER WRITER'S WORK

1. With others in your class, work with Justin's travel paper, reorganizing his points into an argument that attempts to convince his mother to allow him to travel to Europe over his summer vacation. What points would you retain? What new points might you need to make?
2. Use your imagination to write a directive sentence for Justin's argument advocating summer European travel. Map that sentence, and then write the appropriate support sentences.

PRACTICE WITH REVISING ORGANIZATION: YOUR OWN WORK

If the responses to your work include such remarks as "I'm confused," "What does this paragraph have to do with the next one?" or "This doesn't flow," you may need to work on the organization of your paper. Apply the following strategies to a paper that you believe needs to be organized differently and record your work in your dialogue journal.

1. Find a directive sentence or sentences in your introduction or in another early paragraph in your paper. Compare it to the statement of purpose in your Writer's Statement.
2. If you cannot find such a sentence or if the one you find does not reflect the purpose you intend to fulfill, write a new sentence and map it.
3. Ask a classmate to look through your draft for support sentences appropriate to your organizational map and to record them in a response to you.
4. Working from your directive sentence, the map, and the existing support sentences, write any new support sentences you may need, numbering them in the order in which they will appear in the paper.
5. In the margins of your draft, mark the material already in your paper with the number corresponding to the support sentence it will develop. Underline any material you will delete.
6. Write a revision plan that includes your directive sentence and a map that includes the support sentences.

TAKING A SECOND LOOK AT DEVELOPMENT

Adding material that helps accomplish your purpose, maintains the focus of your paper, and explains the ideas in your support sentences is another major revision task. However, once you know what you're trying to accomplish and what points you need to focus upon, you have established a basis for choosing additional material.

When a reader asks for more development, she wants more information. You may think of that as a problem of length, but instead it is a problem of thoroughness. When an idea is not well developed, the reader does not have enough information to understand it. The responses you receive to an underdeveloped paper may include "Tell me more," "I'm not sure I understand," or even the response my daughter's boyfriend recently received on a research paper, "Investigation lacking." You can choose among several strategies to meet readers' requests for more information.

Developing by Adding Details

Adding details is one way to enhance readers' understanding of your ideas. For instance, in Justin's first draft of his literacy autobiography, he wrote this passage.

I've really enjoyed playing the saxophone. I liked being part of an improvisational jazz group, although I never got very good. I find that the sax expresses my sadness in a way that I can't with words or any other form of expression.

In the second draft he added material to explain how the sax helps him to express himself.

Playing the saxophone helps me express my feelings that are part of my life. Better than writing for expressing sad feelings is playing the sax, especially playing jazz. But, I can also express happiness with music. Sometimes the sadness and happiness are mixed, just like words can have two meanings at the same time. I try to understand life through music as well as through words and pictures. It's the greatest when other people understand what I'm trying to say through my playing. When people applaud our band I know that I am being understood. Part of being literate is being able to express yourself so somebody else understands.

ANALYZING FOR DETAILS

How did Justin use details to develop the passage about his enjoyment of the saxophone? Point out the additional details included in the revised passage.

Developing by Adding Examples

The most successful explanations often include examples that can connect with the reader's frame of reference by offering the familiar to explain the unfamiliar. Recently, my daughter tried to explain Indie Rock to me but with little success. Finally, she said, "You know that song by Pavement, 'We Dance,' that I play all the time in the car? That's Indie Rock." Immediately I understood what sort of music she was talking about.

In Natali's paper about curfew, she offers many examples. One exemplifies the dangers that await young people with no curfew; others offer possible solutions to the curfew problem as employed by various cities. Such examples can come from your reading, interviewing, or observations. You may also draw examples from your own experience or knowledge base as Justin did when he discussed his own experiences with interracial friendships in Paper 3. For many readers, those examples add authority to the paper by showing the connection of the writer to his topic.

ANALYZING FOR EXAMPLES

In the following passage from Justin's literacy autobiography, he uses a number of examples. List them in your dialogue journal as you read.

Although my dad left our family when I was three partly because he couldn't advance on his jobs with his lack of reading ability my mom supported me in every way. The most important way was in promoting reading. When I was little she read to me every day. I liked animal stories, so she read the entire Red Stallion series and books like *Bambi*. We had a deal that she would pay for half of any book that I wanted to buy. We used the library most of the time, but if I wanted a book I had to save only half the price from my allowance or paper delivery money. The first book I bought was *Lassie Comes Home*. One thing I liked about stories was that they had a beginning, middle, and end. Even if not everything turned out the way you wanted you could understand from the story why the ending was as it was.

Developing by Adding Authority

Although examples drawn from personal experience can add your voice to a paper, sometimes the authority of an acknowledged expert is needed to develop a paper, most often when you have to convince a skeptical reader. When you choose expert sources, be aware of their credentials and of your readers' standards for authority. You can often find the authoritative opinion that you need through library research, or you may also use information from interviews.

Sally recently proposed a paper about people who try to overcome their fears by taking part in the very activities that cause those fears. She called a number of psychologists, but none would take the time to talk with her. Finally by calling a sky diving school, she found an instructor who had significant experience with people who, sometimes on their therapist's recommendation, took up sky diving to conquer a fear of heights. He was quite willing, even flattered, to share his knowledge and experience. Sally discovered this interview source through perseverance and some creative thinking, and, as a result, she enriched her paper with authority and a touch of the unusual.

ANALYZING FOR AUTHORITY

In drafting Paper 5, Justin went to written sources to find answers to his questions about the extent of a father's influence on his children's success. In his draft, he quotes David Blankenhorn, the chairman of National Fatherhood Initiative and president of the Institute of American Values, who "calls fatherlessness 'the most urgent social problem of our generation.'" Later in that draft, Justin quotes an article from the *Journal of Counseling and Development,* pointing out the effect that family breakup has on fathers. The authors, Janice Wilbur and Michael Wilbur, are associate professors at Boston University. His third authoritative source is an article about the relationships between divorced fathers and their children from *Demography* by Frank Furstenberg, Saul Hoffman, and Laura Shrestha. He has no further information about them.

How authoritative do you find the sources Justin used in Paper 5? What lends them authority or might detract from their authority? What other sources might be accessible to someone on a college campus in a medium-sized city?

CREATING A DEVELOPMENT PACKAGE

When you begin to develop paragraphs, many types of information are available. You may find it helpful to plan a development package, a combination of types of information that can round out a discussion and provide the reader with a thorough treatment of your topic or point. Rather than depending upon one developmental strategy, you may want to combine an example, a quote from an authoritative source, and some details drawn from your own observation or knowledge base. You have then created a development package. As you read the following paragraph from Justin's revised draft of Paper 5, identify the support sentence and the four different sources and authorities he brings together.

Justin's Paper 5, Revised Paragraph, Research Investigation

All that is bad, but it does not indicate that all children of fatherless families are doomed to crime and dropping out of school. What may be of most concern to

```
many people who are growing up successfully without
fathers is that they may repeat the cycle and put their
children at risk of being less successful by falling
into some of these problems that they avoided. According
to Whitehead, children of divorce are "less successful
as adults in the two domains of life--love and work--
that are most essential to happiness. . . . Many
children from disrupted families have a harder time
achieving intimacy in a relationship, forming a stable
marriage" (47). She quotes a study by Wallerstein that
says the "long-term effects of divorce emerge at a time
when young adults are trying to make their own decisions
about love, marriage, and family" (65). She also says
that Nicholas Zill's research shows that girls from
single parent families are at a greater risk for divorce
(66). That's something we learned in a health class in
high school, that statistics show that people from
divorced families are more likely to be divorced
themselves.
```

ANALYZING DEVELOPMENT STRATEGIES

1. What is the point of this paragraph?
2. How effective is Justin's use of material to develop that point?
3. What other development strategies would enhance your understanding of the paragraph?

Consider these same questions as you read the following paper by Dave.

REVISING TO DEVELOP MAIN POINTS

When Dave, a freshman writing student, finished his draft of a paper arguing that beer is not a suitable drink after exercise, he was concerned not only that the paper was short (about 250 words) but also that he needed evidence to back up his claim about beer. Here is his draft.

Dave's Argument Paper, Draft 1

Is Beer a Suitable Fluid Replacement Beverage?

For many Americans, drinking a cold beer is one of life's little pleasures. One can imagine a hot summer day with great numbers of people enjoying outside activities such as basketball, softball, beach volleyball, bicycling, and running. Many of these physically active people enjoy the fellowship of other athletes and, as an enhancement of that experience, along with the need to quench an exercise-induced thirst, will grab an ice-cold beer. But wait! Is beer the beverage their bodies *really* need? Although moderate consumption of alcohol has not been proven harmful, I submit that beer is not suitable as a fluid replacement beverage for two important reasons.

First, the calorie content of beer is nutritionally void of any vitamins, minerals, or other components essential to the well-being of active people. These empty calories also cause the body to override the use of stored energy within itself and process those empty calories, which if done over a prolonged period of time, can lead to fat weight gain--definitely not helpful to an athlete or anyone conscious of their appearance.

Second, but most important of all, is the diuretic effect alcohol has on the human body. While it is true that cold beer is rapidly absorbed by a thirsty, overheated body, the alcohol will cause the body to release more fluid than it takes in, resulting in a net fluid loss which can lead to dehydration. Why drink something that takes more than it gives?

In conclusion, beer cannot be a suitable fluid replacement beverage because it contains nutritionally empty calories and the diuretic effect on the body causes dehydration.

Dave received these comments in response to his essay:

1. "Where does this information come from?" (a request for authority)
2. "Doesn't alcohol have any food value?" (a request for more information)
3. "This paper does not meet the length requirement." (a comment on fulfillment of the assignment)

ANALYZING FOR DEVELOPMENT

When Dave revised his essay, he added a significant amount of information. As you read his revision, identify and list in your dialogue journal the kinds of material he added. How does each kind of evidence aid development by convincing the reader to accept or understand Dave's point better than did the original draft? In his Writer's Statement, Dave says he could come up with two more reasons to support his main idea. Do you think he should do that? Why or why not?

Dave's Argument Paper, Draft 2

Is Beer a Suitable Replacement Beverage?

One of life's little pleasures for many Americans is drinking cold beer. Imagine, if you will, a hot summer day with great numbers of people enjoying recreational sports like softball, basketball, beach volleyball, running, and cycling. As part of the fun and celebration of the moment, as well as the need to quench an exercise-induced thirst, many of these physically active people will reach into their coolers and grab an ice-cold beer. But wait! Is beer the beverage their bodies really need? While beer drinking in the context of celebration and quality of life enhancement should not be eliminated, it is not suitable as a fluid replacement beverage for two important reasons.

Although it is true that beer contains only carbohydrate calories and no fat calories, those carbo calories are derived solely from the alcohol in the beer and have little nutritional value. Charles Williams advised runners in 1983 of the lack of nutrition in alcohol: "While alcoholic beverages may be enjoyable, they do not provide enough nutrients to be categorized in the Basic Four [food groups]. Their major contribution is in the form of calories" (95).

Even though the Basic Four food groups have been updated to become the Food Pyramid, his advice is still valid today. The alcohol, from which the calories are derived, is processed first by the body to the exclusion of any remaining stored fuel (either glycogen or fat). Therefore, no real nutrition is available to restore spent fuel.

The second, and perhaps the most important, reason is that although cold liquids such as beer are rapidly absorbed by a thirsty, overheated body, the diuretic effect of the alcohol will cause the very condition athletes are attempting to avoid: dehydration. Norman Brooks, who describes this effect in his 1987 book *Endurance Running,* states basically that extended bouts of competition in hot conditions can cause a person to become dehydrated due to excessive sweating. Says Brooks, "This stops our body functioning effectively and can lead to heat related stress problems" (77). The late Jim Fixx, whose name became a household word in 1977 with his pioneer work, *The Complete Book of Running,* describes beer also in the context of hot weather exercise:

> After all, it does add weight--it's pure calories--and in addition to impairing coordination, decreasing your ability to process oxygen, and reducing muscle strength, it has . . . an adverse effect on your tolerance to heat. Indeed, studies have shown that even a single bottle of beer can affect your ability to run in hot weather and that the effect lasts for as much as two days (167).

It is easy to see how beer can affect a runner, so it can be shown that beer will bring about a similar effect on participants of other athletic disciplines. After all, dehydration can't tell a runner from a softball player.

In conclusion, one cannot deny that for many active people a cold beer is refreshing and not harmful if consumed in moderation. But when a human body is in need of serious fluid intake, reach for Gatorade or water first. Save the beer for later.

Works Cited

Brooks, Norman. *Endurance Running.* Marlborough: Crowood, 1987.

Fixx, Jim. *The Complete Book of Running.* New York: Random, 1977.

Williams, Charles et al. *Jogging Everyone?* Winston-Salem: Hunter, 1983.

PRACTICE WITH REVISING TO DEVELOP YOUR POINTS

If responses to any of your papers indicate a need for further information or development of your ideas, try the following strategies and record the work in your journal.

1. Choose a paragraph that readers have indicated lacks development, a paragraph that explains a complex idea, or a paragraph that simply seems skimpy to you. Analyze the paragraph for the kinds of information you offer. Do you offer details? Examples? Information from an authority? Personal experience? What kind of information will appeal to your reader?
2. What sources will provide the kind of information you need: your own knowledge and experience, other people who have had similar experiences, experts on the topic, or facts and statistics? Where or how will you obtain this additional information?
3. List the different kinds of information you plan to combine into a "development package."
4. Create a revision plan that incorporates your discoveries about the level of development in your drafts and the need for added material. Or add this information to the revision plans already in progress for your papers.

A FINAL LOOK AT REVISION

As you read Justin's second draft of Paper 5, the research paper on fatherlessness, keep in mind the questions he asks in the Writer's Statement. You may want to make notes about your responses to the questions or about ideas his draft raises about issues in your own work.

Justin's Writer's Statement for Paper 5, Draft 2 for his Course Portfolio

I started out thinking that I might show how the absence of a father didn't really make a difference because it didn't make much difference in my life. But I also wanted practice doing a research paper. So I thought I might find out just what influence the absence of a father does have. I ended up realizing that when a father is absent, many kids are affected badly. There's no way to prove that it is the absence of a father that directly causes all the problems kids have. But it does turn out to be pretty coincidental that kids in trouble often do not have a father present in their homes.

My purpose became to show that while fatherlessness and divorce do not guarantee problems, they don't do kids any good, so the best thing we all can do is try to stay married and raise our children. My audience is other males in my generation, especially those of us who have grown up without our fathers.

My questions are:

1. What was the most convincing information about the negative effects of fatherlessness? Why was it so convincing?
2. The paper got awfully long. Would you take out anything that is not necessary to my purpose? What?
3. I tried to write good support sentences, but I don't think the paper maps very well. Does it all make sense in a good order?
4. I was worried about putting personal information into a research paper. Did the personal material seem okay?
5. If there was anything you didn't understand, what was it? Please ask specific questions about it so I'll know what to add.

Justin's Paper 5, Draft 2, Research Investigation

Fathers for the Future

One of the most talked about problems today is the problem of absentee fathers. All the discussion about the overhaul of the welfare system, crime, and problems in schools seem to come down to pointing a finger at families where the fathers are gone. If you listen to some of the talk on television, the male influence is supposed to be so important that it's a miracle that families without it even survive.

Yet, lots of American kids grow up today without having a father in the house for their entire childhood. Most of those kids go on to successful lives. They do not become criminals, they do not have children out of wedlock, they do not go to jail. If the majority of this broken family generation survives their situation, then the American public might legitimately ask why fatherlessness has been identified as "the most urgent social problem of our generation" (Cose).

That question becomes even more appropriate when the source of that quote is identified as David Blankenhorn, chairman of National Fatherhood Initiative and president of the Institute of American Values, organizations which appear to have a conservative bias. Other conservatives agree with Blankenhorn. William Bennett, former secretary of education and well-known conservative, says in *Commentary* that fatherlessness is one of the three most critical problems in America today. We have come to the point, he says, where we ask prisons to do for young men what their fathers used to do. And an editorial in *Christianity Today* says that because the two-parent marriage is "God's design," the single parent family is "pathological" (Jones 20). As the product of a so-called broken home and as a male who has grown up without a father's influence or interest, I know that I will not become a statistic. I am a college student, hold a job, take part in my family, and will probably have a productive adulthood. It would be easy for me to ignore all the talk about the importance of fatherhood. But because I am a male and because I know that I missed out on things by my dad's absence, I cannot totally discount the concern about fatherhood as a phenomena of the conservatives. Too much evidence exists to show that fatherlessness is a problem. Just because all young men do not fall prey to the problems that can result from it does not mean that it is not a significant problem.

One of the sources of the fatherlessness controversy is a 1992 television show. When sitcom character Murphy Brown, a liberated reporter, decided to have a baby without being married or involving the father in the baby's life, vice president Dan Quayle responded with outrage towards this irresponsible role model and the general immorality on television. A national debate sprung up. Everyone had an opinion. But it was just that, opinion.

The definitive article about the problems of fatherlessness is Barbara Dafoe Whitehead's in *The Atlantic Monthly,* "Dan Quayle Was Right." Her article, according to *U.S. News and World Report,* "summarizes a decade's scholarly research" (Zuckerman 72). Her summary attacks the single parent family on many fronts. But some of her strongest statements concern the future of children who grow up without their fathers. According to a "growing body of scientific evidence," they are, she says, at great disadvantage.

The father-child bond is not what it used to be. Whitehead reports that in 1976 less than half as many fathers as in 1957 said that providing for children was a life goal. The proportion of working men who found marriage and children burdensome and restrictive more than doubled in the same period (58). She cites a National Survey of Children that says that "in disrupted families only one child in six, on average, saw his or her father as often as once a week in the past year. Close to half did not see their father at all in the past year" (65). As time passes, "ten years after a divorce, more than two-thirds of children report not having seen their father for a year" (65). That has been my own experience. Since my dad left us, years ago, I hardly ever see or hear from him. As time passes, I think we just grow farther apart and he just doesn't think about us.

Educational achievement is effected too. Children are more than twice as likely to drop out of high school. Boys drop out more often than girls and are more likely to show aggressive behavior. Children of single parent families are more likely to be late to school, to be truant, to be in trouble at school (66). Whitehead says that the "great educational tragedy of our time" is children failing because they are emotionally unable to perform in school. Principals report, she says, "a dramatic rise in the aggressive, acting-out behavior characteristic of children, especially boys, who are living in single parent families" (77).

The rise in our country's crime rate is also a result of single parent families according to the sources compiled by Whitehead. More than 70 percent of juveniles in state reform institutions come from fatherless homes (77).

"A number of scholarly studies find that even after the groups of subjects are controlled for income, boys from single-mother homes are significantly more likely than others to commit crimes and to wind up in the juvenile justice, court, and penitentiary systems" (77).

All that is bad, but it does not indicate that all children of fatherless families are doomed to crime and dropping out of school. What may be of most concern to many people who are growing up successfully without fathers is that they may repeat the cycle and put their children at risk of being less successful by falling into some of these problems that they avoided. According to Whitehead, children of divorce are "less successful as adults in the two domains of life--love and work--that are most essential to happiness. Many children from disrupted families have a harder time achieving intimacy in a relationship, forming a stable marriage" (47). She quotes a study by Wallerstein that says the "long-term affects of divorce emerge at a time when young adults are trying to make their own decisions about love, marriage, and family" (65). She also says that Nicholas Zill's research shows that girls from single parent families are at a greater risk for divorce (66). That's something we learned in a health class in high school, that statistics show that people from divorced families are more likely to be divorced themselves.

That's one outcome of the discussion of fatherless families that should concern everyone. If being fatherless does affect some people in these ways, as my generation marries and begins raising families, we must remember the risks to our children of subjecting them to divorce and abandonment. We should try to break the cycle.

Works Cited

Cose, Ellis. "The Year of the Father." *Newsweek* 31 Oct. 1994: 61.

Bennett, William J. "What to do about the children." *Commentary* March 1995: 23-29. *InfoTrac.* CD-ROM. February 1996.

Jones, Stanton L. "The Two-Parent Heresy." *Christianity Today* 17 May 1993: 20-21.

Whitehead, Barbara Dafoe. "Dan Quayle Was Right." *The Atlantic Monthly* April 1993: 47-84.

Zuckerman, Mortimer B. "The Crisis of the Kids." *U.S. News and World Report* 12 April 1993: 72.

ANALYZING JUSTIN'S PAPER 5, DRAFT 2, AND A CLASSMATE'S PAPER

1. Use Justin's Writer's Statement to guide your analysis of his paper. Practice strategies you have learned throughout this book to help you in your analysis. For example, identify directive and support sentences and map the paper if that activity would help you to respond to his question about organization. Or analyze his use of sources or development strategies, and list them to see if he has provided a development package. You may want to work in a group with each person taking responsibility for one of his questions and leading the discussion of your response.

   Do the other members of your group agree with your response? What issues will you raise in a whole-class discussion? Record them in your journal. You may want to include this analysis in your own Course Portfolio to support your knowledge of development strategies.

2. Follow the same procedure with a classmate's paper. Include in your response any work such as mapping or descriptive analysis that you have done as preparation for answering her questions.

WORKING PORTFOLIO UPDATE

With others from your class, brainstorm a list of strategies helpful in preparing for various revision tasks. Which of those tasks do you still have to complete as you revise your drafts for your Course Portfolio? In a journal entry, write a revision plan for each paper that describes those tasks and useful strategies for completing them successfully. Be sure to include these materials in your Working Portfolio for possible inclusion in your Course Portfolio.

In the next chapter you will see Justin polish the drafts that he has worked so hard to compose and to revise. Editing his papers for issues of style and usage to make sure his work conforms to the conventions his readers expect and to correct errors, Justin will bring his work to a state of completion that makes it ready for his Course Portfolio.

CHAPTER 12
Editing Your Portfolio Papers

Have you heard the story, perhaps told in your own household, about the parent who walked three miles in the snow each way to school and had only a pencil stub and pad of coarse paper to use for writing? This proverbial tale allows the teller to emphasize his hardships and devotion to learning. A more modern version of this story is the parent who received a failing grade in college on any paper with more than three spelling errors, punctuation mistakes, or grammar miscues. This updated story is often accompanied by a call for a return to the basics. The narrative reads: "Students these days can't write. If teachers only returned to teaching spelling, punctuation, and grammar like they did when I was in school, students would be able to write and get jobs."

These storytellers do not know what researchers about writing have discovered in the past twenty years. Researchers have learned that doing grammar exercises on isolated sentences composed by someone else does not assure that writers will write well. Those exercisers might be able to correct random sentences and might know some grammatical terminology, but they will not necessarily become better writers from that practice or knowledge. So far in this book, you have not focused on spelling, punctuation, grammar, or other conventions of your writing that must be accurate for readers to read your work fluidly and with understanding. You have first been focusing on your purpose, focus, organization, and development of ideas.

Now, however, you need to attend to all the features extolled by these storytellers because you have decided on the pieces of writing that will go into your Course Portfolio to demonstrate your abilities as a writer. Correct spelling, grammar, punctuation, and usage are essential in the finished pieces that exhibit your ability to communicate your ideas.

Although you may have made corrections as your teacher and classmates noticed misspellings, you did not need to worry persistently about spelling as you worked through early drafts. During revision you may well have omitted or changed the very misspelled words that you had originally used, so taking the time to find the correct spelling would not have been worthwhile. Using a spellcheck on your computer, of course, obviates the effort of looking up a word, so you may simply have run the spellcheck on every draft. Ensuring correct spelling through running a spellcheck, looking up a word in the dictionary, or asking another person is absolutely essential now that you are editing revised drafts of the pieces you have selected for your Course Portfolio. The same is true of each type of editing that ensures a paper free of errors.

LOOKING FOR PATTERNS OF ERROR

Most of us competently follow many of the conventions of formal written English. For example, we usually place periods at the ends of sentences, indent paragraphs, make subjects agree in number with verbs, capitalize proper names, and choose the appropriate homonym. Many of us also, however, find that certain conventions pose problems. For example, I check the Modern Language Association style guide each time I document an edited book to remind myself of the proper punctuation in the citation, I depend on my spellcheck to know if *occurred* has both two *c*'s and two *r*'s, and I pause to differentiate before writing *eminent* for "well-regarded" and *imminent* for "soon-to-occur." Like you, I have certain errors that appear again and again in my work. Sometimes the pattern of error occurs because I don't know the convention, but more often the pattern of error represents long-term practice that I must be alert to correct as I edit.

A helpful reader of drafts always looks for patterns of error. Instead of marking with the traditionally dreaded red pen all the errors on a paper, an effective reader searches for repetition of the same error that may indicate the writer's need to learn a certain convention. Rather than add an apostrophe every time that it is missing in a paper, for instance, a reader may note that the writer never includes an apostrophe to show possession. A paper may contain the words "my dads car," "President Lincolns speaking style," "under the tables surface," and "adding the teams score," all nouns or phrases that contain words showing possession. In conventional English, apostrophes belong before or after an *s* on a word showing possession, depending on the singular or plural nature of the word. The writer who consistently omits the apostrophe needs to be alerted to conventional practice and then to pay close attention in his papers until he more automatically follows the convention.

Fortunately, these conventions are not magical. They are practices that readers and writers have accepted over time as helpful ways to facilitate common expectations in written discourse. People in a discourse community, that is, a group of people who speak and write to one another on a regular basis, have agreed to follow common practices to make listening and reading easier for all. Just as we agree to stop at stop signs as we drive cars, we agree to stop at periods that end complete ideas that are labeled sentences. We might alter our agreements—we might stop our cars at round green signs or stop our reading at the placement of two commas—but until we negotiate such change or it evolves over time, we continue with our conventional stop signals.

Conventions do change, though, so we need to be alert to language practices around us. What one year is slang, the next year may be entered into a dictionary as acceptable usage. What was once regarded as grammatically incorrect may become acceptable usage. For example, coordinate conjunctions (words like *and, but, or, nor, for, so,* and *yet* that join or coordinate two independent ideas that could be sentences) used to be taboo at the beginning of a sentence. Now they are more and more acceptable as sentence starters in formal English.

BEING ALERT TO WRITING CONVENTIONS

The best ways to keep abreast of conventions, both traditional and changing, are to read many kinds of texts, to check a reliable handbook, to consult with experienced writers, and to ask readers who are members of the audience for your writing.

Reading many texts reveals the uses of conventions that writers have and are currently employing. The well-known poet e. e. cummings, for example, calls attention to the convention of capitalization of proper nouns by not capitalizing them as his stylistic trademark. bell hooks, a contemporary feminist critic, does the same. As you read this poet and this critic, you might be aware of your reception of unconventional punctuation. What does it do to you as a reader? What would happen to your readers if you omitted capitalization of proper nouns? Why would you choose to do so or not to do so?

Consulting a handbook is another excellent practice when you are unsure of a writing convention. Your class members all may be using the same handbook, or you may have chosen one recommended by someone else. Handbooks are arranged differently, contain various combinations of information, and are written at different levels of difficulty. If the one you are using doesn't serve your needs, you may want to find another. A good handbook should provide answers to many of your questions about grammar, usage, and even style. Although conventions, when practiced, become easier to remember and to use naturally, a handbook is a valuable resource. Libraries and Writing Centers usually contain an array of handbooks for reference if your own handbook does not address your question or if you need more information than it offers.

Faculty and peer tutors in Writing and Learning Centers are excellent resources when you are dealing with errors. These teachers and tutors will not correct your errors but will help you learn to spot the errors and correct them yourself. You may also rely on peers in your writing class, your instructor, or other accomplished writers to help you with editing. Asking another person questions about errors is not a form of cheating but a smart move that shows you care about accuracy and communication with your audience. Be sure not to focus on errors too soon, though, when you go to a writing or learning center or consult with another writer. Sometimes students want to ask about punctuation, for example, before they have revised sufficiently to achieve focus in their papers. Remember that final editing comes after revising.

Audience members for your writing can aid you in identifying acceptable conventions in a discourse community. If your audience is specialized, you may want to question a member of that audience. For example, if you are writing a business letter, your company may have expected formats or sentence length restrictions. If you are writing a newsletter for a youth organization, you will want to consider the conversational tone typical of that organization's written style. Asking a work colleague or a member of the youth organization to help you edit your writing would be smart as you adhere to the conventions of that discourse community's written texts.

WORKING ON EDITING TASKS

As Justin looked at his latest revised drafts, he searched for the errors in conventions that had been noted by his readers and by himself. He found some marked on his papers and some noted in his dialogue journal entries. Four categories emerged as he realized that he had some patterns of errors and some single errors with which he needed help. He discovered the categories when he went to his university's Writing Center to begin what felt like an overwhelming editing task. Justin was afraid that he wouldn't see the errors and that he wouldn't know how to correct them. His peer tutor, who had herself taken the course in which Justin was enrolled, helped him group his errors so that they could talk about them and so that he could consult handbooks for help. Justin's errors in grammar, punctuation, usage, and style appear in the examples.

Grammar

You may have a strong feeling when you hear the word *grammar.* Because so many of us studied grammar through repeated exercises with little context, we often see the consideration of it as a dreaded chore. But grammar is actually an area you know a good deal about without thinking. For example, you know that saying "I want an ice cream cone" makes more sense in English than saying "Cream an want I ice cone." You have been learning and using English grammar, the set of rules by which sentences are made, since you learned to talk.

In writing, however, we are more stringent about certain grammatical constructions than we are in speaking. The punctuation issue in comma splices and run-on sentences, for instance, is pertinent to written form only: although we tend to pause at the end of sentences in speech, we may not signal sharply the end of each sentence. In writing, however, we are expected to signal the end of a sentence as a grammatical construction.

Justin has made some grammatical errors in his drafts. We will consider two of his errors that show up regularly in student writers' papers, so you may recognize these problems in your own writing or in the writing of your peers to which you are responding. Although it is more important to focus on your own problems, you will also be a better responder for other writers if you understand correct grammatical forms. As grammatical problems emerge in drafts in your class, you can check your handbook, ask your instructor, or consult with your classmates or Writing Center tutors about ways to correct the problems. Justin's errors are only representative of those that you may deal with in your own writing and the writing of others.

1. Use of Subject-Verb Agreement

In English the subject and verb in a sentence agree in number. That is, if the subject is singular, the verb is singular; if the subject is plural, the verb is plural. Usually, this agreement is easy to achieve. Sometimes, however, words modifying the subject that come between the subject and verb cause the writer to use a plural verb for a singular subject or a singular verb for a plural subject.

For example, one writer stated, "Each of the members have a credit card." *Of the members* is a prepositional phrase that modifies the subject *each* and comes between the subject *each* and the verb *have*. Although *members* is plural, the subject *each* is singular so that the verb must be singular also. Thus, the correct sentence reads, "Each of the members has a credit card."

Example 1: Paper 3, Draft 2

The first sentence of Justin's Paper 3, Draft 2 contains the sentence, "In our society today, relationships between members of different racial or cultural groups is a big issue." The subject of the sentence, *relationships,* is obviously plural, but the verb is singular. Justin needs to make the subject singular by using the word *relationship* or to make the verb plural by using the word *are.*

Example 2: Paper 5, Draft 2

In the second sentence of Justin's Paper 5, Draft 2, he again has a subject-verb agreement problem: "All the discussion about the overhaul of the welfare system, crime, and problems in schools seem to come down to pointing a finger at families where the fathers are gone." Do you spot the problem? Justin has been swayed into using a plural verb by the series of words in the phrase that modifies the singular subject *discussion.*

Justin could correct the problem by making the subject plural to fit the plural verb: the sentence would read, "All the *discussions* about the overhaul of the welfare system, crime, and problems in schools *seem* to come down to pointing a finger at families where the fathers are gone." Or Justin could correct the problem by making the verb singular to fit the singular subject: this sentence would read, "All the *discussion* about the overhaul of the welfare system, crime, and problems in schools *seems* to come down to pointing a finger at families where the fathers are gone." Justin must decide which change will better express his meaning.

2. Use of the Word *That* with an Indefinite Antecedent

When I used to recite for my sons the proper rules of etiquette for a formal social situation, such as "Face the person to whom you are introducing someone as you say the new person's name," "Accept a dish with your left hand, shift it to your right, and pass with your right," and "Say 'I'm glad to meet you' as you shake hands with a new acquaintance," they would shrug and say, "Oh, we know that, Mom!" But I was never sure what they knew because the word *that* in their reply could have referred to any part of my admonitions, to the fact that I simply wanted them to be polite, or to the general idea that they already knew what I had undoubtedly said before.

Sometimes we use the word *that* to refer to some previous idea or general concept without providing a specific antecedent. The prefix *ante* means *before,* so an antecedent is a word that comes before a pronoun to which the pronoun refers. You might write, "Lancelot was a knight in King Arthur's court. He served Arthur loyally." The pronoun *he* refers back to *Lancelot,* so *Lancelot* is the antecedent of *he*. You might also write, "My family kid one another and play practical jokes. That sometimes offends other people who don't know us well." To what does *that* refer? Does *that* refer to the family, to kidding, to playing practical jokes, or to all of the above? The second sentence would be clearer if it read: "That apparent lack of seriousness sometimes offends other people who don't know us well."

Justin fails to provide clear antecedents for the word *that* in two of his papers. He needs to rework the sentences involved so that they are clear.

Example 1: Paper 3, Draft 2

In Paper 3, Draft 2, Justin writes, "We have spent lots of time together and I have learned a lot about their backgrounds from our friendships. I like having that as a part of my life, and I think it's helped me see the value of other cultures and how they add to our society." What does Justin refer to with the word *that* in the second sentence? Does he mean the time spent together or his learning from friendships? Justin could clarify his meaning by writing, "Having friends from different cultures has helped me value other cultures, especially what they add to American society."

Example 2: Paper 5, Draft 2

In Paper 5, Draft 2, Justin quotes Whitehead about scholarly studies that show boys from single-mother households are more likely to commit crimes and to end up in court and prison. Justin begins his next paragraph with this sentence: "All that is bad, but it does not indicate that all children of fatherless families are doomed to crime and dropping out of school." A clearer sentence might read, "All that evidence is persuasive, but it does not indicate that all children of fatherless families are doomed to crime and dropping out of school." Notice in this sentence that the word *that* modifies the specific noun *evidence* rather than alluding vaguely to the entire previous sentence.

These two grammatical points emerge in Justin's work, so he must attend to them. You will want to look at your instructor's and peers' comments about your grammar to find the points you need to consider. You may have one or both of Justin's problems, but you probably have more of your own. Look for patterns of grammatical error in order to explore ways of correcting your misuses.

Punctuation

Punctuation marks are signals. Quotation marks signal the use of the exact words of a speaker. A colon can signal a series or one clause that amplifies another. A semicolon can mark the separation of two independent clauses. Punctuation can alert readers to the relationship of ideas or structures.

The omission of expected punctuation or the misuse of punctuation marks can interfere with readers' understanding of a text. Readers of Justin's texts alerted him to three punctuation errors that repeatedly got in the way of their understanding of his papers. Justin needed to learn the conventions of punctuation that apply to the three situations noted by his readers.

1. Use of a Comma Between an Introductory Adverbial Clause and the Independent Clause of the Sentence

An independent clause has a subject and a verb and expresses a complete thought. If the independent clause stands alone, it is called a simple sentence. If the independent clause is attached to another independent clause, it is a compound sentence. If the independent clause is attached to a dependent clause, which has a subject and verb but can't stand alone, it is a complex sentence. If two independent clauses are attached to a dependent clause, it is a compound-complex sentence.

Simple sentence:	I like your tie.
Compound sentence:	I like your tie, and I plan to buy one like it.
Complex sentence:	I like your tie because it is red.
Compound-complex sentence:	I like your tie because it is red, and I plan to buy one like it.

The comma helps to separate independent clauses from each other and from dependent clauses in some cases. One case in which the comma separates the independent and dependent clause is when the dependent clause comes at the beginning of the sentence and answers an adverbial question, such as *why, how, under what circumstances,* or *when* about the independent clause. The dependent clause is, therefore, called an introductory adverbial clause. For example, in the sentence "If it rains, we will stay home," the dependent clause *if it rains* tells under what circumstances *we will stay home*. The comma after *rains* separates the introductory adverbial clause from the independent clause *we will stay home*.

Justin had not learned that a comma comes after an introductory adverbial clause. His drafts are replete with examples of sentences in which he omitted the comma after an introductory adverbial clause that modifies the independent clause.

Example 1: Paper 1, Draft 1

"When I was three my dad left my mom, my younger sister, and me to try to find a better job."

Example 2: Paper 1, Draft 1

"Since I was really little she read to me every day."

Example 3: Paper 4, Draft 1

"Although most people may think of traveling as going far away from home I remember that my first travels were not far in physical space but were far in psychological space."

Example 4: Paper 4, Draft 1

"Because we live in the Midwest we went several times to Mammoth Cave and to Chicago, two very different experiences."

Example 5: Paper 5, Draft 1

"If you listen to some of the talk on television the male influence is supposed to be so important that it's a miracle families without it survive."

Do you see the pattern of error? The dependent clauses that begin with *when, since, although, because,* and *if,* all words called subordinate conjunctions, are at the beginning of each sentence. They all answer adverbial questions about the independent clauses: for example, When did his dad leave? Why did they go to Mammoth Cave and Chicago? Under what circumstances would you believe that the male influence is so important in a family? Because these dependent clauses are introductory and adverbial, they are followed by a comma. By Justin's final drafts, some of which will go into his Course Portfolio, he had corrected the punctuation in all of these sentences.

Example 1: Paper 1

"When I was three, my dad left my mom, my younger sister, and me to try to find a better job."

Example 2: Paper 1

"Since I was really little, she read to me every day."

Example 3: Paper 4

"Although most people may think of traveling as going far away from home, I remember that my first travels were not far in physical space but were far in psychological space."

Example 4: Paper 4

"Because we live in the Midwest, we went several times to Mammoth Cave and to Chicago, two very different experiences."

Example 5: Paper 5

"If you listen to some of the talk on television, the male influence is supposed to be so important that it's a miracle families without it survive."

2. Use of an Apostrophe to Show Possession

This use of the apostrophe, mentioned earlier in the chapter, is one that Justin often overlooks.

Example 1: Paper 1, Draft 1

In Paper 1, Draft 1, Justin omitted the apostrophe seven times in words that show possession: sisters, troops, class, dads, guys, dads, and dads. Interestingly, that number reduced to two times in Paper 1, Draft 2, not because Justin added apostrophes but because he often revised in such a way that he no longer used the words in question. This example illustrates the point that editing carefully too early can be a waste of time.

Example 2: Paper 1, Draft 2

The remaining errors in Paper 1, Draft 2 are in the following sentence: "I have pictures of my Boy Scout troops trip to Gatlinburg, Tennessee, my sixth grade class production of *You're a Good Man, Charlie Brown,* and my junior prom." Can you tell where to add the missing apostrophes? Notice that Justin punctuated the rest of the sentence well, using commas around a state address in the middle of a sentence, italicizing the name of a play, and using commas between each part of a series.

Example 3: Paper 5, Draft 1

In Paper 5, Draft 1, Justin again left out the apostrophe to show possession: "A fathers absence can even put a child at higher risk for accidents and injuries." How would you correct this sentence?

3. Use of Punctuation to End a Sentence

Some students do not always signal their readers with an appropriate punctuation mark to show that a complete thought, a sentence, is finished. When writers use a comma or no punctuation to separate two sentences, the error is called a comma splice or a run-on. Your instructor may use the abbreviations *cs* or *ro* to mark instances of such errors.

Justin had several comma splices and run-ons that he needed to edit. He could consider using periods, semicolons, or colons.

Example 1: Paper 1, Draft 2

"Stieglitz also talked about his own photographs within each picture was an item that called for a certain kind of frame around it."

> Period: "Stieglitz also talked about his own photographs. Within each picture was an item that called for a certain kind of frame around it."

Notice that using a period separates the two main ideas properly but does not help the reader understand the relationship of the two ideas.

> Semicolon: "Stieglitz also talked about his own photographs; within each picture was an item that called for a certain kind of frame around it."

Although this alternative is grammatically correct because a semicolon can separate two independent clauses, the semicolon indicates that the clauses are related but does not show in what way they are related.

> Colon: "Stieglitz also talked about his own photographs: within each picture was an item that called for a certain kind of frame around it."

Because a colon after an independent clause signals that the following independent clause explains the first one, the reader of this sentence knows that the clause about the frame is what Stieglitz said about his photographs. The choice of the colon, then, might be the most effective in correcting this sentence.

Example 2: Paper 3, Draft 1

"Gender was mixed, race or obvious cultural background was not usually."

> Period: "Gender was mixed. Race or obvious cultural background was not usually."
>
> Semicolon: "Gender was mixed; race or obvious cultural background was not usually."
>
> Colon: "Gender was mixed: race or obvious cultural background was not usually."

Notice that the period again makes for a correct sentence but does not aid in understanding the relationship of the ideas. The colon, which signals an expansion or focusing of the first clause, is in this case misleading because the second clause is parallel in meaning to the first. The semicolon is, then, probably the best choice because it separates two equally important ideas. The ellipsis, or omission, of *mixed* at the end of the second clause, in fact, shows the intimate relationship of the ideas and the parallel construction of the clauses.

If you want to know more about comma splices or run-on sentences, or if these explanations generated more questions for you about ways to correct comma splices or run-ons, check your handbook or ask a peer tutor or instructor. Before you seek help, identify in your own writing instances of these errors so that you can use your time well in correcting comma splices and run-ons.

Usage

I have a friend who gets really annoyed when she hears a speaker say, "I'm going to lay down for awhile." *Lie* is the appropriate verb for this sentence because *to lie* means to recline or rest. The statement would reflect correct usage if the speaker said, "I'm going to lie down for a while."

Other writers interchange words that actually have different meanings. When a writer claims that a person can be a fair judge in a dispute because the person is uninterested, the writer really means that the person is disinterested, or impartial. *Uninterested* means indifferent or not interested.

Do you know the difference between *farther* and *further*? *Farther* means a greater distance, while *further* means more or to promote. Yet we often read sentences like "We drove further along the road in hopes of finding the motel" or "John is further along in his reading of the novel than I am."

Precise language furthers precise communication. Although some students are convinced that remembering the difference between *credible* and *credulous, council* and *counsel,* and *principle* and *principal* is primarily important for scoring well on tests, choosing the appropriate word contributes to exactness of meaning.

Justin discovered three patterns of usage errors in his drafts. All three types of errors had been noticed by his teacher and by at least some of his peers.

1. Use of the Imprecise Word *Thing*

Justin used the words *thing* and *something* when he could have used more precise language.

Example 1: Paper 1, Draft 1

In Paper 1, Draft 1, Justin wrote in his first paragraph, "I've been avoiding a wreck, using language like Rich but other things, too. Now, however, I'm ready to move toward something, hopefully through my college education." By Paper 1, Draft 2, Justin had replaced *things* and *something* with specifics: "I've been avoiding a wreck, using language like Rich and also pictures and sounds. Now, however, I'm ready to move toward a new stage in my life, hopefully through my college education."

Example 2: Paper 4, Draft 1

Justin reverted to the nonspecific variations of *thing,* however, in Paper 4, Draft 1. Concluding a paragraph on his first travels away from home, Justin wrote, "That great feeling of doing something different and of being on my own is one that I associate with travel even today." Later in the paper he wrote, "One time our neighbor took my family to a travelogue on Greece the slides of the Acropolis touched something in me that connected me with the distant past in a way I can't explain." Although Justin has decided not to include Paper 4 in his Course Portfolio, he wanted to revise parts of the paper for precision: in his journal he decided to use "being in a different place and engaging in new activities" for "doing something different" and "touched a sensibility in me" for "touched something in me." Remembering what he had learned about run-on sentences, he also completed one sentence with *Greece* and began another sentence with *The slides.*

2. Use of *Affect* and *Effect*

Justin is consistent in his misuse of these two terms. In fact, he is fortunate that he has a pattern of error with these words because he can learn or relearn their definitions and correct his misuse. Or, if he simply has difficulty remembering the distinction, he can do a special readthrough of each of his papers looking for instances of the use of either word and checking that he has used the appropriate selection.

Example 1: Paper 5, Draft 1

As you read Justin's work, you probably noticed his multiple incorrect uses of *affect* and *effect*. For example, in Paper 5, Draft 1, he wrote, "Maybe we should look as well at the affect this situation has on the fathers" and " . . . the answer to the question about the affect of absentee fathers is that their absence has an affect on every member of the family." Because the verb *affect* means to influence and the word *effect* means accomplish as a verb and result as a noun, Justin needs to substitute *effect* for *affect* in these sentences.

They read properly when written, "Maybe we should look as well at the effect this situation has on the fathers" and " . . . the answer to the question about the effect of absentee fathers is that their absence has an effect on every member of the family." Because the second sentence is repetitive, Justin might want to make it more concise by writing "Because absentee fathers affect every member of the family, absentee fathers are a significant problem."

3. Use of *Lots* and *a Lot*

When writers want to indicate large numbers, they sometimes rely on vague terms like *lots* and *a lot*. Justin has adopted this fuzzy language in at least three of his drafts.

Example 1: Paper 3, Draft 1

In Paper 3, Draft 1, he writes: "When mother was in London, she was surprised to find lots of Indian curry restaurants and lots of Jamaicans as well. Those cultures are very different from the English and she said they add a lot to the atmosphere of London."

How would you advise Justin to edit his language? Here is one possibility: "When mother was in London, she was surprised by the large numbers of Indian curry restaurants and Jamaican people. The Indian and Jamaican cultures, so different from the English, added significantly to the atmosphere of London." What are some other alternatives?

Example 2: Paper 3, Draft 2

In Paper 3, Draft 2, Justin writes, "We have spent lots of time together and I have learned a lot about their backgrounds from our friendships." In addition to inserting a comma before *and* because it links two independent clauses, Justin needs to consider how to be more precise and, thereby, provide more information for the reader. How much time have the friends spent together and how much has Justin learned about their backgrounds? In a revision Justin might write, "While we spend some of each day and at least one evening a week together, I have learned about their family cultures and their cultural heritages." How else can this be revised?

Style

You probably vary your style of dress depending on the occasion. You wouldn't wear tattered jeans to a formal wedding, a dress suit on a picnic, or pajamas to class. Style applies to writing, too. Sometimes formal diction is appropriate; at other times slang is fine. Sometimes long sentences are understandable; other times short sentences are clearer. At all times, however, you try as a writer to be rhetorically sound, a term that means writing in ways suitable to the purpose, occasion, and audience.

Justin wrote for his peers as he prepared papers for a Course Portfolio that would show his best work. He wanted to provide sufficient evidence, to write clearly, and to persuade his readers about his conclusions. His peers had marked on his papers places where they were confused by his writing. Upon examination, Justin discovered two stylistic matters that he could address to eliminate their confusion.

1. Use of Sentence Variety

Choices about sentence length and kind are dependent on purpose and context. For example, if a writer wishes to show that one idea is not as important as another, she can put that idea in a dependent clause. Or, if a writer wants to emphasize a point, she might put it in a short sentence that follows three or four long sentences. Writers manipulate sentence type and length in order to serve their purposes.

With help from his instructor, Justin saw in three of his drafts that he could combine sentences to show the relationships among ideas.

Example 1: Paper 2, Draft 2

Justin argues that because diversity enriches our lives, cultures should keep this distinctiveness. In Paper 2, Draft 2, he writes, "When I was in high school, my two best friends were Rajesh and an African American guy named Darnell. I learned about sweet potato pie, about Hindu religious customs, about saris, and heard stories about Darnell's slave ancestors." Notice that the main idea in these sentences for the argument that Justin is making is the variety of knowledge

Justin gained from his friends. If Justin subordinates the less important information in the first sentence within the second sentence, he serves the purpose of his argument: "From Rajesh, an Indian, and Darnell, an African American, who were my best friends in high school, I learned about Hindu religious customs, saris, sweet potato pie, and the history of slaves." Justin's expanded knowledge becomes the focus of the new sentence.

Example 2: Paper 1, Draft 2

In Paper 1, Draft 2, Justin writes about photography as a way of understanding the world. He explains, "In third grade the Polaroid Company sponsored a contest in which I won a free camera. I took pictures of my house, my neighborhood, my mom, my sister, and events in our family." The first sentence focuses on the company's sponsorship of a contest, even though Justin's use of the prize is the important idea for his establishment of photography as one of his developing literacies. A revision would focus his lens on his main point: "With a Polaroid camera that I won in a third-grade class, I took pictures of my house, my neighborhood, my mom, my sister, and events in our family."

Example 3: Paper 4, Draft 1

Justin's instructor noted that Justin had used sentence length in an effective way in the second paragraph of Paper 4, Draft 1. In this paragraph Justin explains a psychological dimension of his first overnight away from home alone. He explains, "I remember the scary feeling of being alone but also the exciting feeling of not quite knowing what went on in this new house: just things like locating the bathroom at night, eating different foods at a table where they said grace and talked about politics at dinner, and having a dad who played pool with us were novel. I felt pretty independent." The lengthy first sentence establishes the details of the new environment; the second sentence states succinctly the psychological consequence of that environment, the more important idea for this paragraph. The short length of the second sentence pinpoints our attention on its meaning.

2. Use of Unnecessary Words

Verbose and *wordy* are words that might appear in the margins of your papers if you have not trimmed the fat off your meaty sentences. Because initial drafts reflect early thoughts about a topic, they may contain more words than you need when you reconsider what you want to say.

Example 1: Paper 2, Draft 2

In Paper 2, Draft 2, Justin wrote, "We are in the midst of arguments about such things as affirmative action, and new arguments about busing in some parts of the country." Because Justin wants to emphasize that "We are in the midst of arguments about affirmative action and busing," he can cut unnecessary words.

Sometimes a word is redundant, which means unnecessarily repetitious. For example, you might read "Patricia is a slim, slender woman." Because the definitions of both adjectives are so similar, the writer can choose either *slim* or *slender* and get across the same meaning with fewer words.

Example 2: Paper 5, Draft 1

Justin uses unnecessary words in Paper 5, Draft 1 when he reports on a *Newsweek* article: "The article goes on to say that a 1993 *Atlantic Monthly* article says that kids raised without fathers are 'more likely to drop out of high school, to get pregnant as teenagers, to abuse drugs, and to be in trouble with the law.'" Do you have an editing suggestion for Justin? He might try, "Quoting a 1993 *Atlantic Monthly* article, *Newsweek* relates that children reared without fathers are 'more likely to drop out of high school, to get pregnant as teenagers, to abuse drugs, and to be in trouble with the law.'"

Example 3: Paper 2, Draft 2

Sometimes sentences go on and on. Consider this sentence from Paper 2, Draft 2: "All the African names that people use now, and the lawsuits that Native Americans have started over land and artifacts that belong to them and are important to their religion show that people value their different backgrounds just like many of us enjoy them too." Notice first that Justin is ethnocentric in identifying a homogenous audience of presumably Caucasian readers. In setting up an us-them situation, Justin reveals his own biases, a point that he would need to consider before editing this sentence further. That problem aside, Justin can cut unnecessary words in order to emphasize his meaning: "Increased use of African names and of legal actions to recover important religious artifacts and lands for Native Americans demonstrate how people value different backgrounds."

Example 4: Paper 5, Draft 1

In Paper 5, Draft 1, Justin reports about an article: "But it also says that more academic research is needed and says that lots of people grow up very successfully without their fathers." This wordy sentence can be improved in several possible ways, including the following:

> "Because many young people grow up successfully without their fathers, the article states that more academic research is needed."
>
> "More academic research might explain why many young people grow up successfully without their fathers."

"The article contends that successful development of young people without fathers could be explained by more academic research."

Which of these possibilities is better? Why? Try to think of other alternatives.

PRACTICE WITH IDENTIFYING PATTERNS OF ERROR

Although you will have different patterns of error in your drafts and papers, like Justin you can develop a process that enables you to identify your editing needs. You will want to develop your own process for identifying and tracking errors. As you develop your own process, try each of the following techniques to determine which works best for you.

1. In your journal, make a list of suggestions and markings by your instructor, your peers, and yourself on drafts or in responses to Writer's Statements.
   a. You can create columns such as these.

      Kind of Error   Example of Error   Corrected Example

      If you leave space after identifying each kind of error, you can add multiple instances under the example column so that you begin to recognize the pattern. Including the corrected example supplies you with different ways to correct the same error or reinforcement of the appropriate single way to correct an error.

Kind of Error	*Example of Error*	*Corrected Example*
Run-on sentence	Jonathan missed his train he was so angry!	Jonathan was so angry because he missed his train.
	The last time she was late this time she was even early.	Although she was late last time, she was early this time.
	The general admonished the troops the technique worked to motivate them.	The general's admonition motivated the troops.
No quotation marks around direct quotation	Sit commanded the puppy's owner.	"Sit!" commanded the puppy's owner.
	Lionel Kingston stated evidence indicates that the medicine is toxic.	Lionel Kingston stated, "Evidence indicates that the medicine is toxic."

b. Another technique is to keep a list of the kind of error with references to the placement of the error and its correction.

Kind of Error	*Location of Error*	*Location of Correction*
Dangling modifier	Paper 2, Draft 1, p. 2	Paper 2, Draft 2, p. 3
	Paper 4, Draft 2, p. 1	Paper 4, Draft 3, p. 1

c. A third alternative is to list the kinds of errors in your dialogue journal. Then you can identify by number on your drafts the same kind of error. For example, if your list reads like this one, you would put a number 1 beside each omission of an *s'* for possession of a plural noun in all your drafts. A number 3 would go beside slang terms, and so forth.

1. omission of *s'* for possessive of plural noun
2. sentence fragment
3. slang
4. comma between subject and verb
5. plural subject/singular verb

Each time you note a new error, you add it to your list. Each time you find the error repeated on drafts, you write the number on the draft so that you begin to see the pattern and to watch for the error.

d. You may devise another way of tracking your errors. Do you currently have a way of doing that tracking? Can you think of a way that makes sense for your writing process?

2. As you notice that you are making the same punctuation or grammar error again and again, you can consult your instructor, a peer, a Writing Center tutor, or a written or on-line handbook. For instance, you can ask your peer tutor in the Writing Center to place a checkmark at the end of any line of text that contains a compound sentence with no punctuation. The tutor will be helping you to locate the error, but you will be responsible for punctuating correctly, perhaps asking the tutor to confirm your correction.
3. Referring to the patterns of error listed in your dialogue journal, you can then remember to edit specifically for that error in future papers. As you learn to identify the error yourself, you can correct the problem quickly on your own and, gradually, eliminate that pattern from your writing.

IDENTIFYING RANDOM ERRORS

Sometimes, of course, writers make random errors: they know better but are rushed or less careful than usual. These errors need the same attention as more systematic errors, however, so that final papers follow conventions that make them easy to read.

Example 1: Paper 5, Draft 1

Justin's instructor, for example, circled a punctuation error in Paper 5, Draft 1. The sentence read, "An article called 'The Noncustodial Parent: Dilemmas and Interventions,' says that noncustodial parents experience 'feelings of loss, self-doubt, and ambivalence and a generally diminished sense of their importance as parents.'" Probably Justin put the comma after the article title because he thought he had written a nonessential appositive, a noun that renames a noun immediately before it. That sentence would have read "An article, 'The Noncustodial Parent: Dilemmas and Interventions,' says. . . ." But the present sentence has an incorrect comma between the subject and verb of the sentence, an easily corrected error. Justin simply can remove the comma.

Example 2: Paper 3, Draft 2

In Paper 3, Draft 2, Justin uses the first person but maintains an appropriate register of language. He uses a suitable formality of language for the purpose of the paper, except for one instance. A peer questioned Justin's use of the word *guy* in the second paragraph: "Darnell, an African American guy and Rajesh, whose family came here from India are both my friends." Justin realized that the colloquial designation for his friend didn't fit in this paper, so he eliminated it. Although Justin is usually attuned to levels of formality in language choice, talking about a close friend probably caused him to be inappropriately informal.

PRACTICE WITH LOCATING RANDOM ERRORS

1. Give yourself the gift of enough time to reread drafts several times so that you can correct careless errors that trouble readers. If possible, reread over several days or at least allow some time between each reading.
2. Ask another person to place a checkmark next to a line that contains any kind of error that can be corrected by editing. You can quickly fix typos, correct spelling mistakes, and add omitted words.
3. Develop a process for checking for the random errors that can mar your finished product.

YOUR TURN TO EDIT

Now you have the opportunity to edit those papers that you have revised for your Course Portfolio. This chapter has suggested methods of locating your common patterns of errors and of looking at typos, misspellings, and random errors that your instructor, peers, tutors, or you caught in your earlier drafts. Now you need to apply your editing skills to your own drafts.

1. After you have read a paper several times, finding errors sometimes becomes difficult because of your familiarity with the text. Try a technique that enables you to focus on the sentence and word level so that you can find any last mistakes. Try reading your paper backward, sentence by sentence. In this search you are not reading for comprehension but for the kind of omissions and errors that you might not catch as you read through familiar material.
2. Another technique at this late stage in the editing process is asking a reader to do a reconnaissance mission to locate mistakes. This reader should not suggest changes that qualify as revisions, such as reordering points, including more evidence, or rewriting your conclusion. All you want at this stage is help with pinpointing the type of grammar, punctuation, usage, and stylistic matters that can be improved through editing.
3. Many computer programs used in composition classes have editing components that can indicate suggestions for change. Be sure, however, that you consider the suggestions only in the context of your own paper. For example, some grammar-check programs caution about lengthy sentences, without, of course, knowing the reasons for your choice of length. Although editing programs can call your attention to possible areas of concern, use your own knowledge and judgment about computer help, just as you do with help from your instructor, peers, and other human readers.
4. For each of the papers that you have revised for the Course Portfolio, do a thorough editing. This last step enables you to offer polished, professional work to your readers.

A student told me recently that he didn't have to worry about editing because what he said, not how he said it, was more important. In one sense he is right: meaning is paramount. Yet meaning is created through language choice, sentence construction, and punctuation markers. Correct surface appearance signals ability, care, and respect for readers from which readers can infer much about the writer's care with organization, evidence, and reasoning. Attention to grammar, punctuation, usage, and style indicates a high regard for the substance and importance of the paper.

WORKING PORTFOLIO UPDATE

The readers of your Course Portfolio expect the best that you can offer in your written work. By conscientious and careful editing, you are ready to present your best ideas in their most effective form. As soon as you have edited your revised Course Portfolio entries, you can assemble your Course Portfolio and write your portfolio introduction. Chapter 13 suggests ways to construct and interpret your Course Portfolio so that readers can appreciate what you have accomplished and how you are looking to the future.

CHAPTER 13 Completing Your Course Portfolio

Graduation signals an important point in an education: it signifies that a person has arrived at a certain mark on the continuum of learning. Reaching a mark means completion of one set of goals. In another sense, however, it points forward toward other learning goals. Graduation from school, the ending of one set of goals, is also called commencement, the beginning of the next set of goals and accomplishments. The term *lifelong learning* implies that we all will be graduating and commencing throughout our lifetimes.

As you anticipate the completion of your Course Portfolio for this class, you will reach one mark, one level of accomplishment in your writing. You will receive credit for this class as an indication of your accomplishment. You will have the opportunity to measure your progress toward the goals set for your class and the goals that you set for yourself early in the course. You will graduate from those goals into the next set of goals that you select for your writing.

Your Course Portfolio becomes the site of your accomplishment and the site for launching your next steps as a writer. This chapter presumes that you will continue to write throughout your time at college, that you will write in any job that you have, and that you will use writing in your life in many ways. Your school may acknowledge the centrality of writing by requiring a portfolio to document your learning in general education or in your major. You, however, are the person who must decide the various ways in which you intend to develop your portfolio. This chapter makes some suggestions for developing your own portfolio to mark accomplishments in your lifelong learning.

DOCUMENTING YOUR LEARNING IN THIS COURSE

As you have developed your writing process and created written products, you have generated and received many kinds of written documents: dialogue journal entries, heuristics, proposals, drafts, Writer's Statements, responses to Writer's Statements, e-mail responses to drafts, responses to finished products, and revisions. All this material traces the evolution of your choices as you have written. With this material as evidence, you are ready to affirm what you have accomplished during this term. You are ready to assess for yourself and others the progress you have made toward goals, in other words, your graduation from this class. But you are also ready to determine your next set of goals, the commencement of your writing future. Where do you go next based on what you have accomplished?

Collecting Your Materials

You need to have at hand all the sources of evidence that you may want to include in your Course Portfolio. All term you have been saving the journal entries, written responses to drafts, and other documents that contributed to your papers. Bringing those together is important so that you can see and reread all the material that has emerged during your thinking and writing. Although your instructor may limit what you can include or you may decide to include only your best work in your portfolio, rereading your entire body of writing enables you to develop the points about your writing that you want to make in your portfolio introduction.

You may also want to bring together other writing that you have done at home, in other classes, or on your job. One learning outcome from a class should be that you can apply what you have learned in other contexts. If your personal journal entries have developed from diarylike summaries of the day to reflective pieces on significant events in your life, you may claim progress toward the goal of analysis. If for the first time you received a high mark on a biology lab report, you may attribute part of your success to newly developed organizational skills. If your patient reports at the nursing home have become more understandable, you may claim progress toward clarity in your writing. Your instructor may want you to include only class-generated writing; but if you have an option, you may want to use writing external to the class to develop your self-assessment.

Some students include in their portfolios writing done prior to the class in order to show progress. A report from high school that relied almost exclusively on the ideas of others might contrast well with a paper from your current course that used sources as evidence for your own ideas. A previously written persuasive memo critiqued by your supervisor as rambling may be very different from a position paper praised by your peers and instructor as well focused. Again, the contents of your portfolio may be prescribed by departmental policy or other constraints; if not, you demonstrate ingenuity by using evidence that shows applied learning.

Mining Your Materials

Now that you have all your materials, how can you use them in making choices about the contents of your Course Portfolio? How can they help shape the portfolio essay or letter that introduces the Course Portfolio to your readers? Three steps enable you to use your materials well: (1) make notes as you reread your materials, (2) confer with your classmates, and (3) decide what you want to show through your Course Portfolio about yourself as a writer.

1. Make notes as you reread your materials.

In responses to your writing, do you note recurring comments? Do the comments change over the term? For example, do readers often praise your precise word choice? Do questions about reasons for ordering of your main points change to acknowledgment of clear organization?

Do you notice change in your writing process? In your dialogue journal, do you notice a record of less procrastination before starting a draft, a sense of continued frustration with writing introductions, or a use of more revision strategies over the course of the term?

What do you notice about topic selection? About the length of your responses to the writing of others? About the variety of resources that you used in research work? About the kinds of dialogue journal entries that you made?

At this stage you are conducting research, research into your own materials. Sometimes during research writers have a hypothesis, a tentative idea that they are confirming or refuting during the research process. You may think that you have improved in focusing your writing; yet, in rereading written responses from peers and instructor, you find that from the first to last papers they consistently critique the lack of focus in your writing. You would, therefore, refute your hypothesis about focus.

On the other hand, you may scan your materials with few preconceived notions. You are inquisitive about your own dialogue journal entries: do they show you probing topics, complaining about the workload in writing class, or describing how your peer group worked? Such questions will help you assess how you use your dialogue journal and how it did or did not contribute to the evolution of your papers.

As you review your work, identify the most important points that you see in it. Beside each point list the documents that provide evidence of that point. For example, you might identify "can now get into a topic more quickly." Then you might list an early dialogue journal entry (in which you talked about being blocked when starting Paper 1), a cubing exercise for Paper 2 (in which you discovered the approach you took toward your subject for that paper), an e-mail message from a fellow student (in which she gave you information you requested for Paper 3), and your instructor's response to Paper 4 (in which he praised your multiple drafts that showed significant revising, noting that your quick start on the paper enabled you to have time to revise). Simply asserting something about your accomplishment in your writing is not enough: you will want to have evidence to support your claim about your writing.

2. Confer with your classmates.

Trade your written documents with a peer. Then identify the main features of this person as a writer and her writing based on these materials. You do not need to read everything minutely to be able to help your classmate see distinctive features. If you have read some of this student's work during the semester, you will already have some familiarity with it. If you have not, you provide a fresh eye able to see, perhaps, something that the author might have overlooked about herself.

This exercise can be helpful to the author, but it can also be fun and helpful for you. It is enjoyable to see the fruits of the labors of other writers. And you may learn how to mine your own materials better by noticing what catches your attention in the work of your peer. For example, do you notice that the writer consistently talks with friends about a paper that she is writing? What do you do to stimulate your thinking? Are there effective techniques that you use to prime the pump? How do those practices show up in your materials?

Make a list for your peer of the features that you notice and refer to the written documents that caused you to identify each feature. You may do this exercise in class, or you may want to give yourself more time by meeting outside of class.

3. Decide what you want to show through your Course Portfolio about yourself as a writer.

You may have stipulated aspects of your writing that your instructor wants you to demonstrate in your Course Portfolio, so you will look for those aspects. You may be expected to show skill in focus, organization, development, and editing, for example, so you will look for evidence of those skills.

You may, on the other hand, be asked to provide your best work. In this case, you must develop criteria on which to base your evaluation. For example, if one criterion for a skilled writer is the ability to write in numerous genres, you may want to claim that ability by including in your portfolio a narrative, a critical analysis, a research report, a poem, and an essay. Another skill may be ability to provide useful response to another writer. Responses to peers with their identification of specific ways they used your advice would be evidence here.

Justin's class, for example, has seven criteria that it developed based on departmental goals and class objectives. Justin will be assessing his own writing based on these criteria: (1) knowledge and use of a repertoire of ways to generate ideas, (2) ability to use and synthesize various media sources for writing, (3) knowledge and use of a repertoire of revising strategies, (4) ability to reflect on, analyze, and evaluate own writing, (5) willingness to give and to receive constructive comments, (6) ability to understand and to use conventions of written discourse, and (7) ability to create a portfolio that represents self as writer and learner.

EVALUATING YOUR WORK

A prime feature of the Course Portfolio is the introduction in which you situate and evaluate your writing. Your Course Portfolio is not simply a collection of papers but a persuasive exhibit whose contents demonstrate what you contend in your introduction.

1. Write an introduction for your course portfolio.

This introduction to your work serves as a guide for approaching all the materials in your Course Portfolio. In the introduction you make claims about yourself as a writer and invite readers to explore the written documents that enable you to make those claims. Because most of us are not accustomed to self-assessment, this introduction may take several revisions, just like other papers. You will want peer review and instructor response, if possible, before you place this important document in your Course Portfolio. Later in this chapter you will read some portfolio letters, one form of portfolio introduction, and parts of portfolio letters written by other students as they presented their work to readers of their portfolios.

2. Read drafts of portfolio introductions of classmates.

You can learn from the ways in which peers evaluate their own work. Observe the way that the writer organizes the main points of his introduction, the amount and kinds of evidence, and the tone of the introduction.

You may want to exchange drafts in class. Readers can respond with suggestions or comments about the introduction, perhaps responding to a Writer's

Statement by the author. Are you persuaded by the claim and the evidence? What additional evidence would be necessary for you to agree with a certain claim? Can you help the writer find the evidence within the portfolio materials?

PRESENTING YOUR WORK

At a fancy restaurant you might hear a customer exclaim, "Oh, what a lovely presentation!" Because the customer reacts positively to the way the food is arranged on the plate, she is predisposed to find the food delicious. Although presentation does not substitute for substance, it can provide both ease and satisfaction in approaching the substance.

1. Organize your materials so that they are easily accessible to readers.

Many writers include a table of contents and use tabs to mark the sections of their Course Portfolios. If your portfolio is on-line, you will want to make each section easily accessible. Some readers, like your instructor, may read all of your portfolio. Other readers, like some of your peers, may read only parts, so you need to cater to the needs of each kind of reader, perhaps using summary comments about each paper and its preliminary writing or including only the papers in your portfolio with the preliminary writing and drafts in an appendix.

2. Present the materials neatly.

Because initial impression is so important, your Course Portfolio should be professionally presented. Some writers include only clean copies of their papers, with no instructor comments. Some writers place papers in plastic sleeves, whereas others simply place materials neatly sequenced in a notebook. Although aesthetic considerations may seem unimportant to you, notice how much more positive you feel about a neatly typed paper than one handwritten in pencil, even if the quality of writing in the latter surpasses the former.

PREPARING YOUR PORTFOLIO INTRODUCTION

Your portfolio introduction may be a letter, an essay, or another form stipulated by your teacher or chosen by you. Whatever the form, the introduction allows you to contextualize your body of work and to persuade your readers of your accomplishments. Your introduction should match the format, tone, purpose, and length defined by your instructor or your class. Often portfolio introductions are addressed to the instructor and class as primary readers, but you may have a secondary reader if, for instance, you take this Course Portfolio to your next composition course. You must decide if the introduction will be a letter or an essay, if it will be informal or formal, if it is a description of your work or a persuasive piece, and if it will be a brief survey or a more detailed analysis. As you write your introduction, consider the examples from this chapter for hints about approaches that you may want to take.

Jack prepared a Course Portfolio in his composition class in order to have a record of his work for the term, to assess the progress of his work, and to be evaluated for the course. In his class the portfolio introduction was in the form of a letter to the readers of the portfolio.

Jack's Portfolio Letter

Dear Reader,

This portfolio letter serves as an attempt to evaluate myself as a writer. Comparisons, as the Buddhists believe, are odious, so I won't compare myself to professional writers. I will say that I have been influenced by the beat authors, and I admire their ability to write beautifully without revision. I wanted to do the same, but I found out quickly that I don't think fluidly enough to be a beat writer. Learning this lesson was a major step forward during the semester; I am more comfortable with the need to revise my work to get a presentable piece. I learned a great deal more in this class: how to give and receive criticism without falling apart, how to be more receptive and open to people, and how to define an essay. I was able to find interesting topics, also.

When I came to the class, I thought that writing was going to be easy; I knew drafts weren't necessary if I could think in finished product form. When I turned in my first essay, my instructor showed me a number of ways to improve it. I started revising my paper immediately, but each time that I finished, I found more improvements to make. Writing was suddenly difficult instead of being the breeze that I had forecasted.

Revising has been a chore throughout the course, even to the last piece of writing that I am turning in. I was going over a draft of this letter with

Charlotte, and she said that I could do better by exchanging obscure references with more familiar ones. Specifically, she thought that I should change from the word *Zendo* to *Buddhist* and explain what the beat philosophy means. I received both bits of advice without feeling defensive and even decided that they would make my paper stronger. This willingness to listen to criticism is a change in attitude from as late as March 2, when I said in my dialogue journal that I didn't like other people wanting to change my work. I have been able to accept advice from much of the class; a look behind the finished papers will show entire pages influenced by Melanie, Wendie, and Donna.

Along with their helpful criticisms, my classmates have helped me be a more open person. I am very private by nature and have only recently become aware of the fact that I can never be a published writer if most people don't like what I write about. By pushing myself to be outward with some of our classmates, I have realized one of my personal goals for this class, the one about becoming comfortable with personal interaction, and I also found out what topics could interest some people. Charlotte and Jacqueline have both said that I am more open in class and willing to help with computer problems when asked. Carolyn, Charlotte, Amy, and Tamara all thought that I came up with some interesting topics to explore. They liked mountain climbing, Indian affairs, guitars, building houses out of tires, and beat generation literature. I wasn't able to develop all of these topics because of time constraints, but I do feel good knowing that I have thoughts inside that other people would like to read about.

As I wrap up this biased letter, I must say that everything didn't come up roses: I have been introduced to a whole new grammar, which can only mean that I didn't pay attention in high school. This new attention to detail has been a real thorn in my pride because I haven't even begun to master it. Another problem has been the new genre of the essay. Before hearing Scott Russell Sanders's explanation, I thought that an essay was a type of question asked on a history test; but with the constant exposure I've had all semester, I have grown to admire the skill it takes to be an

```
effective essayist. Becoming one will be my main goal
as I move on to the next English class.

                           Sincerely,

                           Jack
```

Notice that Jack identifies three areas of accomplishment demonstrated in his portfolio. In the last two sentences of the first paragraph, he speaks about revision, receptiveness, and genre definition, adding the point about topics that he later merges with receptiveness. He supports his point about revision by describing his previous attitude based on his admiration of beat writers, by identifying his first personal awareness with Paper 1 that revision is continuous, and by detailing a specific instance of revision of his letter. Jack supports his progress in receiving criticism by contrasting a specific dialogue journal entry, in which he resisted peer suggestion, to evidence from classmates later about his helpfulness to them and about his interesting topic selection. Although he identifies the essay genre as difficult because it is new to him, he expresses an admiration for the skill involved in essay writing, a recognition that implies that Jack knows the characteristics of effective essays.

Although Jack could have usefully drawn on more evidence from his papers, such as pointing to the topics he did develop, his choice of evidence from the remarks of peers is consonant with the main points he is making about openness to the need to revise and to rely on the responses of readers. His point about being open to other people is placed effectively in the context of the way that increased receptivity benefits his writing, the point of the composition course.

Using the metaphor of the rose and thorn, Jack admits that he has more growing to do as a writer. Yet he places remaining problems in the context of the future, indicating that he has already set a main goal for his next English class. When I evaluated Jack's work for the semester, I added to the information from his portfolio letter a statement that Jack made in his retrospection, an overview that each student wrote on the last day of class after the Course Portfolio had been submitted. Jack wrote, "I have a thousand other topics in my head that need to be developed. I can see how a professional essayist might have started his collection of essays for publication, because my portfolio already has four essays in it. These essays aren't publication quality, but they do serve as symbols of what the future might hold." Notice that Jack has progressed even from writing the portfolio letter to the last day of writing in class: he now feels comfortable indirectly comparing his essays to those of a published essayist and not only foresees developing his skill as an essayist, as he had in his portfolio letter, but implies that he, too, may one day publish a collection of essays.

The tone of Jack's portfolio letter is casual. He is openly conversational, another evidence of his newly developed ease in talking with others about his writing. Although some circumstances might demand a more formal tone, Jack's choice is appropriate for his task. Because the genre for the portfolio introduction was a letter, he could use the genre to his advantage in demonstrating his ease in discussing both positives and negatives about his status as a writer at the end of the term.

Portions of Portfolio Letters

When you make claims about your writing process or products in your Course Portfolio, you must provide evidence that supports your claims. As you examine paragraphs from portfolio introductions by students in composition classes like your own, ask the question, "Has the writer provided sufficient evidence that he has the attribute claimed, has made progress toward the stated goal, or has reached a declared objective?" Although you could read the papers cited, were you examining the entire portfolio, each part of the portfolio letter or essay should make its point persuasively.

Example 1

"This portfolio contains several very good examples of my capabilities as a writer. The two papers in which I examined poems by Wole Soyinka nicely illustrate my ability to analyze other people's work. My Literacy Autobiography, as well as my dialogue journal entries, show me writing on a very personal level—a level that is a departure from the more removed style that I generally tend to utilize. The piece on *The Scarlet Letter,* though difficult to write, demonstrates my willingness as a writer to observe literature through different lenses of perspective."

Without a list of class or personal goals, we can surmise from this paragraph that this student wants to make claims about ability to analyze written texts in different ways and to write in a personal style. Although the writer helpfully refers to specific pieces in the portfolio, he does not, however, cue readers specifically about his abilities. For example, what aspects of the two analyses of poetry "nicely illustrate" his ability? Does he use critical language well? Does he unpack complicated poetic structure? Does he recognize literary allusions that reveal meaning in the poems? Also, what marks his autobiography and dialogue journal entries, presumably personal writing for most writers, as "very personal"? Why is the personal rather than the "removed style" important to this course or to this writer? Finally, with the novel, what are the different perspectives used? What does the use of multiple perspectives have to do with the writer's accomplishments in the course?

Notice how each of the following alternatives increases the concrete explanations that will be convincing to readers. (1) "My two analyses of Wole Soyinka's poems illustrate my ability to explain how metaphors function on at least two levels of meaning." (2) "I expanded my stylistic range by adding to my usual removed style some personal writing in my literacy autobiography and in my dialogue journal entries, particularly in the revelations about overcoming the fear of using myself as an example." (3) "My use of feminist and historical perspectives to analyze *The Scarlet Letter* demonstrates my ability to choose from among critical perspectives appropriate lenses for understanding the novel."

ANALYZING EXAMPLE 1

List other suggestions for the writer about how he could revise his paragraph.

Example 2

"Another goal was wanting to apply what I learned to other writing projects. There is no doubt I have been transferring things I've learned about the writing process and myself as a writer to other work. Two weeks ago I sent one proposal off for a Bible study that I'm doing with a co-author. As we tried to hammer out our sample lesson for this first attempt at a joint project, I could say, 'Wait a minute. What are we trying to do right now? Do we need the concept, the specific question, a certain word?' And it kept us far more on track than I have been in other collaborative projects in the past. We didn't kill each other or stop speaking! Then last week when I worked for fourteen hours a day, four days in a row on a paper with another co-author, it was inordinately helpful. In the past on this project, we had had difficulty explaining what we didn't like. Asking things now like, 'What do you hear me saying when you read that?' or stating, "When you say, 'Difficulty in planning,' I hear . . ." led us to change paragraphs and headings, or even to eliminate whole sections."

This writer states immediately that she wants to apply her learning in the writing classroom to other writing sites. She does not, however, state what it is that she is applying; after reading her two examples, a reader can infer that she has learned how to ask questions and make comments that evoke compatible, collaborative composing and revising. The reader, though, does the work in figuring out the point. Although the writer provides two instances and illustrative negotiating language used on those occasions, she could make her case more clearly by generalizing what new knowledge or strategies she is applying.

ANALYZING EXAMPLE 2

What suggestions would you make to this writer about her portfolio letter paragraph? Could she eliminate some unnecessary words while adding more specific cues about what readers should make of her examples?

Example 3

"In Papers 1, 4, and 5, I demonstrate that I can use evidence to prove a point. In Paper 1, I use evidence from my own experience and from two books; in Paper 4, from a film and from two interviews; and in Paper 5, from my own experience, from four magazine articles, and from a television show. One of our class goals was to broaden our base of information sources: I've done that."

The initial sentence in this paragraph promises that the writer will show how he can use evidence effectively, yet the paragraph is about varieties rather than sufficiency of evidence. The last sentence, which identifies the class goal, is closer to helping readers understand why the writer surveys the various sources of evidence used in three of his papers. Does the writer want to contend that the evidence is well used, for example that the evidence from a film and two interviews in Paper 4 was appropriate and sufficient to make his points in the paper? If so, he needs to refer specifically to the paper's main point and the reasons for the suitability and power of the evidence.

ANALYZING EXAMPLE 3

What questions would you ask this writer if you were responding to this paragraph of his portfolio essay?

Example 4

"I've become a better writer in this course: I have learned that brainstorming and cubing help me get started on difficult writing assignments, I've started using e-mail to ask readers about my drafts, and I finally can keep focus in a piece of writing. Now I want to work on other areas: I need to make better choices about organization of my ideas depending on the purpose of my writing, and I have to learn the conventions of punctuation so I can edit better."

What is the main point of this paragraph? A portfolio letter or essay does look at accomplished as well as future objectives, yet by surveying both perspectives in one short paragraph, this writer forgoes specificity. In earlier sections of her essay, perhaps the writer had already referred to specific instances in which she had used brainstorming and cubing to generate ideas, e-mail for soliciting help, and revising to achieve focus. If she is moving here to a forward look, however, she can make clearer the reasons for her next objectives and the ways in which she will progress toward them.

A peer of this writer, who knew the writer's evolution from semester-long experience in the same writing group, wrote on a draft of this portfolio essay: "You could mention that in the past you always tended to use chronological order in your papers, no matter what the topic or purpose. This semester, however, you have revised ineffectively organized papers, using a comparison when you were arguing for childcare in the home rather than in a center and working from the least to most important point when you advocated better advising here on campus. You did get better with punctuation, but with organization and punctuation you still relied on all of us to help you. What are you going to do differently in the future?"

The writer of the portfolio essay might then mention future plans. She could note the introduction to nonfiction class in which she had enrolled the next semester in order to read more nonfiction and, thereby, have exposure to more possibilities for organizing ideas. She might mention that after discovering the Writing Center at the end of this semester, she planned on weekly visits with drafts the next semester, expressly to work on punctuation. She might talk about taking fewer classes in order to give herself enough time to compose and edit papers. In other words, if a writer chooses to mention future objectives, she needs to be specific about ways to make progress toward those objectives.

ANALYZING EXAMPLE 4

What suggestions would you give this writer to improve this paragraph from her portfolio letter?

The Course Portfolio letter or essay contributes to the integration of learning from a writing class: the writer benefits in becoming aware of his progress and future goals; the reader benefits in understanding the writer's self-assessment, accomplishments, and future plans.

JUSTIN'S PORTFOLIO INTRODUCTION

Justin's class wrote portfolio essays to introduce their Course Portfolios. Justin wrote a draft of the essay, a Writer's Statement, and, based on his instructor's response and his own ideas, a revision of the essay.

Justin's Portfolio Introduction, Draft 1

Learning from Myself

I used to get embarrassed when my Aunt Danielle would pat me on the head at our annual family reunion and say, "My, how you've grown!" Because she hadn't seen me in a year, my aunt was thinking about me as I was the year before. Because I looked at myself in the mirror every day, I saw the changes gradually and unconsciously. Sometimes it takes someone else or some special occasion to make a person stop and look at how he has grown. Putting together this Course Portfolio has caused me to conclude that I have grown as a writer during this past term but also that I have a way to go before I'm a mature writer.

One way that I've grown is in my willingness and ability to revise. In the past I felt virtuous if I corrected spelling errors, rewrote a sentence or two, and added an example to a paper. In this class, however, I learned the meaning of revision: sometimes revision requires major change. For example, it's really hard to throw out words and ideas that I've already written because I've often worked hard to come up with those words and ideas. Beginning with Paper 1, my literacy autobiography, though, I have done major revision. I began with information about my dad and about my resentment of his leaving our family. I wrote about why he left and its effect on me. When a reader pointed out that I was writing more about my dad than about myself, I really did make a significant change to talk more about my own development. Another example is Paper 2 where I realized that I had to get other people's ideas to add to my own. In Paper 5 I reorganized my ideas to feature the ways that my research supported my own ideas. In each of these revisions I listened to readers, something I hadn't done much of before.

The greatest benefit of revision is shown in my literacy autobiography. In my writing I've always had a problem with focus. I tend to write like I talk: when a subject comes to my mind, I talk about it even if it isn't connected to the previous conversation. In Paper 1, I revised to focus on myself, especially ways in which I am literate. I explained in some detail why photography and music are ways of expressing literacy. I came up with a focused paper that makes me proud.

A second criterion for our class is ability to use and synthesize various sources for writing. My writing shows improvement in this area when I interview my grandmother and use information from that interview. In the second and third paragraphs of Paper 5 I refer to or quote three sources which are all used to support a point I am making. In that same paper I rely on one substantive source, an article in *The Atlantic Monthly,* but it is the definitive article on my topic. I summarize sometimes and quote only when the author says something particularly well. In my paper on racial groups I integrate my personal experience with my observations to make my point about the need for more research.

I, too, need more work with research, though. My instructor and members of my class pointed out to me that I didn't use the information from my observation as fully as I could, but I am still unsure how to draw conclusions from my own observations. Although I did reading for most of my papers, I don't have a method for taking notes, so I'm sure that I don't use my sources as well as I could. Next semester I am taking another composition class that teaches research methods, so I will improve. Specifically, I want to learn what to do when my sources disagree and how to organize a sociology paper, if I end up majoring in that. They say that the more you learn, the more you know what you don't know. That statement applies to me and research, so although I've made progress this semester, I know that I have much more to learn.

A third area in which I've made improvement this semester concerns a third criterion, ability to understand and use conventions of written discourse. I used to get irritated when anyone commented on my choice of words or use of punctuation. This semester, especially in trying to read the work of other writers in my class, I realize how important editing is. In Dennis's dialogue journal, I've written on four different days that he needs to pay attention to typos because I had trouble even reading his drafts. My teacher helped me by showing me how to find patterns of error. In my case, for example, I omitted the comma after an introductory adverbial clause. In the past I would have dismissed even knowing that language, but learning to identify this kind of clause helped me know much more easily how to punctuate. You will see that in every paper I have corrected punctuation in the final versions.

Lastly, this portfolio demonstrates my "ability to create a portfolio that represents self as writer and learner." You will be able to see in my portfolio that I have improved as a writer during this semester. For Paper 1, for example, I have included pieces of writing that were useful in the development of the paper, demonstrating that I have a process now for making a draft better. Although I have not included all the dialogue journal entries, reader responses, and other materials for the other papers, I have used a similar process for each paper. During this semester I have become less defensive about myself and my writing. Collaboration with people in my class and not getting grades on each paper have made me willing to share my writing and to revise. I see how I can use research to learn more about my own life, like understanding my father and his influence on me. College should give you more information to learn from so you can lead a better life. I understand my dad's decision, what I learned from my high school friends, and how I've developed as a literate person better from this class. I hope that you see that clearly in my portfolio.

I plan to add to this portfolio as I take more classes. My instructor mentioned that some colleges encourage students to make a hypertext portfolio so that they can use it for different purposes. I could see using my portfolio to apply for a job, but since I don't know what I want to be, I need to keep all possibilities open. For example, I want to put in some of my photography, which could be digitalized in a hypertext portfolio. I'll treat the end of each future class like my family reunion as an occasion to see how I've grown as a writer and learner. Starting this portfolio has given me the opportunity to begin this continuous process.

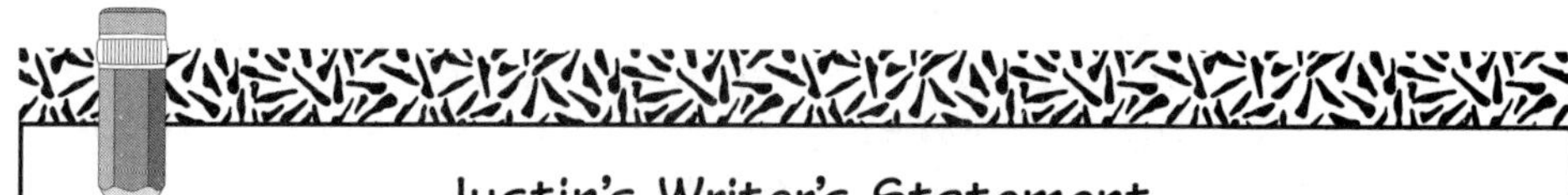

Justin's Writer's Statement for His Portfolio Essay

1. I don't directly quote from very many sources in this essay. I think that I may need to add some direct quotes, even if they seem to show small points. Where do I need to add?
2. I like the way that I started this essay with reference to my aunt's annual comment to me.
3. Do I have too much material about revision? I was able to think of more to write about for this section than the other sections. I'm not sure if I should cut this section or lengthen the others.
4. Do you have any other suggestions about how I can improve this essay?

Responses to Justin's Writer's Statement

Both his instructor and two of his classmates read Justin's draft of his introductory essay and wrote responses.

Instructor's Response

Reading your essay, I am struck by how clearly your voice comes through in those personal passages at which, as you point out, you excel. I am similarly pleased as a reader with the evidence of your progress in your thinking about and understanding of your own writing. Recognizing your penchant for the personal is a valuable insight, because if you aren't deliberate in your purpose, personal material can be a distraction. As you mention about Paper 1, you made that discovery more than once this semester. The issue of the personal has been present all semester and arises in this essay, too. This essay seems a bit informal, less a persuasive piece than a chronicle of your semester. As you revise, think of this piece as a way to convince readers of the success of your work. Muster the strongest evidence possible.

Use convincing evidence, as you do in the concrete support for your growing awareness of revision as a part of your writing process. Showcase that point and others by quoting directly from your papers. In answer to question 1 in your Writer's Statement, I'd suggest pointed direct quotes from a variety of sources, like your dialogue journal entries, your peers' responses to your writing, and early drafts of your papers. Remember our talks in class about levels of abstraction: the more concrete you are in supporting your generalizations about your writing, the more persuaded your readers will be.

Think also about balance. You address four criteria. Should you present roughly the same amount of material for each? And within each discussion consider balance as well. For instance, the development for the "conventions" criterion is lacking. Balance a generality such as "You will see that in every paper I have corrected punctuation in the final versions" with a specific example or two. It's your job to show readers those examples so that they won't have to go searching for them or so that they simply won't be convinced of your case.

Be sure that this last essay points clearly to the materials in the portfolio that can be used to make your case. I look forward to reading your Course Portfolio essay and contents.

Classmates' Responses

Justin's peers also responded to his questions. He learned from them that they wanted to hear more about all his papers, not just the ones in his portfolio: they liked hearing what he had learned from Paper 4 and wondered if he had drawn any conclusions from Paper 2. Their ideas corroborated his instructor's: they wished for more references to parts of his papers and to the dialogue journal entries in which they had participated. One classmate even remembered a comment she had made about Justin's improving punctuation that she thought would be good evidence in the conventions section of his essay.

After returning to his Working Portfolio, Justin identified some references to buttress the claims in his portfolio essay. He decided to keep the same introduction, organizational pattern, and major points but to add direct quotations, reposition his comments about personal experience in Papers 1 and 2, and keep alert to excessive informality. As he benefited from his instructor's and peers' comments, he realized also that his title was certainly erroneous. His revised essay is a strengthened argument.

Justin's Portfolio Essay

Watching Myself Grow

I used to get embarrassed when my Aunt Danielle would pat me on the head at our annual family reunion and say, "My, how you've grown!" Because she hadn't seen me in a year, my aunt was thinking about me as I was the year before. Because I looked at myself in the mirror every day, I saw the changes gradually and unconsciously. Sometimes it takes someone else or some special occasion to make a person stop and look at how he has grown. Putting together this Course Portfolio has caused me to conclude that I have grown as a writer during this past term but also that I have a way to go before I'm a mature writer.

One way that I've grown is in my willingness and ability to revise. In the past I felt virtuous if I corrected spelling errors, rewrote a sentence or two, and added a conclusion to a paper. In this class, however, I have learned the meaning of revision: sometimes revising requires major changes. For example, throwing out words and ideas that I have written is difficult because I have often worked hard to come up with those words and ideas. Finding more examples and doing deeper analysis are also added work.

Beginning with Paper 1, my literacy autobiography, though, I have done major revision. Draft 1 of that paper included extensive information about my father, my father's abandonment of our family, and the effect on me. When a reader pointed out that I was writing more about my dad than about myself, I shifted in a significant change to focus on my own development. For example, I omitted material about my father's background and added in the next draft analysis of ways that photography and music are elements of my developing literacy. Another example is Paper 2 in which I needed to incorporate the views of others with my own. Even in my Writer's Statement for Draft 1, I wrote, "I may have too much about my friends and not enough about the issue of assimilation and the 'elect.'" When my readers indicated that I needed more from the Reed essay, I returned to it for further analysis of Reed's perspectives. Third, in Paper 5 I reorganized my ideas to feature the ways that my research supported my own ideas. In Draft 2, I integrate the ideas of three conservative writers to explain the argument about the dire consequences of fatherlessness, and then I dissect the Whitehead article that summarizes the outcomes of children's lack of contact with fathers. Although I question that all children without fathers are doomed, I state that fathering is important. The authors I quote are shown to support my main contention in my essay.

Even when I did not revise for this class, I identified ways to revise in the future. For example, although I did not choose Paper 4 for my Course Portfolio, it is a good example of the personal essay because it uses original perspectives on the meaning of travel. I had set my purpose as convincing my mother about traveling to Europe, though, so I would have had to reorganize my ideas as evidence and use more sources for the assignment. Even though I did not have time to do this major revising this term, I like my ideas in the paper well enough to revise during another class or some other time.

A second criterion for our class is ability to use and synthesize various sources for writing. My writing shows improvement in this area when I interview my grandmother and use information from that interview. In Paper 1, Draft 2, I supported my contention about the influence of my mother's reading to me on my literacy by using my grandmother's recollection of seeing Mother read the newspaper to me when I was only one month old. After I read reader responses to Paper 2, Draft 1 and did a cubing, I was convinced that I could get more out of Ishmael Reed's article and could synthesize my own ideas more with his. In my final version of the essay, I use my personal examples to support the main point of Reed's with which I agree.

> But I think I agree with the main ideas that Reed is putting across, even though it may be selfish. He thinks that we need to maintain the diversity that comes in a city such as Detroit which has both mosques and a Hispanic population. For those of us who are mainstream American, there is a richness that comes with all those different cultures. When I was in high school, my two best friends were Rajesh, an Indian, and Darnell, an African American. From them I learned about sweet potato pie, about Hindu religious customs, about saris, and about slavery. It's hard to know what they got from me in that way. I would hate to see them and their families become just like everyone else.

In Paper 5 I also show my ability to synthesize sources. In the second and third paragraphs I refer to or quote three sources which are all used to support a point I am making. In that same paper I rely on one substantive source, the definitive article on my topic, from which I derive appropriate references from other published work. In my dialogue journal after I read *The Atlantic Monthly,* I wrote that I can rely on a reputable authority who does what my instructor calls a metastudy to get an overview of sources or I can read multiple sources myself and synthesize. In this case, after I synthesize my own reading, I rely on Whitehead's article for a comprehensive look at my topic.

Even though I show ability in research, I need more work. My instructor and members of my class pointed out that I did not use the information from my observation as fully as I could, but I am still unsure how to draw conclusions from my own observations. Although I did reading for most of my papers, I do not have a method for taking notes, so I am sure that I do not use my sources as well as I could. Next semester I am taking a composition class that teaches research methods, so I will improve. Specifically, I want to learn what to do when my sources disagree and how to organize a sociology paper because I may major in that discipline. The axiom that the more you learn, the more you know what you do not know applies to me and research.

I have progressed toward a third criterion for this class, the ability to understand and use conventions of written discourse. I used to get irritated when anyone commented on my use of punctuation or choice of words. This semester, especially in trying to read the papers of other writers in my class, I realize the importance of editing. In Dennis's dialogue journal, I wrote on four different days that he needed to pay attention to typos because I had had trouble even reading his drafts. My instructor helped me by showing me how to find patterns of error. In my case, for example, I omitted the comma after an introductory adverbial clause. In the past I would not have cared about knowing the definition of a clause, but learning to identify this kind of clause helped me know much more easily how to punctuate. Examples from final drafts of three different papers demonstrate how I now correctly punctuate introductory adverbial clauses: "When I was three, my dad left my mom, my sister, and me to try to find a better job" (Paper 1); "As we grew older, Darnell and I developed separate groups of friends that were not part of our friendship" (Paper 3); and "When my mom graduated from college and got an accounting job, she took a trip she had always wanted to, to London" (Paper 4).

In addition, I learned the advantage of precise words. I was persuaded from the essays and articles that the class read and from reactions of my readers that words like *a lot* and *things* can be replaced with words that tell the reader more. I have even become more conscious in my speaking of using exact words, like saying *articles* or *items* instead of *stuff* and *two, three,* or *four* instead of *several*. Some examples from my revised papers include *photography* and *music* instead of *other things* in Paper 1 and *affected* as a verb instead of *effected* in Paper 5. Here again, I can become even better if I record new vocabulary in my dialogue journal and watch my own essays and reports in the future for places to be precise.

Lastly, this Course Portfolio demonstrates my "ability to create a portfolio that represents self as writer and learner." You will be able to see in my portfolio that I have improved as a writer during this semester. In Paper 1, for example, I have included pieces of writing that were useful in the development of the paper, demonstrating that I have a process now for making a draft better. Although I have not included all the dialogue journal entries, reader responses, and other materials for the other papers, I have used a similar process for each paper. During this semester I have become less defensive about myself and my writing. When my classmate Alex read a draft of this essay, he wrote, "I remember when we read our first drafts. I thought, 'I don't want to read that dude's writing again. He doesn't like to hear about anything bad with his writing.' But, you're OK now. I can say what I actually think about your writing."

Collaboration with people in my class and not getting grades on each paper have made me willing to share my writing and to revise. I see how I can use research to learn more about my own life, like understanding my father and his influence on me. College should give you more information to learn from so you can lead a better life. I understand my dad's decision, what I learned from my high school friends, and how I've developed as a literate person better from this class. I hope that you see that clearly in my portfolio.

I plan to add to this portfolio as I take more classes. My instructor mentioned that some colleges encourage students to make a hypertext portfolio so that they can use it for different purposes. I could see using my portfolio to apply for a job, but since I do not know what I want to be, I need to keep all possibilities open. For example, I want to put in my photography, which could be digitalized in a hypertext portfolio. I will treat the end of each future class like my family reunion as an occasion to see how I've grown as a writer and learner. Starting this portfolio has given me the opportunity to begin this continuous process.

PRACTICE WITH PORTFOLIO INTRODUCTIONS

1. Looking at Justin's Course Portfolio at the conclusion of this book, reread his portfolio essay. Do you remember from reading this textbook or see in his Course Portfolio other claims that he could have made about his learn-

ing during this term? List up to three other claims that he might have made. Beside each claim write at least two examples that would signify his progress. Take examples from different sources, such as his drafts, Writer's Statements, or final pieces of writing.

2. Write a portfolio introduction for your Course Portfolio.
3. Exchange a draft of your portfolio introduction with a classmate.
   a. Underline the main claims in the draft. You will probably find at least three claims, although you may find more if students in your class must show progress toward all class goals.
   b. For each claim, write a number above an example used as evidence. Does each claim have an extended example or multiple examples from different pieces of writing to support it? In the margin of the draft, note where additional examples would be persuasive in making the case for progress toward the goal. If you have access to the writer's papers and other materials, you may find examples to cite as suggested evidence.
4. Answer the Writer's Statement questions for a classmate. When you receive responses to your own Writer's Statement, collect additional examples from your written work if necessary.
5. Revise your portfolio introduction.

COMPLETING YOUR COURSE PORTFOLIO

After you have revised your portfolio introduction, organized your Course Portfolio, and presented your work in a professional and aesthetically pleasing way, you can proudly submit your work for evaluation. Some instructors ask students to assign themselves a grade for the class based on the self-assessment, peer assessment, and instructor assessment that have gone on during the class. If you have conscientiously scrutinized your own learning, you should be able to evaluate yourself in a way that closely matches your instructor's evaluation.

Portfolio learning contributes to fewer surprises when grades are derived at the conclusion of a course. It also enables you to think beyond the grade for one course. Although single grades can signal accomplishment, they are seldom definitive indicators of all the learning that takes place in a course. A Course Portfolio may come closer to representing the breadth and depth of your learning. The Course Portfolio provides the contextual evidence of your learning so that you can refer back to that learning, add to the evidence, and transform your learning as you move into new contexts.

As you look at Justin's Course Portfolio, which follows this concluding chapter, you know from following him in this textbook how much more went into the evolution of his learning than can be shown on the pages of the portfolio. You also know, however, how effectively Justin has demonstrated what he has learned.

As you look at your own Course Portfolio, you know from creating it how much more went into the evolution of your learning than can be represented in its pages. Yet you also know that you have demonstrated in your very best ways the reasons that you are graduating from one set of writing goals to the next. You are ready to begin the next chapter of your own literacy story. Congratulations!

COURSE PORTFOLIO

W100

Justin Cooper

May 25, 1997

Table of Contents

Portfolio Essay

Watching Myself Grow

I used to get embarrassed when my Aunt Danielle would pat me on the head at our annual family reunion and say, "My, how you've grown!" Because she hadn't seen me in a year, my aunt was thinking about me as I was the year before. Because I looked at myself in the mirror every day, I saw the changes gradually and unconsciously. Sometimes it takes someone else or some special occasion to make a person stop and look at how he has grown. Putting together this Course Portfolio has caused me to conclude that I have grown as a writer during this past term but also that I have a way to go before I'm a mature writer.

One way that I've grown is in my willingness and ability to revise. In the past I felt virtuous if I corrected spelling errors, rewrote a sentence or two, and added a conclusion to a paper. In this class, however, I have learned the meaning of revision: sometimes revising requires major changes. For example, throwing out words and ideas that I have written is difficult because I have often worked hard to come up with those words and ideas. Finding more examples and doing deeper analysis are also added work.

Beginning with Paper 1, my literacy autobiography, though, I have done major revision. Draft 1 of that paper included extensive information about my father, my father's abandonment of our family, and the effect on me. When a reader pointed out that I was writing more about my dad than about myself, I shifted in a significant change to focus on my own development. For example, I omitted material about my father's background and added in the next draft analysis of ways that photography and music are elements of my developing literacy. Another example is Paper 2 in which I needed to incorporate the views of others with my own. Even in my Writer's Statement for Draft 1, I wrote, "I may have too much about my friends and not enough about the issue of assimilation and the 'elect.'" When my readers indicated that I needed more from the Reed essay, I returned to it for further analysis of Reed's perspectives. Third, in Paper 5 I reorganized my ideas to feature the ways that my research supported my own ideas. In Draft 2, I integrate the ideas of three conservative writers to explain the argument about the dire consequences of fatherlessness, and then I dissect the Whitehead article that summarizes the outcomes of children's lack of contact with fathers. Although I question that all children without fathers are doomed, I state that fathering is important. The authors I quote are shown to support my main contention in my essay.

Even when I did not revise for this class, I identified ways to revise in the future. For example, although I did not choose Paper 4 for my Course Portfolio, it is a good example of the personal essay because it uses original perspectives on the meaning of travel. I had set my purpose as convincing my mother about traveling to Europe, though, so I would have had to reorganize my ideas as evidence and use more sources for the assignment. Even though I did not have time to do this major revising this term, I like my ideas in the paper well enough to revise during another class or some other time.

A second criterion for our class is ability to use and synthesize various sources for writing. My writing shows improvement in this area when I interview my grandmother and use information from that interview. In Paper 1, Draft 3, I supported my contention about the influence of my mother's reading to me on my literacy by using my grandmother's recollection of seeing Mother read the newspaper to me when I was only one month old. After I read reader responses to Paper 2, Draft 1 and did a cubing, I was convinced that I could get more out of Ishmael Reed's article and could synthesize my own ideas more with his. In my final version of the essay, I use my personal examples to support the main point of Reed's with which I agree.

> But I think I agree with the main ideas that Reed is putting across, even though it may be selfish. He thinks that we need to maintain the diversity that comes in a city such as Detroit which has both mosques and a Hispanic population. For those of us who are mainstream American, there is a richness that comes with all those different cultures. When I was in high school, my two best friends were Rajesh, an Indian, and Darnell, an African American. From them I learned about sweet potato pie, about Hindu

> religious customs, about saris, and about slavery. It's hard to know what they got from me in that way. I would hate to see them and their families become just like everyone else.

In Paper 5 I also show my ability to synthesize sources. In the second and third paragraphs I refer to or quote three sources which are all used to support a point I am making. In that same paper I rely on one substantive source, the definitive article on my topic, from which I derive appropriate references from other published work. In my dialogue journal after I read *The Atlantic Monthly,* I wrote that I can rely on a reputable authority who does what my instructor calls a metastudy to get an overview of sources or I can read multiple sources myself and synthesize. In this case, after I synthesize my own reading, I rely on Whitehead's article for a comprehensive look at my topic.

Even though I show ability in research, I need more work. My instructor and members of my class pointed out that I did not use the information from my observation as fully as I could, but I am still unsure how to draw conclusions from my own observations. Although I did reading for most of my papers, I do not have a method for taking notes, so I am sure that I do not use my sources as well as I could. Next semester I am taking a composition class that teaches research methods, so I will improve. Specifically, I want to learn what to do when my sources disagree and how to organize a sociology paper because I may major in that discipline. The axiom that the more you learn, the more you know what you do not know applies to me and research.

I have progressed toward a third criterion for this class, the ability to understand and use conventions of written discourse. I used to get irritated when anyone commented on my use of punctuation or choice of words. This semester, especially in trying to read the papers of other writers in my class, I realize the importance of editing. In Dennis's dialogue journal, I wrote on four different days that he needed to pay attention to typos because I had had trouble even reading his drafts. My instructor helped me by showing me how to find patterns of error. In my case, for example, I omitted commas after an introductory adverbial clause. In the past I would not have cared about knowing the definition of a clause, but learning to identify this kind of clause helped me know much more easily how to punctuate. Examples from final drafts of three different papers demonstrate how I now correctly punctuate introductory adverbial clauses: "When I was three, my dad left my mother, my sister, and me to try to find a better job." (Paper 1); "As we grew older, Darnell and I developed separate groups of friends that were not part of our friendship" (Paper 3); and "When my mom graduated from college and got an accounting job, she took a trip she had always wanted to, to London" (Paper 4).

In addition, I learned the advantage of precise words. I was persuaded from the essays and articles that the class read and from reactions of my readers that words like *a lot* and *things* can be replaced with words that tell the reader more. I have even become more conscious in my speaking of using exact words, like saying *articles* or *items* instead of *stuff* and *two, three,* or *four* instead of *several*. Some examples from my revised papers include *photography* and *music* instead of *other things* in Paper 1 and *affected* as a verb instead of *effected* in Paper 5. Here again, I can become even better if I record new vocabulary in my dialogue journal and watch my own essays and reports in the future for places to be precise.

Lastly, this Course Portfolio demonstrates my "ability to create a portfolio that represents self as writer and learner." You will be able to see in my portfolio that I have improved as a writer during this semester. In Paper 1, for example, I have included pieces of writing that were useful in the development of the paper, demonstrating that I have a process now for making a draft better. Although I have not included all the dialogue journal entries, reader responses, and other materials for the other papers, I have used a similar process for each paper. During this semester I have become less defensive about myself and my writing. When my classmate Alex read a draft of this essay, he wrote, "I remember when we read our first drafts. I thought, 'I don't want to read that dude's writing again. He doesn't like to hear about anything bad with his writing.' But, you're OK now. I can say what I actually think about your writing."

Collaboration with people in my class and not getting grades on each paper have made me willing to share my writing and to revise. I see how I can use research to learn more about my own life, like understanding my father and his influence on me. College should give you more information to learn from so you can lead a better life. I understand my dad's decision, what I learned from my high school friends, and how I've developed as a literate person better from this class. I hope that you see that clearly in my portfolio.

I plan to add to this portfolio as I take more classes. My instructor mentioned that some colleges encourage students to make a hypertext portfolio so that they can use it for different purposes. I could see using my portfolio to apply for a job, but since I do not know what I want to be, I need to keep all possibilities open. For example, I want to put in my photography, which could be digitalized in a hypertext portfolio. I will treat the end of each future class like my family reunion as an occasion to see how I've grown as a writer and learner. Starting this portfolio has given me the opportunity to begin this continuous process.

Brainstorming for Purpose, Paper 1, Literacy Autobiography

explain to myself why I'm in college

remember how I've been influenced by teachers and other people to be sure in college I hang around people like those who've helped me

convince myself that I am literate

look at my background realistically so I'll make good choices in the future

have fun remembering the past

Dialogue Journal Entry About Audience for Paper 1, Literacy Autobiography

My audience for the literacy autobiography is the other people in the class. I don't know too much about them yet, but I do know that they are all college students. Most of them are about my age though a couple of the women look older, I don't want to guess about that! They have all graduated from high school, I guess, and they must have read some things, and they would probably have heard of some of the things I read or my mom read to me when I was a little kid. This should be a friendly audience because we have to work together after all, at least I want to know about them. I know I shouldn't be nervous about writing about myself, but I am, even if I know a lot about myself. My teacher talked about primary and secondary audience in class. I guess the class is the primary audience, and my teacher is the secondary audience. I'm also interested in what this paper ends up saying. The teacher will probably look at spelling and if I did the assignment right.

Proposal for Paper 1, Draft 1, Literacy Autobiography

1. Topic and perspective: I want to show how my dad's leaving our family when I was very young influenced my developing literacy in important ways. At this stage in my life I want to get over being angry with him.
2. Purpose: I am planning to write chronologically in order to show that I have reacted in different ways to my dad's leaving. My purpose is to show readers how I have gotten to where I am today.
3. Audience: The other members of my class will be reading my papers all term. My professor will even read their reactions to my writing. I want them to understand why I choose some of the topics I do and that I really want to learn something in this class.
4. Evidence: I'll have to remember certain events that symbolize the stages of my development.
   a. My mother used to read to me. I liked to know that my mom would be home every day and would read to me each day. She encouraged me to buy books and to use the library, habits I still have.
   b. A contest that I won for a free camera introduced me to photography, which I love. I understand myself and other people through the camera.
   c. I think that music is a form of literacy. I play the saxophone. Playing the saxophone is a way of expressing feelings.
   d. I'm in many roles myself, but I'm entering a new role now. I'm a college student, and I'd better learn something new here.
5. Probable challenges and ways to meet them:
   a. There are so many events that I could use. I'm going to have to choose only a few events or this paper will get out of hand. Anyway, I have only eight days to write the first draft.
   b. I've always felt funny about writing about myself. I can see, though, how knowing about the other people in this class will help me understand their writing better.

c. Last year my teacher complained that I got off track after I started with a subject. I hope this proposal helps focus me on the topic. I will ask my girlfriend to read my draft to see if I include only points about my main topic.

Writer's Statement for Paper 1, Draft 1, Literacy Autobiography

Diving Away from the Wreck

1. This writing about myself is hard. I have so many memories. I'm not sure which ones I should use. Is the part about soccer and going to eat really about my topic? It includes something about my dad, but I'm not sure it has much to do with my literacy.
2. The audience for this paper is supposed to be the other people in our class. Is this paper interesting to you so far? I want to read other people's papers in my writing group so I can see what they thought would be interesting.
3. I like the specific examples I used in the paragraph about photography. Do you think I need more specific examples anywhere else in the paper?
4. The frame (a term I learned recently that means a way to structure the beginning and end of a paper--I like the term because it is just like photography) for my paper is about dealing with my dad. I think that that is pertinent to what I am doing with my life, but does talking about my dad get me off the topic of my literacy autobiography? I hope not cause I'd have to start over basically.
5. My girlfriend, who read this draft, thinks I need to talk more about writing. Do you think so? I do write pretty well usually. I even won an essay contest in high school. I could write about that and about how I'm doing in other classes with my writing. This paper could get out of hand, though, with too much in it.
6. Do you have any other suggestions about what I should revise?

Paper 1, Draft 1, Literacy Autobiography

Diving Away from the Wreck

My girlfriend likes poetry. When she read some poems to me from a book by Adrienne Rich called *Diving Into the Wreck,* I began thinking about how my life has been the opposite. I've been avoiding a wreck, using language like Rich but other things, too. Now, however, I'm ready to move toward something, hopefully through my college education.

When I was three my dad left my mom, my younger sister, and me to try to find a better job. The trouble was that he never let us know if he found one. My father had dropped out of school when he was sixteen. My mom says that he never really learned to read well, so that he ran into a dead end at each job when his inability kept him from advancing. Although I understand his frustration now I spent most of my younger years mad at my dad for deserting us. My mom has pointed out to me that I tried to be everything he was not: I read everything I could, I did well in school, I was as responsible as could be expected to my mother and sister, and I refused to speak about my father.

My mother supported me in every way. Since I was really little she read to me every day. I liked animal stories, so she read the entire Black Stallion series and books like *Bambi* when I was little and *The Red Pony* when I grew older. She had a deal that she would pay for half of any book that I wanted to buy. We used the library most of the time, but if I wanted a book, I had to save only half the price from my allowance or paper delivery money. I remember that the first book I bought was *Lassie Comes Home,* which I found in the children's section at our local bookstore, Fine Print.

In third grade the Polaroid Company sponsored a contest that led to another way in which I could document my life. I took the free camera given by Polaroid and took pictures of my house, my neighborhood, my mom, my sister, and events in our family. Later I received a Kodak 16 millimeter of my own. I have albums with pictures of Uncle Jims fortieth birthday party, of my sisters room with all the posters of Hootie and the Blowfish, and of the roses that my mom cultivated each year. I have pictures of my Boy Scout troops trip to

Gatlinburg, Tennessee, my sixth grade classes production of *You're a Good Man, Charlie Brown,* and my junior prom. I also liked to take pictures in our town, of people shopping, of homeless people asking for money, and of sidewalk vendors.

I like music, too. I've really enjoyed playing the saxophone. I liked being part of an improvisational jazz group, although I never got very good. I find that the sax expresses my sadness in a way that I can't with words or any other form of expression. Sometimes I wonder if other people feel the deep sadness that I feel sometimes. Not that I'm usually sad, but occasionally I feel really sad for reasons that I'm not sure about. I don't think that this feeling is related just to my dads leaving, but I don't know how else to explain it.

Just so you don't think I'm a morbid person, you should know that I like athletics. My mom says that my dad liked football. She has a high school picture of him in his uniform. I played soccer. Since the goalie seemed to have ultimate responsibility for stopping the other team I decided to be a goalie. By the time I wanted to play, my mom had graduated from college in accounting, so she had a good enough job to pay for the special equipment a goalie needs. When other guys dads came to every game I used to feel cheated, but my mom and sister were always there. My sister didn't understand anything about the game, but she yelled for me anyway. After we'd win we'd stop at Taco Bell for ten soft tacos to go. When we'd lose my mom would insist that we stop anyway, but I'd order something different. I got good in soccer, but I'm not going to play in college because I didn't get a scholarship and I need to work part-time.

I'm now nineteen, and I am a student, a bookstore employee, a roommate, a boyfriend, and still a son and brother. I find it hard to balance my commitments, and I realize that I'm understanding more and more about my dads life. He was only twenty-two when he left us. Probably he just couldn't take all the responsibility when he knew things wouldn't get any better. I hope that I don't cave in under the stress of supporting myself and going to school. It may not seem like much, but I realize that I have to discipline myself now to work toward something. Instead of fighting my memory of my dad, I want to build my own memory for myself and for my family in the future. I want to study how people operate in society, so I'm going to study sociology. My literacy history is already different from my dads and I intend my future to be different, too. I'll let go of being concerned with his decisions and make good ones of my own. I'll use learning toward that goal, so here I come college.

Responses to My Writer's Statement, Draft 1, Literacy Autobiography

1. Is the part about soccer and going to eat pertinent to my literacy story?
2. Is this paper interesting to you as a class member?
3. Do I need more specific examples in the paper?
4. Does talking about my dad get me off the subject of my literacy development?
5. Should I talk more about writing? Can I do so without this paper getting out of hand?
6. Do you have any other suggestions?

Stacey's Responses

1. You're right to ask this question. I play soccer, so I was interested that you do, too. I never played goalie, though. Anyway, the soccer bit shows great support by your mom and sister. It doesn't tell me anything about your literacy, though. Unless you want to say that it took time away from your school work and you didn't do as well in school or something.
2. Yeah, it's interesting. My paper talks about my favorite books from when I was little until now. I try to show how each book says something different about me as a learner. I get writing in by quoting from my diary and from papers I wrote in high school about certain books. My paper may be the opposite of yours. Mine may be too limited. Oh, well, I guess we'll both find out.
3. I like the examples of the first books you read and were read to you. I was surprised that the photography paragraph did seem to belong in your paper. I was convinced by it that the pictures you take are a form of literacy because you tell stories of people's lives by them. You seem to use pictures like some other people use words. If you take out the soccer stuff, you might put in another point with some examples of papers you've written in the past. Are any of them about your dad? That would fit with what you call your frame (yeah, a good term!).
4. I don't think you have to start over even if you take out the soccer and rewrite the last paragraph, which I want to talk about now. Your dad is important, I

know, but you need to emphasize yourself more. The lens of your camera needs to be on yourself. Pretty good use of language, huh!?

5. If you're worried about bragging, don't. Knowing about the essay contest would be helpful. Was your essay published anywhere? What other kinds of writing have you done? Also, I'd be interested if you write music. Is that like writing papers at all?
6. What is your major? Do you know what you want to be when you grow up?! I'm thinking that I should talk about my major in my paper, too, because it will involve lots of reading (I want to be a book critic for a newspaper) and ties to my "book history."

Stephen's Responses

1. Cut the soccer. It just doesn't add to the purpose of this paper.
2. I do like your paper because you seem to be really honest in it. It isn't a lot of BS to fill the assignment. You seem to be working out something in this paper. Sometimes I think you are concentrating on your dad too much. You've already moved beyond your dad in many ways. You can talk about yourself a lot in an autobiography.
3. Do you have any pictures of you writing or reading or something? I'd like to read a description of a picture of you as an example.
4. I hate to revise, so I hesitate to tell you this. But I think you can talk about your dad without making him so important. You can still use your "frame" but you can make yourself the center of the picture.
5. What else do you have to say about writing? I guess one question I've been asking myself is, "What shows I'm literate?" If more about writing shows you are literate, especially when you talk more about yourself, good.
6. I like examples. If you decide to write more about writing, use examples. The photographs you mentioned are good examples of what you're interested in and what you try to do with photography. Maybe you could do the same thing with some of your examples of writing. Hey, I know what you mean about things getting out of hand. Guess you'll have to decide when to stop.

Looping for Paper 1, Literacy Autobiography

Open Freewriting to Begin Looping

Papers I Have Written

I wish I was at home where I have some papers in a box in my closet, but I'll do the best I can from memory. I remember writing a poem in elementary school. It was supposed to be about my family, but I lied. I wrote a poem about a dad, mom, girl, and boy who led the American apple pie sort of life. The teacher really liked it. I never mentioned my dad was gone. I wrote a short story in junior high. I really remember that one. I didn't know we'd have to let other people in class read it. I wrote about being a big stud who had all the girlfriends I wanted. I was so lucky to get Becky Jenkins as a reader. She was too nice to make fun of me, at least to my face. I avoided her like crazy after that though. My best research paper ever was on Alfred Stieglitz, the photographer. He really inspired me. I actually used many sources without copying from any of them. I didn't need to copy because I actually had something to say about him. I talked about the way his ideas about framing pictures came from his purposes in taking the pictures. No one that I read had said what I said before. I'm running out of time. In high school I wrote a poem about learning from other people, especially my music teacher.

Directed Freewriting about the Stieglitz Paper

I remember reading that Stieglitz wrote to Georgia O'Keeffe once about framing her pictures. She had asked why they had to be framed. He had said that paintings might lose some freedom in frames--but there was no other way to protect them for viewers. I remember he wrote to her "Life again!" I like that. Even if life does not have frames around parts of it, art has to.

S. also answered questions about his own photos. He talked about how a single item in the center of a photo could call for a certain kind of frame around it. I wonder why I liked that answer. I think I liked it because I had the same feeling when I took pictures sometimes. I remember one picture of my uncle fishing that needed the big lake and distant trees around it to show that one reason he liked fishing was that he felt a small part of larger nature. I had to use a wide lens to get it all in.

More Directed Freewriting about Frames in Life and in Art

The trouble with life is that you can't choose your frames. In photography you can so you can decide what you want to say about something. You can control things. Being literate means that. You can understand something by seeing it in relation to other things. When you read you compare stuff to your own life. When you write you pick out only certain stuff to tell. What's important about being literate? You need many ways to understand and control life even if life is really uncontrollable.

More Directed Freewriting about Value of an Audience

It's hard to know if you really have anything to say that's worth it. My friend Lucia writes poems that she never shows to anyone because she's sure no one else will like them. I used to be that way about my writing before I was required to enter the essay contest and won it. That's the way with music too. I can play all I want in my basement. But, when people applaud when our band plays I feel it in my bones. I know that my music is being understood. Are you literate if you don't know if anyone else understands you?

Brainstorming List of Photos

my mom reading to my sister when she was little
our band
my uncle fishing
the Tomb of the Unknown Soldier at Arlington
my grandma baking cookies
the sign in front of the library that announces story hours
Maria from Sesame Street when she visited our mall
Melissa Etheridge when we saw her in concert

Directed Freewriting about the Maria Photo

I grew up watching Sesame Street. Maria was as familiar to me as my relatives. In this picture I tried to get Maria surrounded by the kids who had come to see her but also by the stuff for sale in the store window that she was standing in front of. I thought that she was trying to show the kids an alternative to the store's stuff. Learning about letters and numbers would allow them a way past the stuff. They could go beyond the commercial junk to understand something more important. I'm amazed that I thought of that. Did I think of it then or only now?

Cluster for Paper 1, Literacy Autobiography

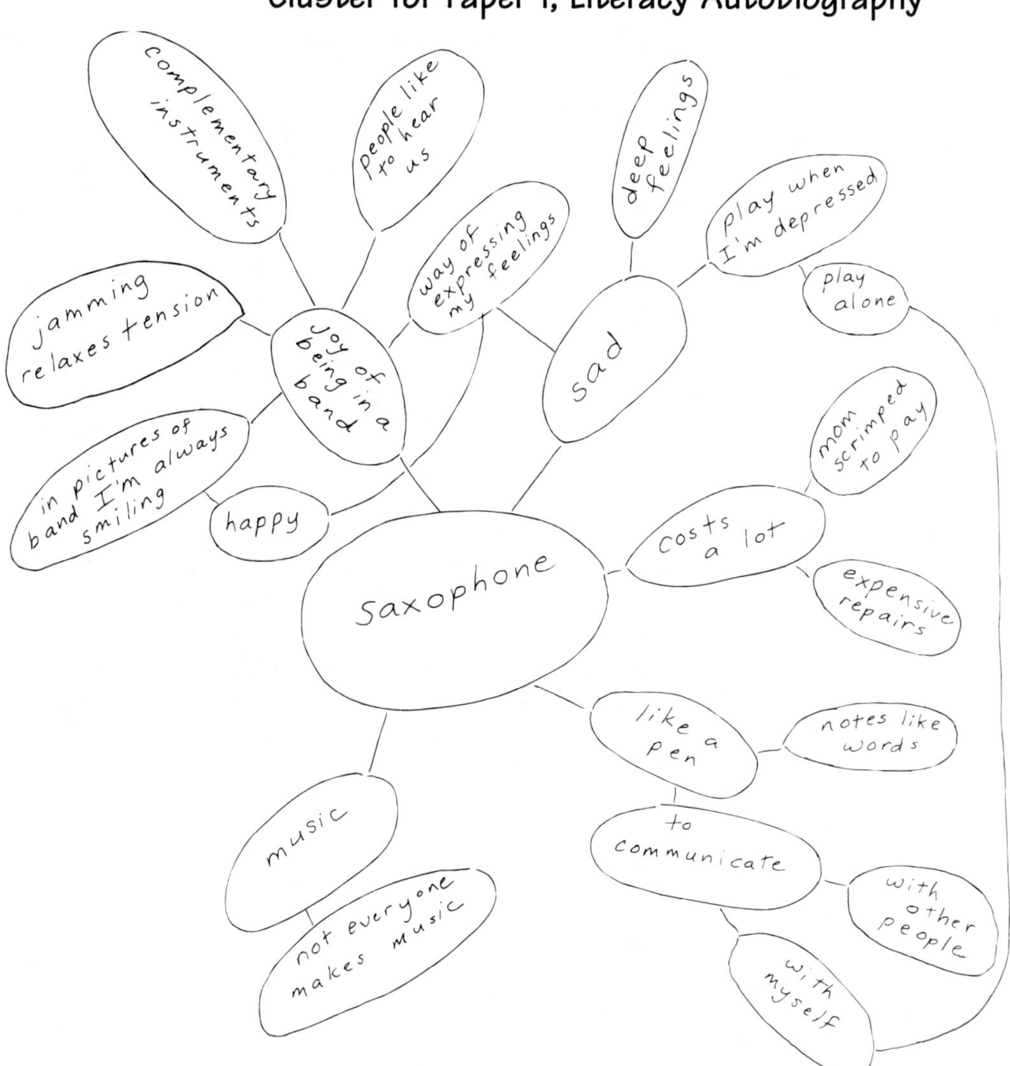

Writer's Statement for Paper 1, Draft 2, Literacy Autobiography

1. I tried to focus more on me than on my dad in this draft. Is the paper more focused on me? Does it say enough about me to give a full picture or to qualify as a literacy autobiography?
2. I left out the soccer stuff and the last part about my dad. I'm not sure I added enough examples like Stephen wanted. I almost think I need to talk to someone about that because I can't remember enough.
3. I like the part about Stieglitz. I have a lot more I could say about what I learned from that paper. But I'm afraid I'd get that part out of balance. It might seem more important than something else.
4. I realize that I haven't talked about the essay contest. It would fit the idea of having other people understand you. But I think I have enough in the essay already. What do you think? Should I include the essay contest stuff?
5. When I read Jackie's draft in class today, I liked the way that she used dialogue. She had actual quotes from people. Do you think that I should use some quotes in my paper? Why?

Paper 1, Draft 2, Literacy Autobiography

Diving Away from the Wreck

My girlfriend likes poetry. When she read some poems to me from a book by Adrienne Rich called *Diving Into the Wreck* I began thinking about how my life has been the opposite. I've been avoiding a wreck, using language like Rich and also pictures and sounds. Now, however, I'm ready to move toward a new stage in my life, hopefully through my college education.

Although my dad left our family when I was three partly because he couldn't advance on his jobs with his lack of reading ability my mom supported me in every way. The most important way was in promoting reading. When I was little she read to me every day. I liked animal stories, so she read the entire Black Stallion series and books like *Bambi.* We had a deal that she would pay for half of any book that I wanted to buy. We used the library most of the time, but if I wanted a book I had to save only half the price from my allowance or paper delivery money. The first book I bought was *Lassie Comes Home.* One thing I liked about stories was that they had a beginning, middle, and end. Even if not everything turned out the way you wanted you could understand from the story why the ending was as it was.

Two experiences with photography taught me that pictures are another way of understanding the world, the goal of all kinds of literacies. In third grade the Polaroid Company sponsored a contest in which I won a free camera. I took pictures of my house, my neighborhood, my mom, my sister, and events in our family. Later I received a Kodak 16 millimeter of my own. I have albums with pictures of Uncle Jim's fortieth birthday party, of my sister's room with all the posters of Hootie and the Blowfish, and of the roses that my mom cultivated each year. I have pictures of my Boy Scout troops trip to Gatlinburg, Tennessee, my sixth grade class production of *You're a Good Man, Charlie Brown,* and my junior prom. I also liked to take pictures of people shopping, of homeless people asking for money, and of sidewalk vendors. When I took many of these pictures I didn't understand why I felt satisfaction taking them.

Writing a research paper on Alfred Stieglitz helped me understand.

In this most original research paper I have written to date, I wrote about the way that Stieglitz talked about framing. He wrote to Georgia O'Keeffe once about framing her pictures. She had asked why they had to be framed. He had said that paintings might lose some freedom in frames--but there was no other way to protect them for viewers. I remember he wrote to her "Life again!" I interpreted that to mean that even if life does not have frames around parts of it art has to be understandable and enduring. Stieglitz also talked about his own photographs within each picture was an item that called for a certain kind of frame around it. I understood what he meant. I remember using a wide lens to get a picture of my uncle fishing that needed the big lake and distant trees around it to show that one reason he liked fishing was that he felt a small part of larger nature. In life you can't choose your frames like I couldn't choose that my dad left me, but in photography you can control what you want to frame. You can understand something by seeing it in relation to other things. Being literate includes comparing what you read to your own life, picking out something particular from your whole life to write about, and taking pictures that mean something. We each need many ways to understand and control life even if life is really uncontrollable.

Another way that I am literate is through music. Playing the saxophone helps me express my feelings that are part of my life. Better than writing for expressing sad feelings is playing the sax, especially playing jazz. But, I can also express happiness with music. Sometimes the sadness and happiness are mixed, just like words can have two meanings at the same time. I try to understand life through music as well as through words and pictures. It's the greatest when other people understand what I'm trying to say through my playing. When people applaud our band I know that I am being understood. Part of being literate is being able to express yourself so somebody else understands.

I'm now nineteen, and I am a student, a bookstore employee, a roommate, a boyfriend, and still a son and brother. I'm not a father yet, but I have the advantage of reading and writing and having other ways of expressing myself and understanding the world that my father did not. My literacy history is already different from my dad's and I intend my future to be different too. I am moving in a positive direction in college as I continue living my literacy.

Transcript of an Interview, Paper 1, Portfolio Draft

I was interested in getting some more information about my dad to understand why he dropped out of school and what he was really like. Also I wanted to learn about how someone else viewed me as I grew up, especially how I liked to read and what I wrote. I interviewed my dad's mother, my Grandma Cooper. She is 64 years old, and she is getting ready to retire from her job as administrative secretary to the librarian at a small college. She likes to read, too, and also likes to cook and to hike in state parks. My grandma is easy to talk to but sometimes it was hard to keep her on the subject.

When I typed up the transcript, I first tried to get it down exactly the way it was on the tape, but that was too hard. So, I would listen and then paraphrase the conversation except where I thought I needed to get it word for word. I know that means I can only quote those places, but I'll just have to be careful.

Me: *M*   Grandma: *G*

M: Grandma, I'm writing a literacy autobiography for my composition course about things I like to do. It's supposed to represent myself and the world. We've been studying that we have lots of sign systems to use to express ourselves. I've written about some of mine.

As I wrote my essay, I started thinking about my dad, so I'm going to ask you some questions about him. I also want to know what we used to do when I was little that influenced the way I read and write now.

So here goes. How come you've always worked in a library and your only son didn't even learn to read very well?

G: Your father didn't like it when I went to work when he was five. Your Grandpa couldn't make enough money for us to pay our bills, so I went to work. I'd had a year of business school and the college had just expanded its library and needed a clerical person. I like to read and liked libraries and I could learn the new job without having to measure up to someone from the past.

Your dad hated the babysitters. He threw tantrums and cried every day when I left him. I think he blamed it on the library, like it was the library that took his mommy away. Later when the first grade class went to get library cards, he refused to get one. His negative attitude toward the library got in the way of him wanting to read, right from the start.

M: I remember that you had books at your house. I remember the Dr. Seuss books. You used to read me *Cat in the Hat.*

G: Those books were from when your dad and aunt grew up. Your dad was always so active that he wouldn't sit still to be read to. He liked to be outside running or throwing the football. I'd sometimes corral him, but he'd talk me into going out back and pitching him a baseball instead of reading to him.

You weren't like that. I remember your mother reading to you from right when you were born. I remember going over to your house and finding her reading the newspaper to you when you were less than a month. She said you needed to hear words and it didn't matter what she read, but you needed to hear it.

M: I remember that you had magnets on your refrigerator to keep my pictures and poems. Wow, what lousy rhymes I wrote, but you always read them out loud like they were from great poets. Were you laughing inside?

G: You said you're learning about how people express themselves. Well, you expressed yourself with words in your poems. You'd write when you were happy and when you were sad. Lots of times you would add pictures, or you said that you sometimes drew a picture first and then wrote words.

M: I still write poetry, but I don't show anyone.

G: I still have my magnets!

M: When Aunt Beth's husband died, I wrote her a letter. I couldn't talk with her, but I could write. Did she ever mention that letter to you?

G: Beth only kept a few sympathy cards, with special notes in them, and your letter. She told me that having a twelve-year-old nephew write the way you did was unbelievable to her.

M: I had been thinking that I take pictures when I'm sad, but I guess that time I wrote. How did my dad show it when he was sad?

G: Mostly, he went away from the house. When Grandpa and I would argue, your dad would go out to the woods behind our house. He had a treehouse there. He never wanted to talk about it.

M: Ok, let's switch subjects. I remember that you took me when I was fourteen to a political debate. I didn't even know who the candidates were. You said that I needed to hear them. Why did you take me?

G: Your Aunt Beth got so self-confident when she was on the debate team in high school. I think that's why she became a lawyer. I believe that we should be good citizens, of course, so we have to know about candidates. But I mostly wanted you to hear how people debate. I thought you needed a way to have confidence at that point in your life.

M: My ninth grade year was a disaster. My grade school teachers liked what I wrote. My ninth grade English teacher bled all over my papers. I couldn't understand the red marks, and I got scared of writing. I even had trouble writing lab reports in biology. I was good at the experiments, but I blocked at writing up results.

G: How did you get past that? I remember that you even won an essay contest later. Was it in your junior or senior year?

M: My mom said I should take pictures. I should take a picture every time I wanted to write something to get myself started. You know, it really worked. When I had a picture to describe, I felt more confident about writing. Oh, I even took pictures when we read *Julius Caesar.* I thought the crowds were so hypocritical when they praised and then booed the same person when their mood changed. I went to a basketball game and took pictures of the supposed fans. They did the same thing. They yelled for the team when they were making hoops. Just let them miss a basket or two in a row, though. The boos were loud. You should have seen the evil looks on some of the faces.

G: How did taking the pictures help?

M: This time I got the pictures developed at one of those one-hour jobs. Then I made a list of words under each picture, whatever came to my mind. I used those words to begin writing about the fickle crowds in the play. I actually tried to write a comparison of the kinds of crowds, but that seemed so farfetched that I dropped it.

Anyway, I learned that for me pictures and words are both important.

G: What was your favorite book that you read in high school?

M: That's easy. I liked *To Kill a Mockingbird.* I probably liked it for different reasons than most people. I tried to imagine what it would be like to be living with my dad instead of my mom. I thought that I'd like a dad just like the attorney in that book. He was smart, cared about his kids, cared about human beings.

G: You are like that, you know. You gave me that book about Rosa Parks and told me that you admired someone who wouldn't let anyone push her around because she was black. Didn't your winning essay argue against hate groups like the Ku Klux Klan and the John Birch Society?

M: You know, from reading about those groups I found out how much I despised them. Then when I started writing, I got real mad. In my essay I argued that groups like that should be outlawed by the Constitution.

G: Well, I'm getting ready to fix dinner. Do you want to ask any more questions?

M: Just one more. If you were me writing this literacy autobiography, what would you think was the best thing to put in?

G: That's a hard one. I guess I'd mention that you show other people how you feel really well in writing. And that you plan to write your Grandmother often while you're away at college!

M: Thanks for the interview, Grandma. I'll be sure to quote you so you'll go down in history as the relative of a famous writer.

Paper 1, Draft 3, Literacy Autobiography

Diving Away from the Wreck

My girlfriend likes poetry. When she read some poems to me from a book by Adrienne Rich called *Diving Into the Wreck,* I began thinking about how my life has been the opposite. I've been avoiding a wreck, using language like Rich and also pictures and sounds. Now, however, I'm ready to move toward a new stage in my life, hopefully through my college education.

Although my dad left our family when I was three partly because he couldn't advance on his jobs with his lack of reading ability, my mom supported me in every way. The most important way was in promoting reading. When I was little, she read to me every day. My grandma recently told me that she remembers seeing my mom reading the newspaper to me when I was less than a month old: my mom said I needed to hear language and it didn't matter what she read. Later I liked animal stories, so she read the entire Black Stallion series and books like *Bambi.* We had a deal that she would pay for half of any book that I wanted to buy. Although we used the library most of the time, if I wanted a book, I had to save only half the price from my allowance or paper delivery money. The first book I bought was *Lassie Comes Home.* One thing I liked about stories was that they had a beginning, middle, and end. Even if not everything turned out the way you wanted, you could understand from the story why the ending was as it was.

Experiences with photography have taught me that pictures are another way of understanding the world, the goal of all kinds of literacies. In third grade the Polaroid Company sponsored a contest in which I won a free camera. I took pictures of my house, neighborhood, mom, and sister. Later with a Kodak 16 millimeter of my own, I filmed Uncle Jim's fiftieth birthday party, my sister's room with all the posters of Hootie and the Blowfish, and the roses my mom cultivated every year. I have pictures of my Boy Scout troop's trip to Gatlinburg, Tennessee, my sixth grade class's production of *You're a Good Man, Charlie Brown,* and my junior prom. Once when I had writer's block, my mom suggested I take pictures to get myself started. Since I had to write about *Julius Caesar,* I thought about the hypocritical crowds who praised and then booed the same person when their mood changed. At a basketball game I took pictures of the supposed fans who did the same thing, yelling for the team when they were making hoops and booing loudly even if they missed only a few baskets. When I got the pictures developed, I wrote a list of words under each one: the words about the fickle crowd got me started writing my paper.

I also liked to take pictures of people shopping, of homeless people asking for money, and of sidewalk vendors. When I took many of these pictures, I didn't understand why I felt satisfaction taking them. Writing a research paper on Alfred Stieglitz helped me understand.

In this most original research paper I have written to date, I wrote about the way that Stieglitz talked about framing. He wrote to Georgia O'Keeffe once about framing her pictures. She had asked why they had to be framed. He had said that paintings might lose some freedom in frames--but there was no other way to protect them for viewers. I remember he wrote to her "Life again!" I interpreted that to mean that even if life does not have frames around parts of it, art has to be understandable and enduring. Stieglitz also talked about his own photographs. Within each picture was an item that called for a certain kind of frame around it. I understood what he meant. I remember using a wide lens to get a picture of my uncle fishing that needed the big lake and distant trees around it to show that one reason he liked fishing was that he felt a small part of larger nature. In life you can't choose your frames like I couldn't choose that my dad left me, but in photography you can control what you want to frame. You can understand something by seeing it in relation to other things. Being literate includes comparing what you read to your own life, picking out something particular from your whole life to write about, and taking pictures that mean something. We each need many ways to understand and control life even if life is really uncontrollable.

Another way that I am literate is through music. Playing the saxophone helps me express my feelings that are part of my life. Better than writing for expressing sad feelings is playing the sax, especially playing jazz. But I can also express happiness with music. Sometimes the sadness and happiness are mixed, just like words can have two meanings at the same time. I try to understand life through music as well as through words and pictures. It's the greatest when other people understand what I'm trying to say through my playing. When people applaud our band, I know that I am being understood. Part of being literate is being able to express yourself so somebody else understands.

I'm now nineteen, and I am a student, a bookstore employee, a roommate, a boyfriend, and still a son and brother. I'm not a father yet, but I have the advantage of reading and writing and having other ways of expressing myself and understanding the world that my father did not. My literacy history is already different from my dad's, and I intend my future to be different, too. I am moving in a positive direction in college as I continue living my literacy.

Revision Analysis, Paper 1

Paper 1--Diving Away from the Wreck--I've done a lot of work on this paper. I got a better focus by leaving out a lot of stuff about my dad and really thinking about my own literacy. I did that by putting the title up over the computer and looking at it again and again. I took out the material that wasn't really related. *Autobiography* means it's about me. This paper is in good shape I think. I hope I can make the others as good.

Revision Plan: I don't know. I think it's very good. All the feedback I have says so too.

Justin's Proposal, Paper 3 Observation

The assignment is to write a paper that addresses a social issue we have read about and that is related to the public life on our campus. The paper must include findings from an observation. I am going to write about assimilation, which I began working with in another paper after reading Ishmael Reed's article, "America: The Multicultural Society." In my last paper I talked about my friendships with people from other races or backgrounds. In my cubing for that paper I also talked about Rodney King and the problem of "getting along". I think that people in my generation do have friends from other backgrounds, but I don't know how much assimilation is really taking place. I also wonder whether or not that is really a good thing, to assimilate. Reed seems to think that we're better off with a mix of differences, but maybe the question is whether we can "get along" when we're so different. Tolerance for the difference might be the issue. But I'm interested in friendships between people of different races and cultures and I think that can be not only about tolerance but appreciation of differences too. So I want to explore that in my next paper. I want to look at that issue on our campus.

As I do all this, I have to remember to stay on the real topic and not go off the track like I did in the other papers. Stephen says he kept asking himself how he knows he's literate, maybe I'll find a question like that to ask.

Justin's Journalistic Questions, Paper 3
Observation

I am going to use the journalistic questions to help me decide about this paper, my planning for the observation.

Who will I observe? I will observe students who are in groups in the student union. I will look at both large and small groups.

What do I want to try to find out? I want to see how people of different backgrounds interact. Do they often spend time together?

When will I do my observations? I will do them at lunchtime and in the late afternoons when students have free time to spend with friends.

Where will I do my observations? In the student union.

Why did I make these choices? I chose to watch groups of students because I want to try to watch people from different backgrounds interacting; I chose the union because lots of international students go there. Also, lots of people gather there to watch sports on the big screen TV. I chose the times because that's when people have free time. I didn't choose the library because lots of people study together who aren't really friends, and I want to know about people who choose to be together.

How . . . I don't know how to do this question.

Writer's Statement for Paper 3, Draft 1, Observation

Note: I included the whole series of Writer's Statements and amendments and my revision plan to show the process I went through in revising this paper. After this first Writer's Statement, I mostly made notes to myself to help me in revision.

Purpose: (Assignment) To write a paper using an observation and talking about a social situation we have read about and that we want to know about on our campus. (My purpose) To show that people of different groups get along when they can relate to each other on a one to one basis.

Audience: I'm not sure. I think it should be other college students who are concerned about relationships between groups in this country and on campus.

Thesis: That people tend to make friends with people from other groups on a one-to-one basis rather than mixing with a lot of other people from a different group.

Process: I began by choosing a topic from an essay I had already written about. I was interested in the issue of cross-cultural or racial friendships. The assignment included conducting an observation and choosing a thinking strategy. I used journalistic questions to help me decide how to do the observation. I conducted it to help me see in our student union if I could see any behavior patterns related to my topic. When I wrote out my observations, I could see that the pattern was that small groups and pairs were more likely to contain mixes. When I thought about my own friendships, I realized that was my pattern too. Then I thought about what would go into my paper, starting with the Rodney King statement. I like to start with a quote. And then I reported what I observed; then I tried to lengthen the paper and go on with the discussion by talking about my friends and about the essay I read by Reed. I tried to stay on the focus of inter-group friendships and I think I did stay on focus and accomplished my purpose better than I did in the first two papers. I also took Stephen's idea of asking a question and decided in this paper to try to stay focused on King's question. I tried to address it in every paragraph. Working on this paper while I'm trying to get my paper on the Reed essay finished has kept my attention on sticking to the topic in this one. I don't want to have to do it over! I feel pretty good about this paper and want to see what other people say about it.

Questions:

Did I use my observations the way I was supposed to? I thought they should be more important in the paper but I didn't know what else to say about them.

Should I have given more information about the Reed essay?

How did my personal experiences work in the paper?

How did the references to "getting along" work to keep me on the topic?

Do you think I would offend anyone with this paper? I am not sure how to refer to people from other groups.

Justin's Interview Plan, Paper 3, Draft 1, Observation

When I wrote that third paper using my observation, I knew that it needed help. I thought I should use my observations more in the paper, but I was also worried about the conclusions I drew. Was I right about people mixing more in small groups than in large ones? I took the advice to go and talk to someone in sociology. My friend Todd told me that Dr. Callahan is an expert on group dynamics, so I went to see her. She told me I had to make an appointment. She seems like a serious woman, so I think I had better really get ready for this interview. My questions are below and I would really like some feedback on them before I go to talk with Dr. Callahan. When I get her ideas, I hope that will help me know what to do with my observations and whether they amount to anything.

Interview Questions:

How did you get your experience and knowledge about group dynamics?

Do you think that most interracial groups are small groups?

How are most intercultural or interracial groups formed?

Are friendships between an American and a person from somewhere else more likely to form before or after that person is assimilated?

What are the main difficulties mixed friendships have to overcome?

Are mixed friendships more common among college students than other people our age?

What is your definition of assimilation?

Do you think assimilation is a good thing for America? For the people being assimilated?

Do you see very many mixed friendships on this campus?

Do you think the union was a good place for my observation?

Writer's Statement Amendment for Paper 3, Draft 2, Observation

This is the worst paper I have ever written. I don't even see what it's about. It goes all over the place, talking about my friends and assimilation and Rodney King and observation. The worst thing is I really am interested in this topic but I don't know what to do with it. I have nothing else to say except help! I revised and I made it worse.

Paper 3, Draft 2, Observation

In our society today, relationships between members of different racial or cultural groups is a big issue. It's on the front page or on the news every day. The big question seems to be the one that Rodney King asked after the LA riots. "Can't we just get along?" One way to try to find that out on a college campus is to watch the people in the student union. That's where people gather to eat snacks or meals and to talk and to watch big screen TV.

This topic is important to everyone first because it's a part of everyone's life, living with people who are from other backgrounds. And also, when a person has experience with friendships with people from other backgrounds and they will find it to be a good thing. Darnell, an African American guy and Rajesh, whose family came here from India are both my friends. We have spent lots of time together and I have learned a lot about their backgrounds from our friendships. I like having that as a part of my life, and I think it's helped me see the value of other cultures and how they add to our society.

But I don't know if other people see the same value. An observation in our student union showed that most people, especially those who gather there in large groups tend to choose the company of people from their own background. Over three observation periods the large groups of people in the union, groups of up to ten people, were more likely to be made up of only one group. As the groups in the observation got smaller they became more likely to be a mixture of two races or cultures, but a mixture of three was not observed.

On the basis of that information it seems as though it might be worthwhile to conduct more research to find out if the integration of America is taking place on an individual basis, among small groups of people or pairs of people. Maybe, if that is true, we are going in the wrong direction to try to create diversity in all parts of our society. Maybe people have to learn to live and work together in small groups instead.

That would mean a gradual assimilation. And assimilation, the merging of the minority group into the dominant group can be both good and bad. It depends on the goal and upon each person's life. According to Dr.

Grace Callahan, assimilation has "both benefits and drawbacks for the dominant and the minority group." Maybe the most important benefit of the merging and friendships of people of different cultures is that it will mean a more authentic blending of groups in our society.

Revision Plan for Paper 3, Draft 3, Observation

Go back to purpose. I think I've had this problem before! Add details. My audience should be students and maybe teachers on this campus. That should help me keep things in perspective. I also don't like my introduction and ending. It's really good on the autobiography, especially the introduction. I want to make this one better.

Writer's Statement, Paper 3, Draft 3, Observation

I'm glad I took out all the material that I did. When Suellen read it, she said that it could still use some more information about the observation, that I should think about the journalistic questions, like when did I do it and how did I do it and why did I do it, and who . . . anyway, she's probably right. It probably means another pass through this draft before this paper is in the final form for the portfolio. But I've still got a little time, and I want it to be right.

Final Writer's Statement Amendment for Paper 3, Draft 3, Observation

I didn't make another pass through this paper, though I probably should. I just ran out of time. But I like the paper. I like the material about my friends and I like the way that the observation does represent the point I have been trying all along to make about one-on-one friendships. Mostly I like the positive note about how we may be slowly making friends and learning to get along.

Paper 3, Draft 3, Observation

Observations on Getting Along

On the front pages of every newspaper in the United States are stories about the difficulties of good relationships between people of different racial or cultural backgrounds. College campuses and college newspapers are no different. The big question everywhere seems to be the one that Rodney King asked after the LA riots, "Can't we just get along?" One way to try to find out whether people are getting along on a college campus is to watch the people in the student union, where people, no matter what their living unit, gather to eat snacks or meals and to talk and to watch big screen TV.

During a recent set of observations in our student union, most people, especially those who gather there in large groups, tended to choose the company of people who appear to be from their own racial or ethnic background. Over three observation periods, set at times of the day or evening when the union is busy, the large groups of up to ten people were more likely to be made up of members of only one racial or ethnic group. However, among the groups recorded in this observation, the smaller the group, the more likely it was to be a mixture of two races or cultures. Friends or couples of two backgrounds were not unusual; but during this set of observations, a group that included three people of obviously different backgrounds was never recorded.

While this small sample from our campus can't really tell us anything definitive, it does have a sort of twofold effect on me. First, I think it's sad that more people don't have the advantage of friends from other cultures. When I was growing up, I had two friends from other backgrounds. Darnell, an African American guy, was my friend from grade school. We've been in and out of each other's houses nearly all our lives. By doing that I've learned about sweet potato pie and I've heard the family stories about their slave ancestors. I understand history better because I have been friends with Darnell. I also understand math better because he has always helped me with my math.

That's how we both got to be friends with Rajesh, our Indian friend. We met in math class. Darnell and I have learned a lot from Rajesh. Some of the things are food and traditions, but also about what it's like to be an immigrant and to want to be a part of this country. Rajesh and his family work hard at their store, and he wants more than anything to be "American." I think that knowing Darnell and me has helped him to get closer to that goal.

Which brings me to the second part of my reaction to the findings from the observation, and that is a hope that people are learning, slowly, to know each other. It's been that way for me and my friends. We are just a small group and we don't really spread our friendship into our other groups of friends. Some people probably think that's wrong, but it is what works for us. For right now, we are friends with each other and we understand each other.

That's what's hopeful about the observation. If people are getting to know each other on a one-to-one basis, that is probably how we spread intergroup relationships into the larger society. Whether people meet and form friendships in college, in their jobs, or later in life in community or church activities, they begin to get to know each other as people. That would make the observation carry a positive note that maybe one of these days, we will all get along.

Justin's Proposal for Paper 5, Research Investigation

Purpose: I will discuss the importance of the absentee father.

Audience: People who still have marrying and having families ahead of them so that they will understand how big a responsibility it is to be the father and have influence over other people's lives.

Sources: I have articles from *Newsweek,* from a counseling journal and *Demography.* I will also use an interview, maybe from my interview with my grandmother or maybe I'll find an expert on family issues. I haven't decided yet.

Concerns: I didn't find the kind of information I was looking for, statistics or factual statements about the effects of absentee fathers on kids. I probably need to do some more looking.

Writer's Statement, Paper 5, Draft 1, Research Investigation

Purpose: To look at the effects of absentee fathers on their families and themselves.

Audience: It's supposed to be young people who can maybe keep from having bad effects on their future families.

Thesis: I have two main points, I think. First I ask just how important a father's influence is. Then towards the end, I say that the absence of a father affects everyone in the family.

Strengths: I think I have a good idea and that it's an important subject. I have experience with the topic and I would like to have some information that would help me to be a better father than mine has been for me. But, as always, I worry about how to put the personal slant into a paper, especially a paper like this that is supposed to be a research paper. This one looks like all my other papers and I think it should be different. I am happy that I think I stayed on a focus this time--how are different family members affected by an absentee father. I did that!

Weaknesses: I think that by talking about all the family members that are affected, I copped out. I don't think I did enough research. I should go get that *Atlantic Monthly* article and I should find out more about the football stadium group. And I really am not happy with using my grandmother. The thing is, I didn't answer the questions I wanted answered. I just wrote a paper and I already knew most of those things, except the effects on the father himself. I read Natali's paper and it looks much more like I think this one should. If I really can't find what I need when I go back to the library, I guess I'll change my topic. And, I know I didn't do all the page numbers for documentation but I will in the next draft.

Questions: My main question is how can I find the right material about this topic? How can I make this more like a research paper? The other important thing to me right now is the age-old problem of how much personal stuff can I put in?

Paper 5, Draft 1, Research Investigation

One of the most talked about problems today is the problem of absentee fathers. All the discussion about the overhaul of the welfare system, crime and problems in schools seems to come down to pointing a finger at families where the fathers are gone. If you listen to some of the talk on television, the male influence is supposed to be so important that it's a miracle families without it survive. But is it really that big of an influence? Who is affected by the absence?

An article in *Newsweek* says that David Blankenhorn, chairman of National Fatherhood Initiative and president of the Institute of American Values, "calls fatherlessness 'the most urgent social problem of our generation.'" The article goes on to say that a 1993 *Atlantic Monthly* article says that kids raised without fathers are "'more likely to drop out of high school, to get pregnant as teenagers, to abuse drugs, and to be in trouble with the law.' They were at higher risk for physical and sexual abuse and an array of emotional problems that would persist into adulthood." A father's absence can even put a child at higher risk for accidents and injuries.

That's a lot of influence to have on a kid. And I'm not sure it's right. The article also says that the research collected about this influence is from the field, people noticing that kids in trouble in school, for instance, are often being raised by their mothers alone. But it also says that more academic research is needed and says that lots of people grow up very successfully without their fathers. I have grown up without my father, and I have never been in any sort of trouble. And I've been thinking about the generation from World War II because lots of men who had families were killed in the war, and you don't read much about all these social problems in the years following that war.

Maybe we should look as well at the effect this situation has on the fathers. In the *Journal of Counseling and Development*, associate professors Janice and Michael Wilbur wrote an article called "The Noncustodial Parent: Dilemmas and Interventions." It says that noncustodial parents experience "feelings of loss, self-doubt, and ambivalence and a generally diminished sense of their importance as parents." If the children are doing well, noncustodial parents feel unneeded. In my life, my father is a noncustodial parent, by choice. He never has tried to be a custodial parent. After he left us, it was a long time before we heard from him. My Grandmother Cooper did, and she would tell us that he asked about us, but I can guess now that he was ashamed. She said he felt like we might be better off without him. But that was for a different reason.

He wasn't very literate. So he thought that he couldn't make a good living, and he couldn't. Then after he left, my mom went on to get a degree, and it would have been hard for him to deal with that. He has remarried now and has two more kids. We haven't met them, though my Grandma has. She says that he has been back to school and has learned to read and write so that he can have his job as a dispatcher for a trucking company. A report in an article in *Demography* says that when parents divorce when the children are young, they frequently give little in monetary or emotional support, and that even when child support is required by law, the child-father tie is no stronger.

Absentee fathers is a big problem today, but the answer to the question about the effect of absentee fathers is that their absence has an effect on every member of the family. It may have an adverse effect upon a family's finances, but it may also encourage the woman to continue her education so she can support the family and find fulfillment outside the home. It may encourage kids to become their own people, not to try to be like their father and to take responsibility at an early age. And it has an effect on the fathers. They may suffer from leaving their families, whatever their reasons, and from not staying in contact with their children. It is possible for children to grow up successfully without their fathers, and we can only hope that they will understand the importance of being a more involved father when their time comes.

Writer's Statement, Paper 5, Draft 2, Research Investigation

I started out thinking that I might show how the absence of a father didn't really make a difference because it didn't make much difference in my life. But I also wanted practice doing a research paper. So I thought I might find out just what influence the absence of a father does have. I ended up realizing that when a father is absent, many kids are affected badly. There's no way to prove that it is the absence of a father that directly causes all the problems kids have. But it does turn out to be pretty coincidental that kids in trouble often do not have a father present in their homes.

My purpose became to show that while fatherlessness and divorce do not guarantee problems, they don't do kids any good, so the best thing we all can do is try to stay married and raise our children. My audience is other males in my generation, especially those of us who have grown up without our fathers.

My questions are:

1. What was the most convincing information about the negative effects of fatherlessness? Why was it so convincing?
2. The paper got awfully long. Would you take out anything that is not necessary to my purpose? What?
3. I tried to write good support sentences, but I don't think the paper maps very well. Does it all make sense in a good order?
4. I was worried about putting personal information into a research paper. Did the personal material seem okay?
5. If there was anything you didn't understand, what was it? Please ask specific questions about it so I'll know what to add.

Paper 5, Draft 2, Research Investigation

Fathers for the Future

One of the most talked about problems today is the problem of absentee fathers. All the discussion about the overhaul of the welfare system, crime, and problems in schools seems to come down to pointing a finger at families where the fathers are gone. If you listen to some of the talk on television, the male influence is supposed to be so important that it's a miracle that families without it even survive.

Yet, lots of American kids grow up today without having a father in the house for their entire childhood. Most of those kids go on to successful lives. They do not become criminals, they do not have children out of wedlock, they do not go to jail. If the majority of this broken-family generation survives their situation, then the American public might legitimately ask why fatherlessness has been identified as "the most urgent social problem of our generation" (Cose).

That question becomes even more appropriate when the source of that quote is identified as David Blankenhorn, chairman of National Fatherhood Initiative and president of the Institute of American Values, organizations which appear to have a conservative bias. Other conservatives agree with Blankenhorn. William Bennett, former secretary of education and well-known conservative, says in Commentary that fatherlessness is one of the three most critical problems in America today. We have come to the point, he says, where we ask prisons to do for young men what their fathers used to do. And an editorial in Christianity Today says that because the two-parent marriage is "God's design," the single parent family is "pathological" (Jones 20). As the product of a so-called broken home and as a male who has grown up without a father's influence or interest, I know that I will not become a statistic. I am a college student, hold a job, take part in my family, and will probably have a productive adulthood. It would be easy for me to ignore all the talk about the importance of fatherhood. But because I am a male and because I know that I missed out on things by my dad's absence, I cannot totally discount the concern about fatherhood as a phenomenon of the conservatives. Too much evidence exists to show that fatherlessness is a problem. Just because all young men do not fall prey to the problems that can result from it does not mean that it is not a significant problem.

One of the sources of the fatherlessness controversy is a 1992 television show. When sitcom character Murphy Brown, a liberated reporter, decided to have a baby without being married or involving the father in the baby's life, vice president Dan Quayle responded with outrage toward this irresponsible role model and the general immorality on television. A national debate sprung up. Everyone had an opinion. But it was just that, opinion.

The definitive article about the problems of fatherlessness is Barbara Dafoe Whitehead's in *The Atlantic Monthly,* "Dan Quayle Was Right." Her article, according to *U.S. News and World Report,* "summarizes a decade's scholarly research" (Zuckerman 72). Her summary attacks the single-parent family on many fronts. But some of her strongest statements concern the future of children who grow up without their fathers. According to a "growing body of scientific evidence," they are, she says, at great disadvantage.

The father-child bond is not what it used to be. Whitehead reports that in 1976 less than half as many fathers as in 1957 said that providing for children was a life goal. The proportion of working men who found marriage and children burdensome and restrictive more than doubled in the same period (58). She cites a National Survey of Children that says that "in disrupted families only one child in six, on average, saw his or her father as often as once a week in the past year. Close to half did not see their father at all in the past year" (65). As time passes, "ten years after a divorce, more than two thirds of children report not having seen their father for a year" (65). That has been my own experience. Since my dad left us, years ago, I hardly ever see or hear from him. As time passes, I think we just grow farther apart and he just doesn't think about us.

Educational achievement is affected, too. Children are more than twice as likely to drop out of high school. Boys drop out more often than girls and are more likely to show aggressive behavior. Children of single-parent families are more likely to be late to school, to be truant, to be in trouble at school (66). Whitehead says that the "great educational tragedy of our time" is children failing because they are emotionally unable to perform in school. Principals report, she says, "a dramatic rise in the aggressive, acting-out behavior characteristic of children, especially boys, who are living in single parent families" (77).

The rise in our country's crime rate is also a result of single-parent families according to the sources compiled by Whitehead. More than 70 percent of juveniles in state reform institutions come from fatherless homes (77).

"A number of scholarly studies find that even after the groups of subjects are controlled for income, boys from single-mother homes are significantly more likely than others to commit crimes and to wind up in the juvenile justice, court, and penitentiary systems" (77).

All that is bad, but it does not indicate that all children of fatherless families are doomed to crime and dropping out of school. What may be of most concern to many people who are growing up successfully without fathers is that they may repeat the cycle and put their children at risk of being less successful by falling into some of these problems that they avoided. According to Whitehead, children of divorce are "less successful as adults in the two domains of life--love and work--that are most essential to happiness. Many children from disrupted families have a harder time achieving intimacy in a relationship, forming a stable marriage" (47). She quotes a study by Wallerstein that says the "long-term affects of divorce emerge at a time when young adults are trying to make their own decisions about love, marriage, and family" (65). She also says that Nicholas Zill's research shows that girls from single-parent families are at a greater risk for divorce (66). That's something we learned in a health class in high school, that statistics show that people from divorced families are more likely to be divorced themselves.

That's one outcome of the discussion of fatherless families that should concern everyone. If being fatherless does affect some people in these ways, as my generation marries and begins raising families, we must remember the risks to our children of subjecting them to divorce and abandonment. We should try to break the cycle.

Works Cited

Cose, Ellis. "The Year of the Father." *Newsweek* 31 Oct. 1994: 61.

Bennett, William J. "What to do about the children." *Commentary* March 1995: 23-29. *InfoTrac*. CD-ROM. February 1996.

Jones, Stanton L. "The Two-Parent Heresy." *Christianity Today* 17 May 1993: 20-21.

Whitehead, Barbara Dafoe. "Dan Quayle Was Right." *The Atlantic Monthly* April 1993: 47-84.

Zuckerman, Mortimer B. "The Crisis of the Kids." *U.S. News and World Report* 12 April 1993: 72.